Free Trade and Faithful Globalization
Saving the Market

Through an analysis of Christian communities in the United States, Canada, and Costa Rica, this book analyzes how religious groups talk about the politics surrounding economic life. Amy Reynolds examines how these Christian organizations speak about trade and the economy as moral and value-laden spaces, deserving ethical reflection and requiring political action. She reveals the ways in which religious communities have asked people to engage in new approaches to thinking about the market and how they have worked to create alternative networks and policies governing economic and social life.

Amy Reynolds is an assistant professor of sociology and the coordinator of the Gender Studies Certificate Program at Wheaton College. She received her PhD in sociology from Princeton University, her MPP in public policy from Georgetown, and her BA in sociology from Harvard University. Before teaching at Wheaton, she was a visiting Fellow at Notre Dame's Kellogg Institute for International Studies. She previously worked for World Relief in El Salvador investigating the coffee industry and alternative markets. Her publications have appeared in the *Journal for the Scientific Study of Religion* and in *Latin American Research Review*.

Cambridge Studies in Social Theory, Religion and Politics

Series Editors

DAVID C. LEEGE, University of Notre Dame
KENNETH D. WALD, University of Florida, Gainesville
RICHARD L. WOOD, University of New Mexico

The most enduring and illuminating bodies of late-nineteenth-century social theory – by Marx, Weber, Durkheim, and others – emphasized the integration of religion, polity, and economy through time and place. Once a staple of classic social theory, however, religion gradually lost the interest of many social scientists during the twentieth century. The emergence of phenomena such as Solidarity in Poland; the dissolution of the Soviet empire; various South American, South African, and South Asian liberation movements; the Christian Right in the United States; and Al Qaeda have reawakened scholarly interest in religiously based political conflict. At the same time, fundamental questions are once again being asked about the role of religion in stable political regimes, public policies, and constitutional orders. The Cambridge Studies in Social Theory, Religion and Politics series produces volumes that study religion and politics by drawing upon classic social theory and more recent social scientific research traditions. Books in the series offer theoretically grounded, comparative, empirical studies that raise "big" questions about a timely subject that has long engaged the best minds in social science.

Titles in the Series

Free Trade and Faithful Globalization

Saving the Market

AMY REYNOLDS
Wheaton College

CAMBRIDGE
UNIVERSITY PRESS

CAMBRIDGE
UNIVERSITY PRESS

University Printing House, Cambridge CB2 8BS, United Kingdom

One Liberty Plaza, 20th Floor, New York, NY 10006, USA

477 Williamstown Road, Port Melbourne, VIC 3207, Australia

4843/24, 2nd Floor, Ansari Road, Daryaganj, Delhi - 110002, India

79 Anson Road, #06-04/06, Singapore 079906

Cambridge University Press is part of the University of Cambridge.

It furthers the University's mission by disseminating knowledge in the pursuit of
education, learning and research at the highest international levels of excellence.

www.cambridge.org
Information on this title: www.cambridge.org/9781107435179

First published 2015
First paperback edition 2017

A catalogue record for this publication is available from the British Library

Library of Congress Cataloging in Publication data
Reynolds, Amy, 1977–
Free trade and faithful globalization : saving the market / Amy Reynolds.
   pages   cm. – (Cambridge studies in social theory, religion and politics)
ISBN 978-1-107-07824-6 (hardback)
1. Free trade – Social aspects.   2. Free trade – Moral and ethical aspects.   3. Economic
development – Religious aspects.   4. Economics – Religious aspects.   I. Title.
HF1713.R46   2015
261.8′5–dc23   2014023786

ISBN 978-1-107-07824-6 Hardback
ISBN 978-1-107-43517-9 Paperback

For Steve

Contents

Tables

Preface and Acknowledgments

In 2002, I ended up spending a semester at the Universidad CentroAmericana "José Simeón Cañas" in El Salvador. Although my Spanish proficiency could have been best described as introductory, through the classes in politics and economics there, I glimpsed some of the variation in what constitutes the social science fields. The boundaries of economics, politics, and sociology differ from place to place; the assumptions scholars share in one institution may not be those shared in another. I had not covered dependency theory in my macro-level economics class at Georgetown, but I discovered this was central to the discussions of economic theory in San Salvador.

During this time, I also was involved in an investigation of the coffee sector in Central America and in evaluating the benefits of membership in fair trade networks for farmers. Working with World Relief Corporation, a Christian relief and development agency, I became interested in issues of global trade as I witnessed how international coffee prices impacted Nicaraguan and El Salvadoran farmers. As I entered the doctoral program at Princeton, issues of trade, development, and the public role of religion occupied most of my attention. This book, which started out as a dissertation, really was born in the coffee fields.

Along the way, many people and institutions have supported and encouraged me. Princeton was a source of strong personal and institutional support. Bob Wuthnow defined what it meant to be an excellent mentor: compassionate, giving, thoughtful, and committed to developing students into scholars. His work on religion and public life has clearly guided, and continues to guide, my own career. The other members of my committee, Viviana Zelizer and Miguel Centeno, prompted me to ask the important questions, related to both life and the dissertation. I'm grateful for their scholarship on economic life, the intersection of culture and economics, globalization, and the ways that they both challenged me to think about economic life in different ways.

As an institution, Princeton provided a wealth of resources for me. The Center for the Study of Religion was critical in its economic and professional support, particularly from Anita Kline and Barbara Bermel. Donna DeFrancisco in the Sociology Department assisted me with a number of projects. I am also very appreciative of the administration under the leadership of President Shirley Tilgman for their efforts to encourage and support female graduate students and lead the way in encouraging family-friendly policies within academia.

Outside of Princeton, the Hauser Center for Nonprofit Organizations at Harvard University provided financial support for my work, as did the Society for the Scientific Study of Religion. The Mustard Seed Foundation, through the Harvey Fellows Program, also provided critical resources for my work and life as a student. A visiting fellowship at the Kellogg Institute for International Studies at the University of Notre Dame was central to allowing me to refine understandings of religion, politics, and economic life within a Costa Rican context, through concentrated time to write and conversations with other colleagues studying religion and public life in Latin America. Chapter 4 is adapted from a paper previously published in the Kellogg Institute Working Paper series (2013), "With or Without CAFTA, We Need a Plan." Multiple grants from Wheaton College (including the Aldeen Grant) gave me the time and resources needed to complete this manuscript, and Provost Stanton Jones, Dean Dorothy Chappell, and the chair of the Sociology and Anthropology Department, Hank Allen, provided additional support for me along the way. I'm also very grateful to Betsy Stokes, and her careful attention to detail, for her assistance in editing the manuscript.

The staff at Cambridge University Press also helped me in the final stages. In particular, Richard Wood did a wonderful job of shepherding me through this process, from the proposal stage to the finished product. His support, encouragement, and critical advice were greatly needed. Anonymous reviewers, copy editors, and the rest of the production team were critical to the completion of the final project.

Those who have engaged in academic conversations with me along the way have shaped this work and the ways that I think about the political economy, trade, and religion. I look forward to decades of continued professional and personal relationships with such colleagues. At Princeton, this included Rebekah Massengill, Michael Lindsay, Conrad Hackett, Christine Percheski, Becky Hsu, Phillip Connor, Jim Gibbon, Carol Ann McGregor, Margarita Mooney, and LiErin Probasco. At Wheaton, I'm indebted to Christine Folch, Larycia Hawkins, Sandra Joireman, Rachel Vanderhill, Winnie Fung, and Leah Anderson for their suggestions on the manuscript as well as their encouragement. Outside of these important institutions, others have also made valuable contributions: Bob Brennaman, Bob Woodberry, Nancy Ammerman, Roman Williams, John Schmalzbauer, Jenny Trinitapoli, Kristin Geraty, Miroslav Volf, Brian Steensland, Philip Goff, Janel Bakker, Steve Clements, and David Swartz.

Lynn and Mike Reynolds have always encouraged me on my journey, and I am truly grateful for the many sacrifices they made to foster my love of learning. To my in-laws, Ruth Anne and Bill Offutt, I am thankful for the hours of childcare and thoughtful conversation they provided during critical stages of this work.

This book would not exist had it not been for the numerous people who gave their time to talk with me about their experiences in the three religious communities under investigation. In addition to those interviewed, Therese Dineen helped me sort through almost forty years of data, allowing me access to the archives of the ecumenical justice coalitions in Canada. Christopher Iosso provided helpful information about the history and texts of the Presbyterian Church. In Costa Rica, the staff at the National Archives spent hours retrieving issues of the *Eco Católico* and photocopying hundreds of pages. I am especially thankful for Miriam de Montoya in the CECOR office, who not only facilitated my work in Costa Rica but also welcomed me into a foreign country.

This work is but one of four fruits of my labor in the last ten years. My thoughtful, talented, and resilient Adrianna Grace; the smashing, compassionate, and dramatic Emily Hope; and the energetic, inquisitive, and assertive Gabriella Joy have kept me grounded. They have made my life rich and exciting, and made the study of sociology increasingly relevant and important. My husband (and fellow sociologist), Stephen Offutt, has shared in this book's journey from its early seeds on the coffee fields of El Salvador in 2002 to its final submission in 2014. He has been my most important intellectual partner, helping me think through big theoretical questions, as well as helping me to catch yet another typo or awkward phrase. He participated in the fieldwork with me and sharpened my analysis. I'm thankful that he pushes me to live life to the fullest and reminds me of the greater purpose of our lives together.

Abbreviations

ACN	Action Canada Network
CACM	Central American Common Market
CA4FTA	Central American 4–Canada Free Trade Agreement
CAFTA	Central America–United States Free Trade Agreement
CAFTA–DR	Central America–Dominican Republic–United States Free Trade Agreement
CCCB	Canadian Conference of Catholic Bishops
CCRDO	Christian Coalition of Relief and Development Organizations
CECOR	Costa Rican Episcopal Conference of Catholic Bishops (Conferencia Episcopal de Costa Rica)
CELAM	Latin American Episcopal Conference of Catholic Bishops (Consejo Episcopal Latinamericano)
CST	Catholic social teaching
EAA	Ecumenical Advocacy Alliance
ECEJ	Ecumenical Coalition for Economic Justice
FTA	free trade agreement
FTAA	Free Trade Area of the Americas
GATT	General Agreement on Tariffs and Trade
ICE	Costa Rican Institute of Electricity
ICCHRLA	Interchurch Coalition on Human Rights in Latin America
IFI	international financial institution
IMF	International Monetary Fund
ISI	import substitution industrialization
ITO	International Trade Organization
MAI	Multilateral Agreement on Investment
NAFTA	North American Free Trade Agreement
PCUSA	Presbyterian Church (USA)
RMALC	Mexican Free Trade Network (Red Mexicana Accion frente al Libre Comercio)

SAP   structural adjustment program
SEDAC   Central American Episcopal Secretariat of Catholic bishops
                   (Secretariado Episcopal de América Central y Panamá)
TNC   transnational corporation
UMAVIDA   Bolivian Association Uniting Hands for Life (Asociación
                   Boliviana Uniendo Manos por la Vida)
UN   United Nations
UNCTAD   United Nations Conference on Trade and Development
VEPS   Catholic vicariate office in San José (Vicaría Episcopal de
                   Pastoral Social)
WARC   World Alliance of Reformed Churches
WCD   World Christian Database
WTO   World Trade Organization

Introduction

Waiting for his next customer, a Costa Rican taxicab driver is parked by the curb. While he waits, he reads an informational pamphlet on the CAFTA-DR, the Central America–Dominican Republic–United States Free Trade Agreement. Although not considered leisurely reading material in the United States, literature on trade agreements was popular in Costa Rica from 2004 to 2008. Citizens disagreed on the potential impact of CAFTA-DR for the country, but all agreed the stakes were high. Former Costa Rican Catholic bishop Ignacio Trejos Picado declared in his protest against CAFTA-DR: "We must always protect life, even when it affects our business and trade ... The church must be on the side of life, and not the culture of death" (2007d). The treaty became the most polarizing issue in the nation's recent history, and the first public referendum ever in the country was held in 2008 to determine the treaty's fate in Costa Rica – with a majority of citizens voting.

Some proponents of economic liberalization around the globe have sought to avoid discussion of the moral questions associated with free trade. They have minimized discourse on the ethics of markets, arguing that economic policies are technical matters, best dictated by values of efficiency and growth. In this book, I focus on one subset of actors who have challenged this view of policies and economic markets. Representing a variety of voices from Christian religious traditions, they have politically engaged issues of globalization, the political economy, and trade policy. By participating in political discourse about market decisions, these religious organizations have produced sacred visions of how economic life should be structured.

Such morally centered discussion of our political economy looms all the more crucial in light of the current vigorous critique of the decades-old rise of economic inequality. How do we measure who are the winners and the losers in the new economy? What does it mean to have equality of opportunity for all? Whose job is it to protect the interests of the most marginal, and what roles do the state and the market play in the process?

Although religious groups are increasingly involved in a number of advocacy efforts in the world, many view them as disconnected from issues related to the political economy (and perhaps, more importantly, consider this perceived distance the proper role). The reality is that many religious communities *do* speak on such political topics and contribute in important ways to public dialogue on the economy. As both Hart (2001) and Wood (2002) have argued, religious groups can play a crucial role in economic and political life through their discourse; such discourse is a central way that they produce the sacred in the economic realm (Wuthnow 1994b). This is true across a range of religious traditions and organizations.

In this book, I follow three Christian organizations that differ in their theologies, audiences, structures, and national locations: Kairos, an ecumenical organization in Canada; the Presbyterian Church (USA), or PCUSA; and the Episcopal Conference of Costa Rica (CECOR), a Catholic council of bishops in Costa Rica. This book is centrally concerned with the ethical and political voice of these organizations when it comes to free trade and free trade agreements. First, I analyze the ethical values they are using to ground their political positions, with special attention to how such values are shaped by religious commitments. I find that even though the groups rely on different religious traditions, they converge on many foundational values they bring to bear on the economy, including responsibility to the community, just relationships among people, and the importance of human dignity and human rights.

Second, I consider how such discourse is produced. Each of these groups has challenged the underlying values of capitalist markets, even as they rely on slightly different sources of moral authority, such as scripture, lived experiences, and tradition. These groups also vary in who has the authority to speak for the group, whether it is the hierarchical structure of Catholic leadership, or a more democratic polity in the case of the PCUSA. As a result, I also consider whether official voices are representative of the membership of these communities.

Third, I investigate how organizations assert and legitimate their moral authority to speak into trade debates, and the different strategies they employ in their political engagement. All of these groups embrace a responsibility to engage political questions, yet they do so in markedly different ways. This reflects different understandings of both the role of economists and policy makers, and the church in the secular realm. Religious actors are not unified in how they conceive of their authority vis-à-vis the state. Different understandings of engagement explain different strategies religious actors employ. Investigating such dynamics is critical for scholars interested in the public roles that religious organizations have – and might have – in our modern society.

METHODOLOGY

To investigate the content, production, and use of religious discourse on trade issues, I have employed a case study approach. Ragin notes that a case study approach is a good way to generate new conceptual schemas and look at the complexity involved in what he terms the "constellations, configurations, and conjunctures" (1987, x). Religious configurations are shaped by the relationship between the church and the state, the type and structure of the religious organization, the theological tradition, and the national context. A case study approach allows one to determine what rhetoric is used in trade debates, how it is formed, and how it is used. Through multiple in-depth cases, I can also make hypotheses about the effect of different organizational variables on discourse and economic engagement. Although this method is not the best for addressing questions about the consequences of different combinations of conditions, it does raise questions and help in explaining and interpreting some of the variation that exists.

Case Selection

Before selecting the cases to be studied in this book, I analyzed a number of religious organizations across the Americas that were involved in trade policy discussions. I selected thirty-one denominations, mission-oriented groups, and ecumenical alliances associated with the Christian tradition in some way (Reynolds 2010). Based on their published statements, these groups fell into four key categories: support of the status quo, no position, cautious critics, and radical reformers. Table A.1 lists the different positions found. Although I do not claim this sample is a representative sample of Christian actors, the organizations do

TABLE A.1 *Overview of Religious Responses to FTAs*

Response to FTAs	Discourse on FTAs	National Location	Religious Tradition	Organization Type
Quiet Support	Rarely speak of trade directly, but endorse increased global capitalism and U.S. power	Mostly the United States	Mainline Protestants and evangelicals	Denominations and political groups
No Official View	Rarely speak of international economic issues	All countries	Mostly evangelical	Denominations
Criticism	Speak about specific policies; discuss development issues	All countries	Catholics, mainline Protestants, and evangelicals	Development groups and Catholic Church
Opposition	Speak about specific policies; discuss technical matters	All countries	Catholics, mainline Protestants, and evangelicals	Political groups and some denominations

capture much of the variance within the broader Christian community. I found that those who are contesting trade are the most vocal, and are producing (and have produced) a lot of discourse about trade and economic life. By contrast, those supportive of the status quo have produced less discourse. As a result, I decided to focus on those publishing, writing, and speaking in critique of the status quo, which included cautious critics and radical reformers.

As also noted in Table A.1, these groups vary by location, tradition, and organization. Organizations in the United States, for example, are more likely than those in Canada and Latin America to be supportive of current international trade policies. Religious traditions are important, but not via a clear pathway (similar to Hart's [1992] finding about individual connections between theological tradition and economic perspectives). Often religious ideas associated with political stances, but groups with similar theological claims vary in their political and economic assumptions. I found that Protestant denominations (especially evangelicals) are less vocal than ecumenical alliances and the Catholic Church. From this exploratory analysis, I determined that national location, theology, and organizational structure all merited further attention.

Three cases were selected to represent three regions within North and Central America: an ecumenical justice coalition in Canada (currently named Kairos), the Presbyterian Church in the United States (PCUSA), and the Costa Rican Conference of Catholic Bishops (CECOR). These cases varied in denominational affiliation (ecumenical, Protestant/Reformed, and Catholic) as well as organizational type (grassroots coalition, democratic denomination, and hierarchical denomination). Table A.2 provides more detail on these selected religious organizations.

All three groups have challenged dominant market paradigms and have been involved in progressive action on the political economy. They have connected religious values with public policies, bringing their religious authority to bear in struggles for progressive economic action in the political realm. Yet they have varied in their action. As a result, these cases offer insight into some of the ways that religious communities have engaged in activism over the scope and ethical outcomes of increasingly liberalized and globalized markets.

Data Collection

Internal texts of the organizations, research reports, policy memos, and official public statements compose the core of this analysis. Utilizing qualitative comparative-analysis software (Atlas.ti), I examined statements from the mid-twentieth century through 2008, although I focused more attention on documents from 1990 to the present. (Chapters 2, 3, and 4 provide further detail on the documents under analysis for each case, and the primary bibliography at the end of the book lists each of these documents that were part of the textual

TABLE A.2 *Religious Case Studies*

Organization	Religious Tradition	Organization Type	National and International Ties	Attitude toward FTA
GATT-Fly/ ECEJ/ Kairos	Ecumenical Liberation theology	Religious coalition (Staff create policies and action)	Canadian	Opposition
PCUSA	Mainline Protestant Reformed	Denomination (Democratic vote determines policies)	United States (connected with international alliances)	Criticism (and opposition)
CECOR	Catholic CST	Representative of the Catholic Church (Bishops are the official voice)	Costa Rica (connected to Latin American conference and under authority of Church)	Criticism (no political position)

analysis). Texts were coded for different references to authority, invocation of values (religious and nonreligious), attitudes about the political economy, and groups' particular political positions on trade. In order to capture the full range of variation in these categories, such coding was done without a defined set of initial codes; by this practice, I induced the prominent elements of discourse for each group.

I complemented this analysis of written texts with participant observation and interviews. The twenty-seven interviews with organizational leaders and individuals specifically dealt with issues of economic and social justice. I attended conferences within both the PCUSA and Kairos dealing with economic justice issues, and I spent time at the CECOR offices in Costa Rica. Preliminary fieldwork started in the fall of 2006, interviews started in the spring of 2007, and all fieldwork was completed by the spring of 2008. I received institutional review board (IRB) approval for the interview process and fieldwork in May 2007. I spent the summer of 2007 in Costa Rica interviewing Catholic leaders and accessing the archives of the Catholic Church. Interviews were conducted mostly in Spanish in Costa Rica and in English in the United States and Canada. In the cases of interviews with male priests and bishops in Costa Rica, I conducted these interviews with a male researcher. Interviews lasted between thirty minutes and two hours (the average length was about an hour). I traveled to various regions in Canada and the United States to speak with members of Kairos and the PCUSA; this included the organizations' respective headquarters in Toronto and Louisville.

Each of these groups spoke on behalf of a particular religious community, so understanding the relationship of organizational leaders with other co-religionists within each group was important. For Kairos, whose members join because of many shared political beliefs, I examined denominational reports and conducted interviews with denominational actors to see how rhetoric produced by Kairos was used. In the case of the PCUSA, I consulted Presbyterian Panel Data (2006b), and I analyzed such data, with the help of a statistical software package (Stata), to determine the representativeness of the official positions of the church. Finally, in the case of the Costa Rican bishops, I consulted a Catholic periodical, *Eco Católico*, which has published a number of nonofficial articles on trade treaties in the past five years, as well as some published texts from an active antitrade Catholic contingency in the country.

BOOK OVERVIEW

To begin, Chapter 1 considers the current knowledge about how values shape economic structures and ideology. Economic sociology has increasingly focused on the idea that markets are cultural constructions. While not seeing values as the only – or even central – shaper of market ideology, I do argue that markets are deeply shaped and molded by underlying foundational values. For example, people within a market may determine the appropriate boundaries of economic behavior, develop regulations to control markets, and/or promote strategies emphasizing individual freedom. I consider how the moral authority of cultural producers matters for such societal discussions. Chapter 1 also examines the contexts in which these organizations operate as they bring their theology to bear on the economy. This includes attention to the role of institutional settings and internal organizational structures.

I turn in the last part of Chapter 1 to an examination of why religion is an especially important voice to consider in discourse about trade. Imbued with moral authority, religious traditions have often engaged in public discourse about political and economic issues. Latin American liberation theology gained attention for its political message and critique of economic systems, and the larger Catholic tradition has dealt with what they deem to be "the social question" for some time. More broadly speaking, the Christian ecumenical movement also has grappled extensively with issues of industrialization, has been important for the Reformed tradition, and has been connected with the Social Gospel in North America. Religious traditions are an important part of the cultural repertoires of the religious organizations that I study here.

Chapters 2, 3, and 4 are case studies of the three religious organizations. Each chapter first focuses on the group's political response to issues of international trade. I then turn to the question of what religious values were used to support positions, how institutional factors influenced the production of discourse, and how such discourse was both employed and received.

In Chapter 2, the reader is introduced to Kairos. Originally founded as GATT-Fly due to their opposition to international trade policy (including the General Agreement on Tariffs and Trade [GATT]) in the 1970s, Kairos has visualized and espoused total reform of the economic system. Protestant denominations, the Catholic Church, Catholic religious orders, and Christian development groups are among the eleven member organizations that make up this coalition committed to social justice and political change.

Kairos has demanded markets that focus on the poor, transparent and democratic systems, and increased state sovereignty in economic management decisions. Their central religious values have remained consistent: solidarity, community, equality, and the sacredness of creation. Just as important as the content of their values, the *practice* of their religion has defined their identity and been maintained by action. They are heavily influenced by the tradition of liberation theology, applying it to their own Canadian context. Although their organizational structure has changed over time, they consistently have been staff-led, allowing key religious actors a high degree of autonomy in their discourse production. Their strong stance against state policies also has been facilitated by their weak connection to the state and influenced by a broader civil society movement.

The PCUSA is the topic of Chapter 3. The PCUSA has leveraged their moral authority in efforts to reform powerful political systems. Governed by institutionalized democratic processes and part of an international Reformed community, the PCUSA is one of the most established mainline denominations, representing about 2–3 percent of the U.S. population. Multiple task forces and programs have dealt with international economic issues since the 1970s. As part of the interfaith community in Washington, DC, they have lobbied against current free trade agreements (FTAs), with discourse intended to both speak to those in power and educate their members. Citing religious values alongside empirical research, they have endorsed more market protection and regulation, an expanded definition of rights to include economic rights, and increased global governance of the economy. Values of God's sovereignty, covenant, and hope have been central to their message.

Chapter 4 follows CECOR in Costa Rica. The Catholic Church enjoys a high level of authority within this society, even as the percentage of Catholics in the population is in decline, with an estimated 70 percent of citizens still claiming a Catholic identity. In the numerous statements issued by the eight bishops who make up this Catholic council, concerns over free trade have involved the fate of the poor, the protection of culture, a power imbalance between negotiating nations, and a lack of dialogue within society over trade. Religious principles of human dignity, solidarity, concern for the poor, and peace have been foundational, with CST a central source of authority. On CAFTA-DR, CECOR has taken a neutral stance, utilizing their position of power to offer a development framework for society, to exist within and alongside trade agreements.

In Chapter 5, I return to the dialogue about moral discourse and the market, using the three case studies to explain why different religious groups have chosen to engage differently in political debates about economic life. In this chapter, I make three central arguments. First, for religious groups that are critical of current economic globalization efforts, a core set of values seems to motivate involvement, with concern for the community being the most central. Second, both national identities and organizational structures are important in explaining the different modes of discourse in which organizations engage. That is, while each of the groups is a transnational actor in some respects, they all engage with national audiences and are influenced by national values. I also suggest that different understandings about the role of religion and the role of economists have lent themselves to three very different styles of engagement in political life – from influencing the values of debate to crafting actual policy. Chapter 5 provides a more generalized typology of engagement, highlighting the different ways religion can be used as a frame, lens, or practice to guide economic policy decisions.

In Chapter 6, I focus on the implications of this research for both religious practitioners and political activists. Beyond the organizations profiled in this book, a host of other religious organizations are seeking economic change. I suggest four specific actions that such groups should prioritize: emphasizing the Christian notion of community, using their prophetic voices, personalizing market activity, and working ecumenically.

Religious groups are clearly active on economic issues; the case of trade policy provides an example of how such groups have framed economic issues as religious concerns. Religious organizations are important actors when it comes to the moral space of globalization, as they raise attention to the ethical issues involved in crafting markets. Far from being relegated to the private domain, such organizations create spaces to discuss the common good, human dignity, and their relationship to market policies. These conversations, although not sufficient for political change, are essential to the cause of democratic politics and are a vital way that religious communities are engaged in public life. As FTAs continue to proliferate, understanding what religious communities can bring to the public dialogue – as well as the challenges and processes they confront in creating discourse – is central for scientists and activists alike in the construction of richer democratic discourse over economic policy decisions in today's globalized world.

I

Producing Market Discourse

Rowan Williams [Anglican archbishop of Canterbury] called for a challenge to "naive confidence in free trade." ... The archbishop would do well to hearken to the advice of his own top spiritual leader. "Render therefore unto Caesar the things which are Caesar's; and unto God the things that are God's," said Jesus, thus making clear his belief that church and state should stick to their core competencies.
— *The Economist* (2005)

Economists are often charged with decisions regarding economic policies ranging from human development agendas to macroeconomic stability. And as articulated in this epigraph from *The Economist*, such decisions and policies are often viewed as the private domain of technical experts, and markets themselves as purely technical structures. But markets are social constructions. They are inescapably composed of people, as well as the products of particular historical processes and specific political action.

How markets should function, and how they should be constructed, is therefore often contested. Throughout time, the economic status quo has been open to debate. In the current phase of increasing economic liberalization and globalization, questions are increasingly being raised about previously accepted free-market principles. Such questions often lead to public discourse. A premise of this book is that such discourse can influence, facilitate, and drive social-economic change.

In this book, I analyze the discourse of religious actors surrounding free trade and free trade agreements, current policies being debated in the public realm. Religious voices historically have been vocal in challenging market paradigms. Although *The Economist* targeted Archbishop Williams, many other religious actors could have been called out instead. Religious communities have been involved in discursive action on the economy, and insisting it be otherwise is unlikely to silence them. The resources of religious groups can give them special authority to speak to the value-laden nature of markets. As described

9

in the Introduction, this book follows three specific religious actors: Kairos in Canada; the Presbyterian Church (USA), or PCUSA, in the United States; and the Episcopal Conference of Costa Rica (CECOR), the Catholic council of bishops in Costa Rica.

These three cases reveal how religious actors are using their moral authority to speak into market life, as they engage in discourse on the political structures and social consequences of markets. As also noted in the Introduction, I focus on three central questions. First, how is religion (and religious ideas) used within economic discourse? Second, how is this discourse produced and legitimated, and who has agency in this process? Finally, how are organizations engaging in trade debates, and how do they legitimate their authority?

Before delving into the moral and political discourse of religious actors, in this chapter I argue that religious actors must be considered as actors that have the potential to re-image market life. Agreeing with other economic sociologists, I first examine the ways that social and political ideas have shaped the structure of markets. That is, particular moral sentiments have been articulated to support change in economic structures; concrete political actions often support certain market values over others. In this section, I also examine the ways the current market dynamics came to be. Second, I argue that discourse itself should be considered an important political action, even as it is not a sufficient action for political change. Rarely have scholars examined the importance of religious actors, and their discourse, in economic policy. But religious actors play an important role in shaping sacred conceptions of the market. Given the importance of such actors and their discourse, I conclude this chapter with attention to some of the different organizational, national, and cultural factors that influence and shape the discursive involvement of religious communities toward the political economy. This includes a discussion of some of the different ways Christian communities have thought about political and social engagement in modern history, and nuances among different theological traditions.

THE STRUCTURE OF ECONOMIC MARKETS

The Values of Modern Market Life

If we define markets as social constructions, we must accept that they are full of moral ideas and assumptions about the allocation of goods. Many have problematized the separate spheres or hostile worlds logic that would designate the economic market as merely an efficient structure for the exchange of goods and services. As economic sociologists Fourcade and Healy (2007) suggest, moral understandings are a part of foundational market values, and are important in the governance and evaluations of markets as well.

Although some would frame markets as merely technical structures for the allocation of goods, historically scholars have long recognized the connection between market structures and other aspects of the social life. Even when attention has not focused on these underlying principles and the debates over what markets should be (a focus of this book), people have drawn the connection between market structures and other aspects of the social life. Hirschman (1977) outlined some of the various perspectives scholars have had regarding markets, noting the ways that markets have been framed as having either "civilizing" or "destructive" effects on human characteristics and values.

Yet often the underlying values embedded in the economy are not articulated, which allows them to go unexamined, unnoticed, and uncontested. Questions of personal ethics become the focus of ethical behavior in the marketplace (Zelizer 2007), and participation within systems is rarely questioned. Many principles, such as efficiency and productivity, are sometimes cast as natural and necessary, even when they are neither (Fourcade and Healy 2007). Such values often develop into what Lamont and Thévenot describe as "repertoires of evaluation." These are the cultural tools or resources that people within a particular community have available to them (2000, 8–9).

In modern market society, ideas of individualism and the free-market are often paramount, even though variance among countries exists. Adam Smith is often heralded as a champion of such individualism and unrestrained capitalism. Yet he recognized a moral foundation must be in place for a just and liberal economy, to protect against individualism. He warned, for example, against private interests that focused on maximizing profits: "To be anxious, or to be laying a plot either to gain or save a single shilling, would degrade the most vulgar tradesman in the opinion of all his neighbors" ([1790] 2009, 200).

The principle of individualism was developed and re-imagined over time. Wuthnow (1989) argues that individualism, alongside other principles essential to capitalism's vitality (rationalization, pluralism, discretion), gained support as a market principle primarily when capitalism began to challenge existing economic systems.[1] This suggests that even widely accepted modern values once required legitimation and arguments for their support.

Discussions about the foundational principles of market life emerge in development debates. Questions about how to define growth, and what type of growth to encourage, bring normative values into policy analysis and technical decisions (Best and Widmaeir 2006). A variety of developmental indicators, produced by groups like the World Bank, offer rubrics to determine how different aspects of growth – economic, educational, social, health-related – should be measured and weighted against one another. Development discussions open wide the door for the philosophical defense of a certain framework's legitimacy. As Best (2005) articulates, such discussions often require proponents of various models to defend the principles embedded within different systems (for example, the heightened moral discipline or responsibility of individuals required under

---

[1] This is not to say that individualism was first championed in support of capitalism, as Wuthnow (1989) points out that earlier cultural episodes (Enlightenment, Protestant Reformation) each helped to develop notions of individual autonomy that were used to support economic change.

capitalism). I find that religious actors are challenging the underlying commitment to individualism they see within current international trade debates and growing economic globalization. Individualism is increasingly contrasted with values of community in modern society (Wuthnow 1989), and religious traditions offer alternative foundational market principles centered on community.

Within the fields of economic and cultural sociology, there has been renewed attention to questions of how different values and repertoires come to play not only in shaping larger economic understandings about economic systems, but also in how markets are governed and evaluated. What types of issues should be governed by market logic, and when should other prevailing logics be more important? Studies that look at corporate social concern, ethical investments, informal economic networks, and the gift economy are just some examples. When does ethical behavior need to be enforced, instead of allowing the market to be governed by its own internal logic? In the area of free trade policy – the focus of this book – the issues of child labor and working conditions are areas of contestation. Debate surrounds not only the type of regulation that should occur, but also which actors should be involved in regulation.

Finally, it is worth considering the way moral evaluations of individuals and individual actions enter into the legitimation of various market systems. Do those who suffer economically in current systems merit such an outcome? Market regulations are laden with moral understandings about what transactions are appropriate for what people, based largely on measures of the moral worth of different individuals and the nature of relationships among them. Such values and assumptions are evident in debates over economic policies. Take, for instance, the welfare system in the United States. Since the inception of welfare relief and guaranteed minimum assistance, there have been questions about which recipients are morally worthy of such support from the state (Katz 1986). Government welfare policies were designed to include only the "deserving" poor (Steensland 2007), a judgment based on the situation and often the moral choices of the individual. Following from the work of Skocpol (1992) that addresses the ascription and achievement of moral status, Mohr (1994) examined the way that certain groups have obtained moral worth (mothers, soldiers, and the disabled) while other groups have not (tramps and indigents). These groups have been the objects of varying charitable interactions, with different sets of unwritten regulations pertaining to how each should be treated.

Values about people and the appropriate interactions among them are made at various levels within the marketplace. This includes the decisions about the type of market system to support and create, the regulations to guide behavior, the scope/power given to the market to regulate itself, and the moral evaluations of individuals (especially those who are marginalized). Further, markets are predicated upon moral foundations. The current free-market system gives the highest value to principles of individualism, efficacy, and growth. Successful free-market institutions embrace these values, and at an international level, global courts and governance institutions endorse them. The spread of free trade in the twentieth century is not a story of the unbridled market "coming to life" and of growing technical and scientific advancement. It is a story of political actors implementing treaties and regulations, policies that serve to enforce certain foundational principles over others.

Institutional Tools of Modern Capitalism

How is the modern market constructed? To be sure, modern capitalism does rely in part on an emphasis on individualism, as noted previously. But the story of the twentieth and twenty-first century is hardly one about the continual rise of individual and economic liberalization. Although such liberalization has increased since the 1980s, the twentieth century witnessed a back-and-forth relationship among states and other actors when it came to the regulation and management of the market. Both the beginning and the end of the twentieth century boasted a similar mantra about the possibilities wrought by the freedom and power of global markets. However, after the economic destruction prompted by two world wars and the Great Depression, a series of international organizations came into existence to lend management to this world economy. At the Bretton Woods conference in 1944, three bodies were proposed for dealing with finance, development, and trade: the International Monetary Fund (IMF), the World Bank, and the International Trade Organization (ITO). These bodies were meant to operate in conjunction with other global institutions, and the ITO was to be located within the United Nations' Economic and Social Council (UNCTAD 2004).

Due to the ultimate rejection (primarily from the United States) of the Havana Charter (the mandating document for the ITO), the creation of ITO failed. The General Agreement on Tariffs and Trade (GATT) became the de facto trade-governing organization at an international level. The product of negotiations by states to reduce trade tariffs, GATT sought to liberalize access to markets, mandate reciprocity between nations, provide for nondiscriminatory treatment of countries, and increase transparency among states over protectionism (Dunkley 2000). Yet in having GATT become the de facto agreement, much was lost for which the ITO initially provided. The ITO covered issues like business practices, investment, and public enterprises (Dunkly 2000, 27). It would have given countries more autonomy is thinking about foreign investment. As trade economist Bhagwati (2008) notes, prior to this agreement, states could apply different trade standards, and the ITO was based on the idea that signatories of an international, multilateral policy would all get the same treatment. The adoption of GATT as the governing system liberalized trade without the social provisions intended with an ITO based at the United Nations.

Until the 1980s, even as global institutions encouraged values of efficiency, liberalization, and growth, trade decisions were largely controlled by individual states. Many developing countries, although they adopted goals of more liberalized trades, continued to use protectionist measures without much contestation. The Uruguay Rounds of GATT (1986–1994) changed some of these dynamics, as they limited state decision-making power and included more developing countries in the process. These GATT rounds took place at the time the world was moving toward a more free-market approach and away from states' management of their economies, as symbolized by the leadership of Reagan and Thatcher (Yergin and Stanislaw 1998). The conclusion of the Uruguay Rounds witnessed the formation of the World Trade Organization (WTO) in 1995. Dunkley (2000) argues that the Uruguay Rounds opened the negotiating table to a host of new concerns: customs procedures, marketing of exports and imports, administrative practices, uses of state authority for protectionist measures, and the contentious issue of subsidies. Central to these proceedings were measures meant to eliminate technical barriers to trade, thus expanding free trade to include regulations against barriers other than tariffs. Fligstein describes this phenomenon as "negative integration"; barriers to trade were removed, without new regulations being produced (2004, 183). In place of the state, the market gained more power; with the increased power of the market, the importance of business actors also rose. Faith in economic progressivism and the "scientific management of society" (Nelson 2001, 113–114) waned. As the confidence in states and governments to manage the economy decreased, self-interest (with its promise of economic growth) became more accepted as the dominant attitude of all sectors. States played less of a role in providing for their citizens; increased exposure to markets in Latin America, for example, has been associated with decreased state involvement (Kaufman and Segura-Ubiergo 2001; Wibbels and Arce 2003).

Yet free trade was regulated, even as economic liberalization grew. Bilateral agreements emerged during this time, with the Canada–United States Free Trade Agreement in 1987 being among the first. Bhagwati, a proponent of economic liberalization and freer trade, notes that free trade agreements (FTAs) are better referred to as PTAs (preferential trade agreements), and notes the ways in which they actually work against free trade. Article 24 of the GATT enabled such agreements, although Bhagwati says the purpose was not to encourage them, but rather to call countries to be more accountable and official about any side deals that were being made (in an effort to limit, not encourage, such arrangements). As an economist, his critiques of FTAs deal with efficiency and issues of trade diversion (Bhagwati 2008); however, he also notes that such FTAs (especially between developing countries and world powers) are vehicles for nontrade issues to be legislated, often under pressure from lobbyists within the more powerful countries.

Free trade agreements, with their emphasis on decreased state regulations of the economy, meant less regulation and more power for transnational corporations (TNCs). Truly global enterprises formed, as these organizations were able to thrive. Rodrik (1997) argues that globalization has made more stark the difference between who can and cannot cross borders, noting that as capital and companies move more freely, migration and the movement of labor have actually been restricted. That is, liberalization privileges capitalism and business over the rights and freedom of people. As Nelson argues, the modern market "advances the pursuit of self-interest in appropriate domains" (2001, 9). Many social scientists have raised concerns about global governance. For example, states have lost some of their power to regulate the market with the growth of global capitalism; at the same time, the international arena lacks mechanisms for actors such as firms and other social groups to make appeals regarding fairness (Fligstein 2004). Debates emerge over the consequences of this lack of governance, who benefits, and who has the most power in the new global economy.

Free trade, then, is a misnomer for the new economic structure. At best, global trade "is made of hierarchies and these in turn reflect both historical legacies and political realities" (Centeno and Cohen 2010, 53). Markets, as Fligstein asserts, depend on an extensive infrastructure to exist (rule of law, property rights, rules of exchange, courts, rules) (2004, 192). Such infrastructures have increased in recent years. Alongside such growth is increasing acceptance that the self-interest of business is best for economic growth, reflecting a changing priority of what was economically valuable; and in the name of growth and efficiency, the world has witnessed a proliferation of FTAs and globalized businesses.

But, at worst, FTAs are not just about the hierarchical relationships between unequal partners, but also about the ways those relationships are further exploited. In protesting FTAs, then, a number of concerns often come together. Actors may be concerned about philosophies promoting more unregulated markets and lower trade costs. They also may be concerned about the de facto powers that are regulating economic life – large countries over small in the growing number of FTAs, businesses with strong lobbying powers within those larger countries, and the power of businesses vis-à-vis states within the market itself.

THE IMPORTANCE OF DISCOURSE FOR POLITICAL LIFE

Discourse Defined

Viewing markets as social constructions places the emphasis on the various political, social, and cultural contexts in which markets are produced. Markets exist within particular cultural contexts. Culture is made up in part of norms and articulated beliefs, and public discourse is one place where such norms and beliefs are articulated (or rearticulated). Put simply, discourse is the conversation – whether published in print, broadcast on television, or preached from the pulpit – that exists publicly about a topic. Wuthnow has suggested that *moral* discourse be considered "modes of reasoning and talking that define things as legitimate according to a set of values about the way things ought to be" (1996, 52). Moral discourse about the market revolves around the values and shared understandings about what is just and appropriate. Such discourse prescribes value to activities and individuals based on a larger conception of the good (Massengill and Reynolds 2010). This discourse allows people to identify the actions necessary and the appropriate behavior required; as Wuthnow further notes, it both describes and composes the context of current cultural conditions (1989, 15). Discourse is a profoundly cultural enterprise in its act of creating meaning. Indeed, without shared assumptions, perceptions of the world, and meaningful symbols, no one could act at all in the political realm (Wood 2002, 154).

Such discourse shapes our understandings of oneself and others, our practices in the world, and our engagement in community. My focus in this book is to understand how discourse (specifically religious discourse) shapes political engagement on issues of economic life; this engagement is based in part on understandings of identity. According to Alexander (2003), it is cultural codes that often impact our engagement and identity. Lakoff notes that public discourse not only shapes identity, but is also a strategic act to define the moral life (2006).

Public discourse often occurs outside of, official government institutions and formal legal pronouncements. Such unofficial discourse is usually not carefully examined. But politics happens in a variety of arenas, and these all can be considered discursive spaces – outlets for expression, analysis, and the shaping of ideas. Wood (2002) highlights the importance of not just the government, but of political society and civil society as well in shaping public spaces. These public discursive spaces allow for fundamental categories to be nuanced and concepts to be linked with one another (Wuthnow 1989). What happens in civil society, for example, has the potential to shape political identities, attitudes, and solidarities, all with implications for political mobilization (Wood 2002, 127).

The political discourse that occurs within the public realm is extremely important in shaping a society and its practices and identity. It is within political discourse that we most often find questions of the economic and the moral (sometimes religiously based, sometimes not) coming together, as Lichterman's study of progressive religious communities supports (2005). It is a place where people articulate their moral visions for society. As Wood argues, "such a moral vision does not replace the political power needed to change society but rather provides an ethical critique that can open up the status quo to alternatives promoted politically" (2002, 162).

Some of this happens outside the formal political sector. Weber stressed that civil society actors, through their discourse, have at times spurred market regulation (Swedberg 1998; Weber 1958). More recently, Bartley's study of certification systems (2007) finds that conflicts among actors, given voice through civil discourse, resulted in changes to voluntary regulation through certification efforts. The political climate inhibited more structural level change via public policies. Civil society can restrict the market, regulate business actors, and lead voluntary efforts to support or discourage certain actions.

This practice of discourse is also political in the way it builds the democracy. Cohen and Arato (1992) assert that discourse can provide actors with conflicting value systems a space for dialogue and for entertaining the views of others as valid. Making connections between values and public action is a collective process, and public discourse that brings people together to discuss the common good and the "just society" is vital to strong democracies (Hart 2001, 3–4). Through discursive acts, citizens confront their own conceptions of the good and explore their universality, which is crucial to a healthy democracy.

Such discourse is all the more important given the lack of a robust public discourse around issues of ethics and the economy. Technical discourse seems to dominate most political discussions, and the underlying moral or ethical values that guide our technical and economic decisions are not acknowledged. Hart notes that a discussion of the ethical values that should guide our actions is often missing from progressive political discourse. He further argues that "the capacity to express moral outrage, universal claims of justice, and visions of a better society is essential if progressive political initiatives are to prosper – or deserve to prosper" (2001, 4). Fostering moral discourse among political actors is itself a type of political action. It is only when new repertoires and unique ideas are articulated in the public realm that they have the ability to shape the imaginations of its citizens.

However, in much of the moral-political discourse, attention to religious communities is minimal at best, and absent at worst. This seems ironic, given the active role of many religious communities in such discourse. Hart, for example, notes that religion may be one of the few sources of "transcendent talk, using standards of values that are grounded in things outside of normal life ... and giving these standards a morally binding quality" (2001, 18). Eliasoph (1998) has also argued that religion is important in that it can provide the vocabulary to discuss larger value concerns. The three religious organizations in this book use religious values to talk about public life and economics; they rely on ideas such as community, solidarity, and covenant, using their religious identities as a source of authority.

Experience reveals that religious actors have historically served as such a source. In the last section of this chapter, I highlight the content of some key theological trajectories within the Christian faith (traditions that are utilized in varying degrees by the three case studies profiled in this book). Hofrenning (1995), in his study of U.S. politics, finds that it was often religious actors who brought in new political ideas and ideas outside the mainstream. This is not a claim that religious actors are leading the public dialogue, but that they often are involved in articulating new visions and igniting the moral imagination of citizens.

Religious organizations have power in part because they provide collective values that can be used by followers to engage the market. This "sacred canopy" of religion (Berger 1967) has the potential to shape economic understanding by declaring basic values about human interaction. Although Berger ultimately challenges whether this sacred canopy can hold up in the modern age, his argument assumes that religion can and has shaped our understanding of other social spheres and institutions. Secondly, values need to be embodied to have power within communities. As Lichterman argues, "a group needs much more than an incisive, articulate analysis of social problems in order to be a good conduit of consciousness raising. Groups need the *customs* that can welcome people to social criticism instead of scaring all but those already convinced" (2005, 4). Religious organizations should be examined for their discursive power not just because they can provide collective values, but also because they often provide communities in which such values exist alongside collectively shared rituals. Wood (1999), in his study of local justice efforts through the faith-based PICO organization, also noted that the power of religious ideas was largely based in the ways the ideas were enacted through practice.

But religious values do not automatically translate into economic values; such connections are nonexistent for many. Wuthnow (1994a) argues that most people, for example, take the economic system as given, using religion mostly to make sense of their reality. Such connections have to be made, and public discourse is one place where this can happen, making it all the more important. Steensland, in his study of mainline religious activists, argues that it is precisely their religious voices in the public realm that may be the most important part of the activism in which they engage; he sees their strength in "their role in raising theological informed moral questions about hunger, poverty, work, and the American economy" (2002, 231).

RELIGIOUS ACTORS AND THE PRODUCTION OF POLITICAL DISCOURSE

Given that values are never produced without actors, attention must focus on *who* is producing the discourse, and under what context and for whom it is being produced. Key actors involved in producing discourse are often interpreting the moral values of a community. Wuthnow has noted this repeatedly (1987, 1989, 1994b). He states,

As something not simply affirmed subjectively or internalized unconsciously but produced collectively, culture depends on social resources, and the availability and distribution of these resources is likely to play a major role in influencing the direction of cultural change ... The fact that cultural change comes about not so much from the experiences of masses of individuals but as the result of culture-producing organizations has been deemphasized in the classical theoretical literature.   (Wuthnow 1989, 539)

Organizational Context

We must consider the organizational context of the actors who are producing religious-political discourse to understand the discursive power actors hold. Organizational structures determine not only who has the authority to make decisions about ideology and discourse but also the procedures for such decisions. Wuthnow notes that "although [clergy] play a very important role in producing public religion, their roles differ depending on the organizational context in which they occur" (1994b, 7). Another contextual feature of organizations is their resources: finances, networks, cultural capital, and moral authority, all of which must be mobilized in cultural production.

In this book, I am looking specifically at religious hierarchies (Wuthnow 1994b).[2] There is a wide variation among hierarchies in how authority is delegated and how those in authority are selected; the cases in this book are selected in part to address that diversity. In the Catholic Church, for example, the Vatican appoints priests to serve as national bishops who produce influential discourse. One man can stay in power for many decades, and bishops lead under the authority of the Vatican. By contrast, in many Protestant bodies, the congregation has power to select their own leaders (and policies). Different levels of professional training are required to have religious authority in different settings. In ecumenical bodies, often no official religious training is required, and less authority may be granted to those who have official credentials.

A high degree of centralization and an emphasis on formal authority, however, do not equate to consistent stances over time. All religious context is variable, as individual personalities may hold a lot of power in directing an organization. Palacios (2007) has noted the different types of themes that different Fathers of the Catholic Church have developed. Within a localized context, Catholic Churches often pursue different agendas. Biography is important within religious communities, as it is more generally within social movements (Jasper 1992). Individual agents and their decisions and actions are often crucial to moments of change, even as the power wielded by these individuals remains largely a product of organizational structure.

Even in formal organizations, structures change over time. The experience of liberation theology in the Latin American Catholic Church prompted significant changes within Catholic authority structures there. As *comunidades de base*, or base communities, developed through this movement in the 1960s, citizens had more authority in interpreting and applying Catholic thought than they previously had held. As people read and discussed scripture and theology, they were effectively redefining and restructuring understandings of Catholic authority in their lives and communities. Even in one of the most centralized religious organizations – the global Catholic Church – changes in individual biographies and in organizational structures can bring about variation, reflected in the religious discourse.

Training of leaders and the requirements for authority are also important organizational issues. Different groups value various qualifications differently, and such qualifications can determine who is involved in producing religious teaching and discourse. Mehta and Winship (2010) have developed the concept of moral capability, which is determined by a person's place in a hierarchical

---

[2] In discussing hierarchies, Wuthnow notes four important sources of variation among them: the degree of centralization, the amount of emphasis on trained clergy, a rational/legal versus charismatic sense of authority, and a this-worldly versus other-worldly focus.

framework, her training, and her moral intentions. Within the cases that follow, I examine what gives groups and individuals such moral capabilities that they can speak with authority. The structures of authority, the people in authority, and group understandings of authority are interwoven and have strong implications for the sacred productions of organizations.

As discussed in Chapter 5, the question of religious authority has to differentiate between authority inside and outside the organization, which is connected to ideas of religious authority and state authority. That is, some of the sources that are authoritative for these religious communities – sacred texts, tradition, rationality, reason, community – translate more readily into secular authority than others.

The larger institutional context is part of understanding the organizational context. Organizations that are made up of individuals exist within larger societal institutions. As Friedland and Alford (1991) contend, these three levels – individuals, organizations, and institutions – operate in relationship with each other. Far from seeing organizations as autonomous actors, these authors argue for a conception of *embodied* organizations, which are governed not only by the resources at their disposal or even their leaders, but also by other individuals interacting with the organization, including members of the general public.

Institutional settings include the broader society as well as other organizations, such as other culture-producing institutions and elites (Wuthnow 1989, 547). Religious organizations have institutional relationships with the government, and these relationships impact the public role of such organizations. In her study of Catholic Church bodies throughout Latin America, Hagopian (2009b) argues for a number of key organizational factors that impact how churches will focus their political attention. The political risk that a church faces within a particular climate impacts which political issues they will emphasize (and which they will not). In some states, the church might be officially sanctioned; in others, it may be in conflict with the state over its public role. Burns (1990) argues that the political constraints upon religious actors are important shapers of the ideologies they adapt. For example, the move within the Catholic Church to treat social and political issues as distinct from religious ones was prompted by deteriorating relationships between the Catholic Church and European secular states. It was only in the beginning of the twentieth century, under the papacy of Leo XIII (1878–1903), that the church accepted and promoted such a division. It was in part a move to avoid conflict with governments (Burns 1990).

These relationships matter in terms of how groups identify their intended audiences, and how they try to engage society. As I argue in Chapter 5, their structural location as actors within their national societies is important to understanding how their religious authority translates into secular authority. While the PCUSA, for example, seeks to reform by speaking to those in power, Kairos engages in a more critical prophetic voice, and CECOR speaks from an official position of state authority. From organizations with a voice in the official political sector, we might expect different types of strategic action than from those holding more marginal positions within a society. As scholars of social movements have noted, regulations and structures of states often determine what sorts of political opportunities activists have; within a state, those with stronger relationships with the government may have more venues for political action available.

The National and International Context of Organizations

In focusing on the producers of discourse, it is also important to think about the context (and audience) of such discourse. I have selected cases from three different national contexts and, in so doing, am able to hypothesize some of the ways that national identity and location matter for the production of discourse. Each of these religious hierarchies is located within a specific national context. Yet despite the importance of national boundaries, religious organizations are positioned internationally as well, as part of a transnational network of actors (Lechner and Boli 2005). National religious bodies are connected with similar religious communities in different locations and often receive instruction or guidance from international bodies. These global networks can provide information to actors that can influence their perspectives and their taken-for-granted assumptions; this is especially important when it comes to issues of national politics related to the international political economy (such as free trade agreements).

Increasing global connectedness does not necessarily mean that national context has become less important. Rather, the national location of religious actors matters in important ways. In particular, these actors rely on different public repertories, they have different audiences toward which their discourse is directed, and they are linked with different national governmental actors and other power brokers. Their repertoires are influenced both by the national society in which they are located and by national and international theological traditions. Their audiences are primarily individuals within their national borders, but organizations also speak as a part of international bodies to a more global audience.

Nations often prioritize different values systems; or, as Lamont and Thévenot (2000) describe it, they have different repertoires. These authors argue that different cultural repertoires exist in different national contexts; people evaluate social life based on those values that are best articulated in their national toolkits. Using such a framework, Boltanski and Thevénot (2006) discuss the different grammars of worth and orders of justification people employ. They argue that differences across national contexts are perhaps best understood as a difference in the tools that are readily available to citizens, versus distinct cultures with disparate values. For example, they note that people in France are more likely to use the rhetoric and logic of civic solidarity than those in the United States, in large part because that framework is accessible within their national society.

As a result, religious bodies (and other social actors) within these nations speak in varied contexts and adjust their discourse to their unique national situations. In looking specifically at the issue of abortion rights, a cross-national study of Germany and the United States finds that similar religious groups in these varied settings speak about the topic differently. Ferree, Gamson, Gerhards, and Rucht (2002) find that religious discourse differs based in part on the different political opportunity structures. Appeals to "morality" are more prevalent in the United States, while appeals to "life" are more common in Germany.

Discourse varies not just because of opportunity structures, but also because of the experiences groups have within specific national and local contexts. Palacios (2007) argues that churches' responses have differed depending on the problems within particular geographical settings. He notes, "The social justice doctrine of the [Catholic] Church arises out of real life situations of poverty, violence, discrimination, hate, etc." (2007, 212–213). Much like the emerging literature on lived religion suggests, religious life is lived out in particular contexts. This reality in part led the Catholic Church to assert in Vatican II (1962–1965) that national churches were to articulate a theology for their particular setting (Casanova 1994; Wilde 2007). Protestant bodies, likewise, retain national autonomy, even as they enter into more global alliances,[3] where important national differences (often between the global north and global south) persist.

Different partnerships with governments and different views of the state among nationals have led to different conceptions of religion's national role among the religious actors in each country. Palacios (2007) provides yet another case, finding that the Catholic Church in Mexico has opted for an ecclesial approach to problems, while the U.S. Catholic Church has been more focused on social ministry. He argues that the historical-political development of the countries allows different political opportunities for religious actors, with implications for how actors may bring their faith into the public square. Doctrines of the separation of church and state as well as a strong civil society have prompted the U.S. Church to make social justice part of its structures, while in Mexico, with a weaker civil society and a more contentious church-state relationship, the Church has been "limited [in] imagination" in terms of how doctrine may move into the political sphere (2007, 228–30). Hagopian (2009b) finds that variation (among different national Catholic Church bodies in Latin America) is less about differences in the Church's position on an issue, and more about which aspect the Church chooses to prioritize in light of its political context.

The same type of variation, as discussed in more detail within the different case studies, exists in the cases being examined here. Past research, for example, finds that those in the United States are more likely than others to rely on individualistic assumptions or market evaluations (Lipset 1990; Lamont and

---

[3] For example, the World Council of Churches, the World Alliance of Reformed Churches, or the Lausanne Congress.

Thévenot 2000). Although appeals to the common good are common across many countries, Lamont and Thévenot have found that this concept often has different connotations in different settings; for example, in the United States (as compared to France), the common good is often seen less as a concept in itself, and more as a "coalition of interests" (2000, 13–14).

International networks are a central way in which such nationalistic influences are tempered. As mentioned previously, global networks provide actors with information that can influence their perspectives and assumptions. Smith (1996), in his analysis of the Central America peace movement, shows how international networks of religious actors across borders mobilized churches in the United States to protest U.S. intervention in Central America, in large part through providing information. Likewise, Woodberry (2012) argues that missionaries during African colonialism played a vital role in sharing information, bringing details of the political and human rights violations occurring in the Congo and other colonies to churches in the West, who then protested such inhumane treatment. I find a similar dynamic to be at work for the cases here, as networks are extremely important in transferring information and informing action. National identities, international alliances, and transnational networks all influence discursive strategies, specifically as it relates to trade and the global economy.

CULTURAL RESOURCES OF RELIGIOUS TRADITIONS

Religion's emphasis on the transcendent offers unique authoritative resources when it comes to political discourse and provides cultural materials for a value-laden public dialogue (Hart 2001). The following chapters examine the nature of the warrants and values that religious organizations use in their political engagement over trade. Such warrants and values draw in part from religious traditions, especially those historically engaged with the political world. Given that "cultural traditions provide the raw material for creating and revising the means and ends of protest – but also for determining the boundary between means and ends" (Jasper 1997, 83), it is not surprising that religious groups rely on sacred texts and historical theological narratives.

Although there is variation both between and within Protestant and Catholic bodies in terms of theological traditions, given historical realities, pieces of the Catholic tradition are important to most Christian communities, which these cases affirm. In both Catholic social teaching (CST) and the more renegade liberation theology, theologians have engaged questions of capitalism and the political economy. Catholic and non-Catholic actors alike reference their conclusions. Just as Hart (1992) finds that people use similar theologies to support diverse economic positions, different actors utilize Catholic teaching in different ways. Among Protestants, different traditions have supported varied views of the world. For example, Presbyterians are influenced by the American Reformed intellectual tradition, with a this-worldly emphasis on engaging one's social world. The Lutheran tradition, while calling for engagement, accentuates the difference between the sacred and the secular, and employs more of a separate spheres mentality.

H. Richard Neibuhr's *Christ and Culture* (1951) is still widely referenced for its typology of how Christians engage with the world and the larger culture. He proposed five models: Christ against culture, Christ of culture, Christ above culture, Christ and culture in paradox, and Christ transforming culture. In terms of religious groups seeking to assert their moral authority in the public realm, the ideas of Christ of culture, Christ above culture, and Christ transforming culture are perhaps the most pertinent.[4] Christ of culture emphasizes the agreement between Christ and culture, with its attention to the teachings of Christ; comparatively, Christ above culture holds that Christ represents the fullness of what society could and should look like. Christ transforming culture does see some opposition between Christ and culture, but seeks to find a way for culture to be involved in redemption and true reformation.

These distinctions speak not only on the proper role of religious communities in social (and economic) life, but also to the proper role of economic authorities. Chapter 5 details the different understandings of religious communities when it comes to their role, and the role of others, in the economic realm. In that chapter, I describe three models that exist: religion as a framework to shape policy, religion as a lens to evaluate policy, and religion as practices to dictate policy.

Catholic Social Teaching

The canon of CST begins in 1891, with the publication of *Rerum Novarum* under Pope Leo XIII. Regarded as the first social encyclical, it was penned after the Enlightenment, when the Catholic Church was no longer part of the ruling elite (Burns 1990). When the Church retreated from temporal affairs, it began the task of reframing its public role (Burns 1992). Social issues were deemed distinct from "faith and morals," and created a hierarchy where social issues were less central than those of personal faith (Burns 1992).

Yet social issues were still validated as worthy of religious attention. Since the emergence of CST, the Catholic Church has written volumes on how to relate personal faith to issues of social importance, including the political economy. Undeniable is that CST has consistently voiced criticisms against the capitalist system and has often taken a centrist position between capitalism and socialism, pointing out the flaws with both systems (Hug 2005). Human dignity, the social nature of humans, the common good, subsidiarity, solidarity, a preferential option for the poor, and social justice are the core principles of CST (Coleman

---

[4] The idea of Christ against culture pits religion against the customs of society; the idea of Christ and culture in paradox relies on a more Lutheran understanding of the separate nature of religion and politics, much like the sentiment expressed in the opening quotation of this chapter from *The Economist*.

2005). Human dignity is at the center of this theology, and Pope Pius XI declared its importance for economic and social life in *Quadragesimo Anno* (1931), written in the midst of economic depression (Palacios 2007). Human dignity is about understanding the nature, rights, and responsibilities of people, and it is predicated on the assumption that humans are embedded in families, groups, and society itself (Coleman 2005). Linking the nature of the individual to the trinitarian nature of God, people are defined as relational – they cannot be understood outside of their relationships. Recent work such as a declaration on economic justice by the U.S. Conference of Catholic Bishops (1986) links the notion of dignity with vocation, viewing humans as coworkers with God in His mission for the world.

The common good is also crucial to CST. *Rerum Novarum* named this as a central principle of the Church. Barbieri suggests that the common good is the "linchpin" of CST, noting its foundational connection with subsequent principles of subsidiarity, solidarity, and a preferential option for the poor (2001, 728). Within CST, the global nature of the common good has become increasingly important. Two encyclicals of Pope John XXIII (1958–1963), *Mater et Magistra* (1961) and *Pacem in Terris* (1963) – as well as *Guadium et Spes*, one of the constitutions set forth from the Second Vatican Council – are examples of this increased attention to international global community (Barbieri 2001).

The Catholic notion of subsidiarity builds on principles of dignity and the common good and has direct implications for public policy and economic life. Subsidiarity is about the power of the local and the responsibility of the global; it demands that decisions be made at the most local level possible yet references the responsibility of the state or national government to ensure basic welfare. In other words, the state should empower other groups to fulfill their special roles. Monsma (2006) has connected this Catholic idea of subsidiarity to sphere sovereignty as employed by the Reformed tradition. Sphere sovereignty also suggests that the state and other groups each have their own complementary roles to fulfill.

Social justice is perhaps the central discipline of CST, drawing heavily on the idea of solidarity. "Justice" is a positive idea within CST, as people are called to actions that "enhance human dignity and the love of neighbor" (Cima and Schubeck 2001, 224). Justice is relational in CST, and rights are always tied with obligations. The teaching promotes action within communities and the world (Palacios 2007).

Liberation Theology

In some ways, liberation theology is simply an extension of CST, although it differs significantly from traditional CST. At its core, it is a political ideology that makes claims about what economic and political life should look like; social issues are the substance of this approach, and not a secondary concern. Daudelin and Hewitt (1995) argue that it is best characterized as a social movement within the Catholic Church. That said, focusing on the political nature of liberation theology could obscure the pastoral focus also present in this line of thought (Mainwaring and Wilde 1989), and so these two goals must be considered together.

It was in Latin America in the middle of the twentieth century that bishops encouraged the local priests and faithful to become more engaged with issues of economic justice (prompting some of the institutional changes wrought by Vatican II [1962–1965]). In the 1960s, the Latin American Catholic Church lost its monopoly in the region; Protestant evangelization and Marxism attracted growing numbers of the impoverished population (Wilde 2007). Engaging the poor and unchurched within Latin America was necessary for Catholic vitality, and in 1967, Pope Paul VI (1963–1978) produced *Populorum Progressio*, which Smith (1991) and Nuñez (1985) argue took the most radical stand on social issues to date within the Catholic Church. (More generally, Paul VI's reign is known for its pronouncements against capitalism [Burns 1992].)

For the theologians at the center of the movement, the focus was not centrally about doctrine but about the actions that produce true liberation. Secondary, and following liberating action, comes reflection on the actions taken (Smith 1991). Gustavo Gutiérrez, often considered the father of liberationist thought, called for a reflection that challenged the standard understanding of theology's role. Theology, though a source of wisdom and knowledge, was chiefly useful to "interpret historical events with the intention of revealing and proclaiming their profound meaning" (Gutiérrez [1973] 2006, 10). In addition to the view of religion as largely an issue of practice, three central themes run throughout liberation theology: an emphasis on the poor as God's people (and so the need for solidarity with them), attention to the work of Christ in the world, and a focus on the role of sin and conflict in society.

Solidarity is a core value in CST, as established in Vatican II. This Catholic solidarity has been called a "middle way between liberal capitalism and state socialism" (Palacios 2007, 44), for it sees society as a whole yet comprised of autonomous individuals. It expands on the notions of justice and equality, concerning itself not only with the suffering of one's neighbor but also the story behind the suffering. Solidarity is linked with the Catholic Church's "preferential option for the poor" and was described by Pope John Paul II as an indispensable part of God's "divine plan, both on the level of individuals and on the level of national and international society" (The Vatican 1987, Part 40). However, a more profound concept of solidarity has been strongly heralded by many liberationists, and Palacios finds that it is the principle most developed in regard to their efforts at social justice (2007, 38–39). The liberationist notion of solidarity that brought the Catholic Church into poor communities throughout Latin America moved from the CST "middle way" toward sympathies with socialism (Palacios 2007, 51).

Liberation theology is a contextual theology that engages one's social situation. Salvation cannot be understood outside of one's political and social context, and no dichotomy exists between the sacred and the profane. As Gutiérrez notes, there are not two histories in the world but rather "one human destiny: His [Christ's] redemptive work embraces all the dimensions of existence and brings them to their fullness" ([1973] 2006, 86). According to liberation theology, economic and political systems are central to the Christian salvific story of the cross, and the work of Christ in the world is integrally connected with the person of Christ incarnate.

Sin and conflict are central theological ideas for liberationists. In calling the church to be on the side of "oppressed classes" and "dominated peoples" [1973] 2006, 174, Gutiérrez argues that suffering and poverty are the result of sin in the world – in this case, sin committed by the whole of society. The Church must "subvert an order of injustice" (Gutiérrez [1973] 2006, 174). An emphasis on sin and conflict is one reason early liberationists were linked with Marxism. As Smith notes, liberationist thought was connected with Marxist-inspired economic logic; he argues, "the diffusion of dependency theory was rapid within the Church" (1991, 147). Dependency theory analyzed the larger international political economy in terms of class conflict and struggle. It links advances in development with underdevelopment, and differentiates between those countries in the center and those in the periphery.

Liberation theology arose in a developing-country context. It was and is a theology for those who are oppressed by the political and economic order, who see themselves involved personally in the class struggles against the powerful. Yet such a theology has gained support from those with more power in the social structure as well. Carney (2001) has discussed the crisis of faith, a *via negativa*, that occurs for many of privilege as they engage liberation theology. Today one of the theological questions for Kairos is what it means to embrace liberation theology within the context of the developed world (which is addressed in Chapter 2).

Lutherans and State Engagement

The Lutheran legacy is one where faith and action are closely linked. Two realms of life exist, the world and the church, and God operates in different ways in dealing with those in this world and those in the church. Luther recognized that God's sovereignty was at play in both of these areas. For Luther, the justice and love of God were ideas that could not be separated (Forrester 1997, 207). Sigrun Kahl has examined the ways that Lutheran perspectives in Europe shaped the structure of welfare states, and play an important part in many of the structures that exist throughout the West today. Luther, she argues, was involved in writing the first Protestant poor law for Wittenberg in 1520. Although ideas of the undeserving poor were part of this system, the history of working with the government and collaborating with the state was central. Luther's ideas about the importance of the state recast poor relief as entitlement over charity (Kahl 2009). Compared with other groups, it seems that the earliest Lutheran witness supported state action more than many of the free churches in Europe (Manow and van Kersbergen 2009). Although the two realms of the world and the church are separate, the Lutheran tradition often emphasizes one's need to be obedient to authorities in both places (causing Neibuhr to see it as an example of Christ and culture in paradox).

One source of contestation within the tradition seems to be the question of supporting state efforts to help the poor or supporting religious institutions involved in welfare provision. Lutherans have relied on this tradition to support both increased states and religious institutional action, even as the influence of the Lutheran church has been less within the United States than in Europe (Noll 1992). We have examples, in Canada, for example, where the Lutheran church was active in calling for more action by the state, and more links between faith and action with society (Lind and Mihevc 1994). Yet in the United States, we find that the Lutheran church, generally speaking, is perhaps the least supportive of the welfare state and welfare spending within the mainline Protestant tradition (Hertzke 1988, 142).

The Reformed Tradition

The Reformed tradition offers a number of intellectual resources regarding the role of religion in the world, resources utilized by the PCUSA, as detailed in Chapter 3. Within the larger Protestant community, it is Calvin's legacy of Reformed thought that is often considered the intellectual side of the church. This tradition grants increased authority to scripture and to the principles of the Reformation (including endorsement of individuals' intellectual interpretation of scripture). It also has had a key role in the development of societal structures within the United States, including colleges and governing institutions.

There are differences, especially among some of the various ethnic traditions that came together within the American Reformed community, concerning what constitutes the essence of the Reformed tradition. At its heart, adherents ascribe to Luther's statements of "faith alone," "grace alone," and "scripture alone." Women and men are fallen individuals, following from Calvin's ideas about original sin. God's sovereignty is central. Such beliefs produce attention to the necessity for God's grace and finally to the concept of God's election over and above individual choice. Boice argues that Reformed theology "tends to put reality together and thus make sense of life as other systems of theology do not" (1985, 301). Although there is variation on many hermeneutical questions of how to interpret and apply scripture, there is often a high view of scripture among members of this community. Related to the social questions, there also has been an emphasis on the work of Christians in this world as well – activity should be meaningful. Neibuhr saw Calvin and his followers pursuing a model of Christ transforming culture.

Weber's popular thesis linking Calvinism and the rise of capitalism argues that a Reformed ethic promoted savings and hard work (1958). Yet in spite of its endorsement of a strong work ethic, the Reformed tradition recognized that industrialization caused social ills. So, intellectual and institutional engagement of this issue was especially important to Presbyterians and other Reformed actors. They established institutions to provide social services to society and saw welfare provision as part of the church's role.

Unlike a more Catholic perspective, Reformed churches saw their main role as contributing to civil society, raising up voluntary organizations to promote social change. The Confession of 1967, a central document for the PCUSA that was implemented shortly after Vatican II, redefined the relationship between scripture and social action. It emphasized the social ethic as part of the faith. Come ([1983] 2001) has argued that the declaration of the social ethic as part of God's reconciling plan was the most significant aspect of the creed, as the work of Christ and the person of Christ became more integrally connected. Context also became important for this tradition as actors engaged their world and scripture was conceived of as a living document that adjusted to new occasions (Coalter 1999).

Protestant Ecumenicalism in Social Engagement

Though it has a shorter history and less authority, and lacks one central story, the Protestant tradition offers important discursive tools for religious actors. Scripture and experience tend to occupy a more central role than they do within Catholic settings, although interpretation of these scriptures and experiences is more open to debate. Still, alongside the debate is a thriving ecumenical movement that tends to minimize doctrinal differences for the sake of important social issues.

The Federal Council of Churches (FCC), a Protestant ecumenical body, was created in 1908, and with it came the development of the Social Creed. The creed called for increased protection of workers, renewed attention to rights, increased wages, and a more equitable division of profits. Most scholars agree that current ecumenical efforts within Christianity largely began with the 1908 formation of the FCC (Wilde 2007) and are now an important part of the Protestant tradition. To be fair, although evangelicalism as a movement in the United States was not institutionalized until the 1940s, many leaders within denominations that would join the evangelical movement were not part of the FCC (Carpenter 2013). The early twentieth century witnessed discussions on Canada over the idea of one united Protestant body, with the United Church of Canada[5] becoming a reality in 1925. Historian Mark Noll notes that the hopes for this new national body were ambitious, especially in terms of their engagement with society (1992, 281–282).

---

[5] The four denominations that came together to form this merger were the Methodist Church of Canada, the Presbyterian Church in Canada, the Congregational Union, and the Association of Local Union Churches.

The principles embodied in the Social Creed were bringing churches together as early as the late 1800s to address contemporary social problems in the United States. Poverty, inequality, and crime were central foci of the church discourse. Issues associated with industrialism supported the increased involvement of churches in social matters. Evans (2001) argues that the Social Creed was evidence of such an ecumenical alliance united around social reform.

The creed also served as an important catalyst for the growth of the Social Gospel movement. Those associated with the Social Gospel movement were a subset of the larger Protestant world and even of those adopting the Social Creed. At the same time, the Social Creed indicated increased reception of the principles behind the Social Gospel within the broader Protestant community. Spurred in part by Social Gospel efforts, the beginning of the twentieth century witnessed many new ecumenical alliances that still exist today.

In fact, Protestant efforts with welfare provision in the United States were such that Steensland finds they historically have been the largest nonprofit providers for the poor (2002) and among the most vocal critics of the economic systems in place, even though the media often did not cover these groups. The Presbyterian Church in the United States (PCUSA), the focus of Chapter 3, fits squarely within the ecumenical Protestant community and their efforts toward social engagement. Hopkins (1940) finds that the PCUSA was the first Protestant body to have paid staff working on Social Gospel efforts; he argues that they served an important role in bringing other Protestant churches toward more social engagement.

In more recent history, mainline Protestant churches have continued to engage social questions, even as the Social Gospel movement never ultimately reached its goals. As Thuesen notes, many in the ecumenical movements have a "perennial confidence . . . in the reforming power of denominational institutions" (2002, 27). Thuesen goes on to argue that within this ecumenical movement, there is a commitment both to cooperation and tolerance of ethical differences, as well as a commitment to a strong public role for the church.

CONCLUSION

Values are one aspect of culture that can significantly influence how people think about economic markets, market behaviors, and market agreements. At the same time, economic and political activity can redefine or reinforce certain values. Norms and values play a role in a number of ways, from establishing the foundational understandings people have about economics, exchange, and the community to regulating action within markets and setting boundaries on what transactions should enter into what realm. Discussion that occurs within a wide range of spaces in the public arena is itself a political act often meant to challenge, reify, or redefine systems within society.

This discourse does not just occur but is constructed and expressed by cultural producers. These producers are impacted as institutional settings constrain and direct their ultimate cultural products. The political and economic context of organizations is especially important to understanding how values are brought to bear on the economy. The position of an organization influences not only how the members experience the economy, but also how they understand economic dynamics and realities.

Religious organizations have some unique resources as cultural producers of economic discourse. Religion serves as a source of collective values that have implications for the market, and it provides networks that influence how groups understand the market. Especially in times of economic change, religious traditions have historically engaged political and economic concerns. Yet within the academic literature, questions still remain about how religious values are being translated into economic values. Understanding how religious organizations produce and use sacred economic discourse aids in our understanding not only of the processes of market construction but also of the factors that influence how actors participate in these processes.

2

Too Flawed for Reform: The Canadian Christian Struggle for an Alternative Economic Order

> In our analysis, more economic independence for Canada is essential if we are to be able to stand in solidarity with other peoples seeking independence and social justice.
>
> – Dillon (1987, 11)

This thesis was explored in a 1987 self-reliance conference hosted for civil society actors by GATT-Fly, a Canadian interchurch coalition protesting the nature of Canada's participation in the international economy. GATT-Fly's very first staff member, John Dillon, publicly argued for economic policy alternatives "to move closer to the top of the [national] agenda" (2007). Although the form of Canadian ecumenical efforts has changed significantly over time, with Kairos today replacing the work of GATT-Fly, Canadian interchurch coalitions represent a sustained example of modern religious activism surrounding trade policy.

What most stands out about these coalitions is their early critical engagement with trade policy. At a time when many citizens were naïve about the effects of globalism, GATT-Fly was not only advocating for an alternative economic order within both Canada and the international community, but also raising and directing resources toward producing new research on the topic. Their 1987 self-reliance conference prompted them that same year to produce the *Free Trade Dossier*, which contained research on alternatives to current international trade paradigms. It secured GATT-Fly's position as a research engine for the larger anti–free trade movement.

GATT-Fly (1973–1990) evolved into the Ecumenical Coalition for Economic Justice (ECEJ) (1990–2001) and eventually merged with other religious coalitions to form Kairos (2001–present). Although several Protestant churches (the Anglican, Presbyterian, Lutheran, and United Church of Canada denominations) and the Roman Catholic Church supported the creation of GATT-Fly, the ecumenical coalition and its later editions have never been traditional religious bodies. The size and breadth of the coalitions, for instance, would be hard to pin down, as would be their specific leadership structures. GATT-Fly and ECEJ, as independent organizations, had a high level of autonomy. As Kairos, however, they have become more formally connected to their religious support-ers. Today, even though staff members are the creators of most discourse produced by the organization, policy is meant to represent the denominational members, and religious volunteers remain the life of the movement. Starting with Dillon as the sole staff member in 1973, the group has employed at most four staff members at a time to work on economic justice issues. Volunteer committees provide feedback on staff-produced materials, and a board of denominational leaders serves as a clearinghouse to approve policies passed by the coalition. The endorsing denominations also provide the bulk of the group's financial support.

In this chapter, I use personal interviews as well as information from eighty-eight internal and public documents to explore the historical development and political stance of GATT-Fly, ECEJ, and Kairos since the 1970s. As evidenced by their prolific discourse – including not only research reports and policy state-ments but also news briefings, calls for action, periodicals, worship resources, and other internal documents – they have consistently endorsed markets that focused on the poor, transparent political processes, and autonomous regulation of state economies. This opposition to the economic order has been facilitated by a cadre of religious activists who have enjoyed significant freedom within the organizations. Crucial to the theology that has guided the coalitions are the moral understandings of solidarity, community, empowerment, equality, and the sacredness of creation. Also important is their Canadian context, which has naturally changed over the years. Throughout their existence, several organiza-tional factors have been important to these groups, including close personal networks with partners outside their borders and a flexible relationship with strong churches. Such factors have guided the organizations to be politically vocal and often critical of the status quo. Today, Kairos remains a marginal community within the larger Canadian Christian church setting.

SELF-SUFFICIENCY AS ECONOMIC JUSTICE

Policy Activism through Education and Empowerment

Although there have been changes in the political alternatives the coalitions (GATT-Fly, ECEJ, and now Kairos) have advocated in their forty-one-year history, their basic political stance has stayed consistent. GATT-Fly's purpose was to protest the General Agreement on Tariffs and Trade (GATT) and other international development policy. Members were among the first, both in inter-national religious circles and in Canadian civil society, to speak extensively and critically about the trade policies developing from GATT. They critiqued both the powerful role of wealthy countries within GATT, as well as the consequences of trade liberalization for developing countries.

Joe Gunn, a long-time member of the coalitions and recent co-chair of the Kairos board, attested to this in an interview. In describing the activism of GATT-Fly in its beginning stages (the 1970s and 1980s), he noted, "A lot of people in Canada were trying to point out these issues [concerns about free trade agreements, or FTAs], and they did, and they had colleague organizations. . . . But for the most part I don't think it had sunk in at the church level, so I would guess the Canadians were further ahead on these trade issues than many, many others" (2008).

In protest of the export-oriented model supported by GATT, GATT-Fly pushed for countries to be independent and more inwardly focused in their development. Self-reliance was the staple of GATT-Fly's early agenda; it called for governments to manage their own economies, to run supply-management boards, and to reject the prioritization of exports. However, "By self-reliance we do not mean autarchy, that is absolute self sufficiency in everything," the coalition argued. "We do mean a planned economy in which meeting the **basic needs of everyone** comes first and in which doing this from domestic production is preferred" (GATT-Fly 1985b, 4).

Because of early disillusionments, GATT-Fly's emphasis soon shifted from lobbying international organizations and the government in order to change international dynamics, to educating and empowering workers through grass-roots action. One of GATT-Fly's first projects in the 1970s, for instance, cen-tered on raising the international price of sugar. But the subsequent increase in international sugar prices was judged a failure, as it did not produce real economic change for poor farmers. GATT-Fly changed its approach, proposing instead an entirely new alternative economic order that would increase the power enjoyed by the small sugar farmers. Along these lines, Dillon wrote *Limitations of the Trade Issue* (1973) and the *New International Economic Order* (1976). GATT-Fly also produced *Paying the Piper: How Working People Are Saddled with the Debt from Huge Resource Projects while the Banks and Corporate "Pipers" Call the Tune* (1977), and *The Power to Choose: Canada's Energy Options* (1981). These publications and the research behind them were meant to be part of a praxis-reflection model, by which an oppressed class of people are encouraged to creatively pursue their own liberation. *Ah-Hah: A New Approach to Popular Education* (1983a) was the clearest example of this type of discourse from GATT-Fly; it was a guide for grassroots education seminars that would promote a message of self-reliance.

These and other publications (such as *Canada's Food Trade: By Bread Alone?* [1978a] and *Canada's Food: The Road to Self-Reliance* [1979]) set the stage for GATT-Fly's self-reliance conference. In 1987, they released a report, *Building Self-Reliance in Canada*. That same year, GATT-Fly initiated the Pro-Canada Network (renamed as the Action Canada Network [ACN] in 1991) an alliance opposing free trade.[1] Within

---

[1] Howlett (1994) argues that this alliance had its start with the Canada–United States FTA negotia-tions. Indeed, the events did coincide and clearly were linked.

the ACN, GATT-Fly's role as a research engine solidified. Their monthly *Free Trade Dossier* was changed to the *Pro-Canada Dossier* in March of 1989 and came under the jurisdiction of ACN.

GATT-Fly continued to identify themselves as key architects of the self-reliance alternative. As they stated in their own history, "While a number of Third World economists such as Clive Thomas and Samir Amin had developed and advocated self-reliance for Third World economies, GATT-Fly ... was one of the first to apply this analysis to industrialized economies like Canada's" (Howlett 1994, 106). They were clearly concerned with the fate of those outside their borders, but a more independent and empowered Canada, they argued, could better stand in solidarity with other countries in resisting an export-oriented, free-market system. Their 1987 conference, for instance, included other civil society organizations such as Mexican antitrade activists.

By 1990, when the organization became ECEJ, *Economic Justice Reports* had become a central focus of their work. These publications continued the research and information dissemination GATT-Fly had become known for and included a report on intellectual property rights (1993b), an action kit against Free Trade Area of the Americas (FTAA) (1994), and background papers on a number of initiatives. Some of the more public and widely distributed reports included *Challenging the Free Trade in Canada: The Real Story* by John Dillon (1996) and *Recolonization or Liberation: The Bonds of Structural Adjustment and Struggles for Emancipation* by ECEJ (1990b). Symbolizing an increasing commitment to church linkages, staff also produced pieces in the *Economic Justice Reports* that dealt exclusively with the theology of the movement.

After the Canada–United States FTA had been expanded in 1994 into the North American Free Frade Agreement (NAFTA), global talks began for the FTAA. As NAFTA went into effect, ECEJ produced their action kit on the "Economic Integration of the Americas." This set of resources, directed at mobilizing people against the FTAA, insisted that such an agreement would have detrimental impacts on health care, labor unions, intellectual property rights, labor and work, the environment, and the status of women. Through utilizing resources from partners outside the North – such as the Mexican Free Trade Network (RMALC) – ECEJ made a clear statement about the negative impacts of NAFTA. They asserted that under NAFTA, the democratic process had been undermined as energy reserves were exploited and drained, health and safety standards lowered, water diverted, and family farms threatened.

In the 1980s and early 1990s, FTAs were a hot topic of political conversation and controversial debate within Canada. But since then, political temperatures on the topic have cooled. Kairos has continued to protest FTAs and their production process, but they have been less vocal against the free trade model more generally. Action alerts were issued against the FTAA in 2004, the World Trade Organization (WTO) in 2005, and the CA4FTA in 2006; such alerts called for changes to FTAs, but did not clearly reject the treaties. Dillon explained this shift in approach: "I think if you go back through things that we did as ECEJ, you would discern very clear statements that say we were always against NAFTA or against the free trade agreement bilaterally, etc. Today you probably wouldn't get a national church body in Canada taking such a clear position" (Dillon 2007). And so Kairos, now aligned with these same church bodies, has traded in insistence on foundational changes in market structures for restrictions and boundaries within the established system. A key concern, for instance, has been chapter 11, a section of NAFTA reproduced in other FTAs, that grants transnational corporations increased legal power in their interactions with national states. The clause has proved costly to many developing states in court proceedings and lawsuits from corporations, so Kairos has called for restrictions on its application.

The Shift to Grassroots Action

As described previously, the organization that was GATT-Fly, then ECEJ, and now Kairos underwent an early shift from an international policy focus to a grassroots emphasis on the oppressed. Ruttan (1987) referred to this initial shift as one from a functionalist to a voluntaristic perspective; that is, GATT-Fly shifted their view that systems could be reformed to one that characterized the system itself as victimizing the poor. Although the group never rejected government lobbying, such political efforts have been a small part of their overall strategy. The importance of such efforts, however, has increased under Kairos.

Renewed attention by Kairos to lobbying was in part due to a new organizational identity. ECEJ and GATT-Fly had not claimed to represent any particular church policy; the coalitions were intended to develop new and controversial ideas, on particular economic topics, in order to facilitate discussion about change. Kairos, by contrast, was officially meant to represent the church, and the coalition has increased its petitioning of the state as a result. This is not to suggest that their petitioning has shown more potential for success than in the past but rather that Kairos has employed different strategies than did their predecessors in trying to speak to those in power.

Part of the reason the coalitions centrally relied on grassroots mobilization instead of governmental lobbying is because they sought a high degree of change. Since GATT-Fly was formed, the coalitions have declared that small reforms would not suffice; they wanted to see a total *re*-creation of the economic order. Consequently, their research has been driven by this ambitious renovation of society. A central goal of their efforts has been to provide an alternative voice to neoliberalism not found in the dominant scholarship, a voice that calls for nothing less than radical change – which naturally entails conflict. Dillon recounted how this rejection of mere reform was both practical and based on experience, giving an example from attempts to reform the World Bank.

Wolfowitz announced three initiatives. One was the SAPRI, Structural Adjustment Participatory Review Initiative.... The other was the World Commission on Dams, and the third was the Extractive Industries Review.... And each of these cases came out with a report. And in every case, you can document quite clearly, the Bank didn't change policies in any fundamental way.... [Initially], one could give the benefit of the doubt that maybe the World Bank can be reformed. Then you go through the era and see that all of the effort put into these inquiries didn't pay off in any fundamental change. (2007)

Yet, after nearly 40 years of business as usual in trade politics, is Kairos losing hope for significant change? On the contrary, even as they have focused their energy on restrictions and boundaries, the coalitions' activists are still hopeful that an alternative economic order could exist. In our 2007 interview, Dillon pointed to the fact that radical change could still be on the horizon and that Kairos wants to be there to usher it in:

Now you've got a very exciting situation.... Southern governments – Argentina, Bolivia, Venezuela, Ecuador, and Brazil to a lesser extent, are leaving aside the bank [World Bank] and the Fund [International Monetary Fund, or IMF]. They're not even participating in it. So a couple of weeks ago when I was up testifying at the Commons Committee, I said, "You know, it's not without possibility that the era of these institutions is coming to an end, and Canada should be prepared to engage in a constructive debate." But what will replace them? ... Very few groups have actually sat down and written, I admit, a utopian-sounding documentation of what a new international financial system might look like. But that's where we *want* to be. (2007)

This utopian vision, according to Kairos, must include markets that serve the poor rather than elites, the recognition that FTAs and their negotiation process threaten democracy, and the endorsement of limited global governance and strong states.

Free Markets Lead to Exploitation of the Poor

The interchurch coalitions have argued that the poor in developing nations and within Canada are hurt by free trade. They have asserted that markets must be government regulated, according to moral values and practices. Free markets, they assert, fail to protect the poor from immoral practices of powerful elites. In addition, FTAs grant even more power to the elite and business sectors over the state, adding to economic inequality and the disadvantaged position of the poor.

Some marginalized groups have received special notice in the coalitions' discussions of human rights, especially women, for whom free markets have been not only been harmful but also sites of violence. The work of Kairos in Mexico, for instance, examines the economic and physical burdens of women working in *maquilas*. Kairos's *Global Economic Justice* reports (produced under the direction of Rusa Jeremic) have noted that the agricultural crisis has disproportionately affected women. In rural settings, women are the primary caregivers yet often deal with harsh working conditions and face discrimination regarding financial access to credit.

For the coalitions, the authority to lift the burdens off the shoulders of the poor comes from the top. They have rejected the idea of markets as autonomous, seeing them rather as subject to the principles of *God's* economy. This idea has been strongly reinforced by the Jubilee Movement. As Cormie (2004) noted, and I expand upon later in the chapter, three key aspects of the Jubilee Movement[2] stressed by the coalitions have been release from bondage (empowerment of people), redistribution of wealth (promoting God's economy and community), and a renewal of the earth (ecological concern for creation). Although Jubilee theology was not in place until the late 1990s, its ideas and theology were quickly embraced by the coalitions and drew upon values already shared by those active in their work. An explicit example of this theology can be found in a 1999 *Economic Justice Report*:

> When God created His economy, He made us its custodian. He therefore not only gave us the right to use the economy, but also the duty to take care of and account for it properly.... Every 50th year was the jubilee year (Leviticus 25:9–15). This was set aside for the redistribution of wealth among people of Israel ... widespread inequality and oppression were against God's will. The sabbatical and jubilee years were set to restore economic justice. The verse rejects perpetual bondage, and Christians should reject policies that in effect create the same.   (ECEJ 2000b, 15)

Market restriction would be the key to enforcing this Jubilee theology, as the poor are powerless to shape the decisions of society and to guarantee their own rights. In an ethical reflection piece produced for the *Economic Justice Report*, ECEJ stated,

> While the denominations may emphasize different aspects of the issues raised by free trade, a basic Christian principle shared by every church involved with ECEJ asserts that the common good of people takes priority over the private accumulation of profits. Therefore the basic question addressed by this report concerns whether the existing FTA or the proposed NAFTA *enhance or inhibit the ability of ordinary people*, and of governments, to provide for the common good, understood in terms of adequate food, shelter, clothing, employment, education and health care.   (italics added; ECEJ 1991, 1)

More recently, and framed by a Canadian emphasis on social welfare and human rights, Kairos has called on the government to endorse a "rights-based framework [for trade and FTAs] that incorporates a vision of trade embodying its legal international human rights obligations" (Jeremic 2006b, 2).

Although their discourse has become less oppositional to the government, the inclusion of human rights is nothing new. At the beginning of the coalitions'

---

[2] The Jubilee 2000 movement was a global movement supported by faith communities around the world centered on canceling debt payments for the poorest countries. The Canadian Ecumenical Jubilee Initiative was a Canadian interchurch coalition (later rolled into Kairos) founded to deal specifically with this issue.

history, GATT-Fly argued that the FTAs being proposed in the 1980s would "jeopardize both our ability to defend the rights of workers, family farmers, and the unemployed in Canada and our ability to stand in solidarity with the oppressed workers and peasants of the Third World" (GATT-Fly 1985b, 2).

Beyond market regulation, the coalitions have called for actual redistribution, enforced by the state and international governing bodies, to guarantee more economic power for the poor. High levels of economic inequality, such as low wages and harsh working conditions at the hands of transnational corporations, demanded severe state intervention. FTAs, however, challenge the power of states to perform their duty "to redistribute income and mitigate the inequality inherent in the market through social spending" (ECEJ 1999a, 8). At GATT-Fly's self-reliance conference, they also called for a "progressive redistribution of income so that all families and individuals have sufficient income to purchase those goods and services that they collectively produce" (Dillon 1987, 10). Bill Luttrell, a former coalition member and key actor in the development of the self-reliance model, spoke on behalf of GATT-Fly at the conference:

In order to achieve this end to material poverty ... a redistribution of income will be necessary, away from the rich and to the poorest. This in turn is linked practically with the need for a tax system in this country which is truly progressive.... Whether or not incomes above a certain level must be eliminated altogether, and if so at what level, may be debated within the context of self-reliance. (1987, 30)

And, in addition to the failure of the free market to provide for economic needs, the coalitions have argued that a free market has too much power over people's vocational decisions. As agricultural work became less profitable and sustainable in Central America under liberalization, many who were previously working the land were forced to migrate or change careers. A 2004 *Global Economic Justice Report* reveals this emphasis on agricultural workers:

When we keep farmers and farm workers at the centre of our analysis, it is clear that a just and viable alternative to the crisis cannot be left to the devices of the market nor solved through a magic formula.... What is needed is a holistic, people-centered approach that brings together key components of local, national and global agriculture trade.

(Kairos 2004b, 11)

GATT-Fly began with a comparatively meager effort to change international sugar prices on behalf of the poor. But since their judgment that the system was inherently flawed, they have advocated nothing less than total reform of the economic system through research, education, and engagement in civil society alliances – especially at the grassroots level.

Free Trade Suppresses Democracy and the Development of States

A second set of political critiques has pertained to the ways that FTAs are negotiated and enforced; values of empowerment and community have been especially central here. The coalitions have diagnosed current FTAs as chiefly beneficial to developed states and transnational corporations (TNCs) and shamefully unenforced in their few democratic standards. They have called for all developing states and the people within them to have more decision-making power.

One of their central complaints has decried trade-negotiation processes where international financial institutions (IFIs), TNCs, and the United States have dominated the proceedings. GATT-Fly initially analyzed trade in light of other international economic conditions and flawed programs; trade agreements were part of a larger package, including structural adjustment programs (SAPs), which took away national autonomy from governments, often forcing them to privatize public institutions. A 1995 book by John Mihevc (now a part of Kairos), *The Market Tells Them So: The World Bank and Economic Fundamentalism in Africa*, was an indictment of such programs. In it, Mihevc linked the World Bank with a political fundamentalism that promotes a certain ideology all must follow, an ideology that has proven detrimental for developing states.

The argument of the coalitions has been that the democratic negotiating process between states is thwarted as IFIs and organizations like the WTO conspire to squelch the voices of developing states by intentionally leaving them out of the process. A comic ECEJ distributed in their 1994 FTAA action kit illustrated this point. The final caption argues that "the transparency in the Ministerial meetings is such that you can't see anything" (ECEJ 1994). This conspiracy theory applied not only to how trade negotiations were crafted but also to how trade was regulated. ECEJ contended, "A secretive, unelected international commission that favours industry over the environment will rule on trade disputes and give a voice to corporations that is denied to environment-protection organizations and the general public" (ECEJ 1994). ECEJ wanted to see a greater role for nonfinancial international civil society organizations, asserting that the International Human Rights Charter or the United Nations (UN) should arbitrate what is legal and illegal in accords. In *Recolonization or Liberation*, they recognized that these bodies have the power to convene and enforce: "An agreement among all the world's nations must be sought, presumably through the UN General Assembly, to create a new international monetary order" (ECEJ 1990b, 84).

In addition to a more equitable decision-making process among states in drafting trade agreements, ECEJ also called for more democratic processes among individuals within states. They rejected the notion that economists are best equipped to make economic policy decisions and considered this an affront to people's sovereignty. Empowerment and solidarity can be achieved only when people have an increased role in trade decisions.

In demanding a stronger voice for the poor, the coalitions called for more international governance but were wary of allowing nongovernmental organizations, including themselves, to represent citizen voices. Dillon explained the risk: "To set oneself up and say, 'We're a spokesperson for the masses and masses of people' is a little bit dangerous and self-aggrandizing" (2007). He noted Kairos's preference to be part of a "broad coalition" and their fondness for grassroots empowerment through democracy. Their 1999 letter to the government reveals these priorities:

We urge the Canadian government to ensure that the process of developing, adopting and implementing an integration agreement is transparent and accountable; that is, it must be open to public scrutiny and input, through meaningful parliamentary review and broad civil society consultation, prior to, during and following the negotiation process.

(ECEJ and ICCHRLA 1999)

Kairos further argued when discussing CA4FTA that without public participation, democracy would not be upheld.

Because negotiations have been held in near secrecy for over four years, the democratic process has been brought into question. *Where are Canada's true commitments to transparency, accountability and democracy* without any healthy public debate, hearings with human rights experts, or participation of affected Central Americans?

(Kairos 2006c, 2)

Although concerns of developing, indigenous people are not at the core of the coalitions' arguments, they have argued that such groups have been more politically marginalized than others. The indigenous have suffered abuses by governments denying them due process (for example, in confiscating their land). In addition, they miss out on basic resources granted to others. Kairos argued in a report from the recent Mexican delegation that indigenous land and natural resources were at risk as trade infrastructures were being increasingly altered to attract investment. Such alterations paid little attention to questions of citizen and human rights. All citizens within developing states, then, require stronger voices in the trade negotiation and enforcement processes (Kairos 2005c).

Free Trade Erodes Domestic Economies

Dismissing the laissez-faire attitude of government, the coalitions have sought to increase the power of governments within their own borders, arguing that states *should* have the sovereignty to manage their own economies, establish business rules and regulations, and decide their own country's path for development. For GATT-Fly and ECEJ, self-reliance was the solution to these concerns of state sovereignty. GATT-Fly hosted the 1987 conference to promote this alternative and was the key group advocating for such an approach.

Self-reliance requires that states provide for the basic needs of all people, and this means supply-management boards and state involvement in production and distribution processes. (Canada has supply-management boards for eggs, poultry, dairy, and wheat; farmers receive subsidies and accepted quotas.) Consequently, self-reliance rejects export-oriented models of development encouraged by free trade. Self-reliance also requires that imports and production be controlled in order to meet domestic need. Additionally, as Bill Luttrell of GATT-Fly argued, self-reliance would "replace private ownership for most of our enterprises, including the most powerful, with some sort of social ownership and control" (1987, 31).

More than an internal insurance policy, self-reliance was also meant to be a sign of solidarity with other countries; a self-reliant Canadian state would be better positioned to help developing states seek their own independence. Dillon argued in his presentation at the self-reliance conference, "More economic independence for Canada is essential if we are to be able to stand in solidarity with other peoples seeking independence and social justice" (Dillon 1987). Herberto Castillo, president of the Mexican Workers' Party, also spoke at the conference to "share with [citizens in Canada] the Mexican peoples' struggle for independence and self-determination" (Dillon 1987, 11). The final statement from the 1987 conference declared, "The struggle for sovereignty, independence, and self-determination has our full solidarity" (GATT-Fly 1987, 45).

Agreeing with dependency theorists, GATT-Fly (and later ECEJ and Kairos) rejected economic models that reinforced the peripheral status of some states, wary of the impacts of such models on agriculture. In a 1996 letter to the Canadian government, ECEJ expressed these concerns:

We are extremely disturbed by evidence that agricultural production is being transformed from one aimed at meeting local food needs to export agri-business, thereby creating food dependency, undermining traditional cultures, rapidly degrading the soil, as well as endangering the local population through intensive use of agricultural chemicals.

(Vandervennen 1996)

Kairos has not pushed as hard for self-reliance as the former coalitions did, but they have critiqued the export-oriented model and called for states to manage their own economies. In place of advocating for supply-management boards, Kairos has protested regulations that would threaten social programs and publicly managed systems (such as communications) that many states own. As for FTAs, Canadian public opinion has now largely accepted the free trade model, so Kairos works to limit the power that these agreements have and to bring some power back to the states. According to Rusa Jeremic, the head of the Global Economic Justice division within Kairos (until 2009), food sovereignty has remained a central issue for Kairos, since states should be able to decide their own agricultural policy. About the current FTAs, she complained, "The other big thing about the model is policy constraints. . . . You are constrained to decide what is the best path for your country's development" (2008).

Although the free trade model has been critiqued from the beginning, the coalitions' true villains have always been the TNCs. The central focus of Kairos in trade debates has been how many FTAs (including NAFTA, through its chapter 11) govern the rights of states to give preferential treatment to domestic businesses, making the practice of discrimination against multinational or foreign corporations illegal. Kairos has criticized this power of the TNCs to sue states when their governments' decisions threaten the TNCs' business interests. In their 2005 Mexican delegation report, Kairos discussed the difficulties faced by a small town in Mexico:

Community activists in Cerro de San Pedro and San Luis Potosí have successfully used the court to halt Metallica's operations. Regardless, the company is still trying to undermine these victories. Most disturbing, Metallica Resources has publicly threatened to use NAFTA's notorious Chapter 11 to sue the Mexican government.... We are extremely concerned about Canadian corporate activity abroad. This case demonstrates the need for Canada to implement binding obligations for corporations.   (Kairos 2005c, 14)

Depicting TNCs as greedy and gaining power has been part of identifying these business actors as villains to be vanquished. This view of a divided society and broken structure – including the emphasis on the sins of TNCs – follows out of the emphasis on sin and conflict found in liberation theology.[3] Free trade is ultimately a problem because, as Rusa Jeremic has argued, "The free trade model is designed to facilitate corporate access into communities ... to grant companies more power than local governments or people" (2008).

THE CENTRAL ROLE OF LIBERATION THEOLOGY

Shared Values, Shared Perspective

Even though Kairos and its predecessors did not have a code of theological doctrines, from the outset the coalitions have been faith-based, with a religious identity. As they have developed within their Canadian context, religious emphases from within the liberationist tradition – namely, *solidarity*, *empowerment*, and the *sacredness of the earth* – have been core values. The roles of personal experience and individual perspective also have been extremely important for the coalitions, just as one would find in liberation theology.

The coalitions' religious identity, however, has never been *based* in liberation theology – or any particular theology. True to form, it is defined more by moral practice than doctrinal creed. In an initial identity statement, GATT-Fly asserted, "We believe all who struggle for justice are God's children doing God's work" (GATT-Fly 1984, 1). Still, as liberation theology gained momentum in the early 1970s (the term was adopted by Gutiérrez in 1971) and had not yet been institutionally prohibited, it wielded a real influence.[4] Tony Clarke, in our 2007 interview, described the environment at that time:

---

[3] Sawchuk (2004) has suggested that this more liberal Catholic theology has emphasized a conflictual view of the world, while a more theologically conservative Catholic theology accentuates peace and easier resolution.

[4] Although some ideas that developed from liberation theology were welcomed into Catholic doctrine (see note 7), other aspects (often viewed as more Marxist) were censured in the 1980s by the Vatican, leading to a marginalization of the theology among Christians.

When I came in '72 you could feel it; you could feel something was in the air. There was something qualitatively different about some of the discourse that was going on at the time. And the fact that [the conference at] Medellín had occurred, that the Latin American bishops had pretty well embraced the basic tenets of liberation theology. And some of us read and interpreted ... *Justice in the World*[5] [as] kind of a signal to move very much in that direction.

Gregory Baum, a Jesuit theologian and intellectual leader of the movement, argued that Christians have a "commitment to look upon society from the perspective of the poor, the weak, and the marginalized" (Baum 1991, 59; Carney 2001, 82). Citing this quotation, Carney has suggested that for Baum, Christians should read society from the perspective of its victims.[6] For Canadian economic justice efforts, part of their religious practice was to seek out just a perspective.

Yet even with this emphasis on liberationist thought, the organizations have avoided theologically naming the influence, at least partly to avoid conflict and distraction. Cormie argues that the coalitions initially made explicit decisions to reject theology:

Ironically though, the specialized disciplines of theology played almost no part in the work of the coalitions. In other words, sustained reflection on the bible, tradition, and signs of the times, or engagement in current debates among theological scholars and church officials, was not a priority. Theological literacy was not part of anyone's job requirements. Theological reflection on the struggles for justice was not part of anyone's job definition. In fact, some early coalition pioneers explicitly rejected theology, on the grounds that denominational differences concerning abstract doctrines could only disrupt ecumenical agreement on practical justice issues and collaboration in practice. (2004, 301)

Solidarity

Among Kairos's values, solidarity is paramount, as Mihevc affirmed:

Well, I think the dominant theological principle that we try to espouse, and I think most of our members support, is the solidarity with our partners. You know, the solidarity, you have to really listen to the voices of your southern partners who are most affected by these policies. So we put a lot of emphasis on bringing our partners here to speaking engagements. ... We try for that model of partnership. And that is fundamental, I think – the root theological principle as well.   (2008)

Solidarity, in its simplest form, describes a shared set of interests that brings unity to a group. For the coalitions, it has been about sharing burdens – by

---

[5] Document produced by the 1971 Synod of Bishops.
[6] This "preferential option for the poor," as it has come to be known, is now an official expression of Catholic social teaching.

granting authority to their partners and working collaboratively with other groups in civil society. For example, they have pursued goals together with groups like the RMALC as they protested neoliberalism's growth within Mexico.

One way that the coalitions have promoted solidarity is through the act of using research created not just *about* but *by* their partners. In their 1994 FTAA action kit, for example, they borrowed several selections from other actors, such as a narrative story from author Joan Atlin and the American Friends Service Committee, a free trade comic from the Mexican Free Trade Network, and fact reports based on evidence from the Canadian Environmental Law Association and Oxfam Canada. All of these were then adapted as ECEJ materials, sometimes presented in new ways and sometimes simply redistributed in their original format.

Another aspect of solidarity has been expressed through the coalitions' inviting those outside Canada to speak for themselves rather than to be merely spoken about. Ten Days for World Development, yet another church coalition formed in 1972 that was devoted to education within Canada on social issues, hosted an annual action campaign that brought non-Canadian voices to Canada to speak on issues of inequality and development.[7] This empowerment of overlooked voices goes back to the beginnings of GATT-Fly. Hearing from sugar farmers in the 1970s was the only way the coalition could realize that international price increases in sugar were not helping the poor (Ruttan 1987).

Solidarity, of course, cannot be achieved without a wider prospective, so the coalitions have prioritized presenting global concerns to Canadians in relevant ways. This means that efforts and funds are invested in gathering information about global conditions firsthand. At the same time, cooperation must be maintained with their partners in Canada and abroad. A recent Kairos report from a delegation sent to Mexico (2005c) highlighted this balanced practice: "At the request of the Broad Opposition Front, KAIROS sent a delegation of church leaders to investigate the situation in Cerro de San Pedro." The Broad Opposition Front is a partner of Kairos, and discourse about their request was used to help legitimate Kairos's action in Mexico.

A 1999 letter to the trade minister of Canada, written jointly by ECEJ and another coalition, the Interchurch Committee on Human Rights in Latin America (ICCHRLA), began in a similar manner, emphasizing both solidarity with the poor as well as with partner organizations and the churches within them: "Indeed, the member churches of ICCHRLA and ECEJ share the profound concerns of the Mexican church, human rights, labour and other citizens' organizations about the negative impact in Mexico of liberalization policies" (ECEJ and ICCHRLA 1999). Another letter on human rights written

---

[7] Cole-Arnal (1998) highlights how this practice of bringing outsiders to speak is founded in contextual theology.

in 1996 described ECEJ "as Canadian churches working together in solidarity with our Central American partners" (Vandervennen 1996). Kairos's discourse continues this emphasis on solidarity; photo galleries on their Web site showcase Canadians working alongside each other as well as alongside non-Canadian partners.

For the coalitions, solidarity is also about a rejection of hierarchy. During worship at the Social Justice Institute, a weekend cohosted by Kairos, one of the hymns selected was "Bring Forth the KinDom of Justice." This song is an adaptation of the popular hymn, "Bring Forth the Kingdom of Justice." The concept of a king, a male figure of power, has been replaced with the image of family relationship, subtly but effectively undermining the hierarchical scheme. No longer is the king bringing justice with him; rather the family is working together to bring justice about. This equalizing, familial image identifies how Kairos defines their target audience. It includes the poor and marginalized as well as influential coalition workers and Canadian citizens, as portrayed in the liturgy for a *Becoming Kairos* service:

> As we gather in this KAIROS circle,
> we remember 'all our relations'
> our Southern partners, our Aboriginal partners, our local community networks,
> our board members, our staff members, our committee members,
> our friends along the way,
> and this sacred earth
> where we walk our journey.   (Kairos 2003a)

In an early piece describing their identity, GATT-Fly outlined clearly whom they officially see as partners: "GATT-Fly focuses on support for 'popular groups.' These are groups whose members have organized themselves to struggle against the economic injustice they suffer. They include democratic trade unions, family and peasant farm organizations, and organizations of native people" (GATT-Fly 1984, 1). Kairos suggested that the organization should listen "to appeals coming from our sisters and brothers in Southern churches for strengthened solidarity and collaboration" (Kairos 2003d, 19). To that end, Dillon noted that the coalitions participated in "other kinds of international meetings where you actually sat down and listened and dialogued with representatives of communities most impacted. There was always an effort to make that part of the praxis" (Dillon 2007).

Must solidarity always entail a dissolution of hierarchy? Yes, in the view of the coalitions. This ideology has heavily influenced whom they have chosen as partners in their efforts, though the group would certainly protest this claim.[8] They have been in solidarity with a broad coalition – but mainly with those

---

[8] Hildebrand (1987), a scholar from inside the organization, for example, states that they do not start with an ideological view but rather are driven first by their desire to relieve the sufferings of the poor.

struggling for an alternative order that deconstructs lines of authority. By their own admission, some groups, some churches, some poor, and some in the South are not legitimate voices. Mihevc explained how they have selected and developed partnerships by seeking to understand the group's ideology:

What's their starting point, what are their basic principles in terms of who they're listening to? Are they really, really listening to or hearing what is going on in the South around the impact of these policies? I think a number of southern theologians I've read or talked to . . . are also blind to what is going on in their own midst. They're kind of above it or detached from it, and they come up with positions that frankly reflect a more elitist, dominant perspective. . . . You know, of course, we are selective about who we talk to and who we choose to listen to and who we choose to partner with. But you know, we have a number of partners we've been working with for years, and you know, those are the ones we trust, and we kind of share a similar analysis. But that's our starting point. (2008)

Empowerment and Equality

Closely related to the coalitions' concept of solidarity is that of empowerment – especially empowerment of those voices currently ignored, with the goal of attaining equality among persons. A significant part of empowerment toward equality has been the enforcement of human rights and the strengthening of the political power of underrepresented people.

But economic sharing, within a community, also has been part of such an empowerment. The idea of community was developed theologically within the organization under the Jubilee Movement of the late 1990s. Mihevc argued that the vision behind the work of the coalitions was "articulated very well in the whole Jubilee Movement. . . . It was very much touted and led by the churches who really picked it up" (2008). Community was about serving and empowering people, and the coalitions ultimately wanted to equip people to share in *oikos*, or the "economy of God." Several Kairos reports, for example, use this phrase to frame their identity, declaring that "as people of faith, we have a vision motivated by the economy of God, an economy of life and abundance that promotes sharing, globalized solidarity, dignity of persons, and care for the integrity of creation" (Kairos 2005e).

If God's economy thrives within community, it is starved out by exclusion. "Exclusion and powerlessness are themes that run throughout biblical history. They are very closely bound up to notions of community and solidarity" (ECEJ 2000b, 2). The coalitions associated these sins with their own mandated action: "We are invited to participate in the building of the kingdom. As we look at the forces of globalization, it is important to ask how we are being asked to participate and who participates in the key decisions that affect our lives" (ECEJ 2000b, 2).

The notion of "God's economy," however, does not show up in most of their research and has been chiefly utilized when theological justification was

needed – such as when Kairos was lobbying on behalf of their partner
churches. In a 2002 letter to Canadian Prime Minister Chrétien, they argued,
"In the Christian Bible, as well as the scriptures of older faith traditions, just
economic relations among peoples and communities are the backbone of a just
and peaceful society" (Smith 2002).

What *is* emphasized, not only in their work within civil society but also within
their organization through their own policies, is the concept of equality. GATT-
Fly explains their own remuneration system and hierarchy, which rejects traditional power structures:

The staff of GATT-Fly try to work as a collective. Responsibility for tasks is generally
shared among two or more staff people, one with principal responsibility and the other(s)
acting in a support role. This, and the fact that Administrative Committee members are
usually involved, is the major reason we haven't named specific authors for our publications. . . . All staff are ranked equally for the purposes of determining base salaries and all are
considered by the Administrative Committee to operate at a similar level of responsibility.
Actual salaries do vary, but only according to the number of family members dependent
upon a staff person (the less dependents, the lower the salary). Routine office tasks such as
typing, answering the telephone and receiving visitors are shared.   (GATT-Fly 1984, 2)

Sacredness of Creation

More common than theological-economic references in the coalitions' discourse
has been references to the value and sacredness of God's creation. True to
antihierarchical priorities, however, it has been people's familial relationship
with a suffering earth – rather than the more traditional, authority-laced concept
of "dominion" over the earth – that has been emphasized. Individuals are linked
to creation in a meaningful, supernatural way, and the protection of each relates
to the other. In explaining their emphasis on the earth, an early ECEJ piece lays
out the theological underpinnings of the movement, relying on the discourse of a
liberation theologian:

Brasilian theologian Leonardo Boff links the cry of the poor with the cry of the earth. Both
stem from wounds that are bleeding. . . . "*The first, the wound of poverty and wretched-
ness, tears the social fabric of millions and millions of poor people the world over. The
second, the systematic aggression against the Earth, destroys the equilibrium of the
planet. . . . Both lines of reflection and action stem from a cry: the cry of the poor for
life, liberty and beauty in the case of liberation theology (Exodus 3:7); the cry of the earth
groaning under oppression in that of ecology (Romans 8:22–3). Both seek liberation."* . . .
For us it means a time to adopt a stance of radical listening to our indigenous brothers and
sisters to help us understand how the cry of the poor and the earth are the same cry and to
teach us how to respond.   (italics added; ECEJ 2000b, 4)

Although they have been much more likely to make appeals to protecting the
environment without a discussion of God, the coalitions have judiciously used

the powerful image of a Creator behind the environment. In the previously mentioned theological reflection of ECEJ, they wrote,

"Claiming to be wise [humanity] became fools; and they exchanged the glory of the immortal God for images resembling a mortal human being or birds or four-footed animals and reptiles … they exchanged the truth about God for a lie and worshipped and served the creature rather than the Creator, who is blessed forever" (Rom 1:22, 25). Essentially what we are talking about is humanity's stance in relation to the created order. When we don't recognise or appreciate God's role as creator and liberator, then we construct idols that enslave us. And that is precisely the theology of economic globalization as it is being imposed on us today.   (2000b, 3)

The theological connections among ecology, social justice, and biblical quotations are not often articulated clearly by the coalitions in their discourse. In the previous example, although the Apostle Paul is quoted, it is not in reference to economic issues, but creation; the authors then vaguely contrast creation with an overextension of the market. Letting the market govern life is equated with a rejection of the Creator and of natural order. Here and in other places, harm against the earth often has been described as idolatry and market worship, and subsequently associated with sin.

The use of creation and Creator imagery has changed throughout the tenure of the coalitions. An intentional link between the environment and the poor was enunciated earlier on and still receives support throughout the organization. Yet more recent efforts on creation also place more weight on the earth as a material entity in need of repair.

Concern about creation is expressed less through logical and research-oriented work (such as biblical exegesis and quoting established theologians) and more through imagery. Paul Hansen, an active coalition member, former chair of Kairos, and priest in the Redemptorist order, suggested to me that some of the more intimate understandings of creation receive more support from women: "Many of the women religious right now are moving more towards earth, creation-centered kinds of things, than human rights kinds of things. The men tend to be in the human rights kinds of things, and see the earth as fluffy-feeffy kind of stuff" (2007). Although it is hard to access if this is indeed the case, women are well represented throughout the leadership of the organization. In earlier stages, men held most of the discursive and creative power within organization. However, at the time of this research, the head of the Global Economic Justice division (Rusa Jeremic), the head of the Latin American affairs (Rachel Warden), and the executive director (Mary Corkery) were female. The board of denominational officials has consistently shown gender balance in its leadership.

An example from Kairos worship materials shows how the group reflects concern for creation and the identity of the movement itself through symbols and imagery. Kairos has made suggestions to churches as they plan their physical environment for worship:

Consider creating a garden which represents the diversity of your KAIROS community, place of worship, and wider community. The garden will also honour the strength of the "grassroots" work of KAIROS.... With the gardeners in your community, choose suitable cuttings or small bedding plants, soil, and container or outside bed. Consider using plants native to your local eco-system.   (Kairos 2003a)

For an even stronger association with the earth as an image of Kairos's mission as well as an entity apart from the people themselves, consider the litany entitled "Act of Greening," produced by Kairos:

> *One: God the Giver,*
> *Who fashioned the garden of creation,*
> *Who promised a reign of justice that would flourish as a watered garden,*
> *Who urged friends to stay awake in the garden of Gethsemane*
> We come before you today.
> We have walked well-worn pathways
> in the journey of justice-making.
> We carry the harvest of many generations of labourers for justice
> from all corners of the earth.
> We are aware and thankful
> for those who have walked before us.
> *In this act of greening,*
> *we offer to You and to each other*
> *a vision of our common future*
> *as we grow united in our holy task of repairing the world.*
>
> (italics added; Kairos 2003a)

Creation imagery, then, present throughout the life of the coalitions, has changed with the times as the popularity of liberation theology has changed and as gender-specific preferences have shifted. Consistent, though, has been the groups' consideration of environmental impacts as well as human ones.

The Context of Canadian Values

Though the coalitions pursue a global perspective and solidarity with their neighbors and partners, it cannot be denied that they exist within a Canadian context. Naturally, the question has emerged within the movement of what it means for liberation theology to be adapted to the Canadian experience. Coalition members have had to recognize their position as quite different from that of the poor in Latin America. Hansen explained some of the challenges of this clash of contexts:

During the 1970s ... those of us who were involved in justice, you know, were kept alive by the literature of liberation theology. That's how I stayed alive in this culture. It was not our theology, and that's why we're in trouble now. We should have had a theology based on Joseph and his multicolored dream coat.... Joseph lived in the empire of Pharaoh and crafted an alternative vision, etc. That should have been our theology, not a Moses liberation theology from Pharaoh. We are living in Pharaoh's court. How do you keep the disciple of Jesus alive in Pharaoh's court. You see? And so we weren't astute enough to pick up on all of that. Our cultural analysis wasn't, this culture wasn't strong enough. We were totally dedicated to Latin America; our theologians became Latin American theologians. (2007)

Hansen believed that the coalitions had not yet sufficiently adapted their theology – born out of Latin America – to their Canadian context. Perhaps this continuing process of adaptation explains Kairos's lack of a well-defined religious creed. An emphasis on theology (as it emerges in the Latin American liberationist setting) continues to frame their moral values, and this is reflected in their religious discourse. Also, the religious identity of the coalitions has been clarified and embraced over time. But the coalitions have still lacked a fully developed contextual theology.[9]

Recent efforts to reflect upon the coalitions' context and history have borne some fruit. The volume by Lind and Mihevc (1994) referenced in this chapter, with stories from each of the coalitions, presents itself as a product of those efforts, called the Canadian Theological Reflection Project. Still, a shared history is not the same as a shared theology.

Cormie (2004) pointed out the potential of the Jubilee Movement to serve as a base of shared theology. He noted how international church bodies, such as the Vatican and the World Council of Churches, have been using the idea of the jubilee, connecting the biblical concept both with cancellation of debt and with relief work in poor countries. However, this has been relatively recent (starting in the late 1990s) and has not been fully incorporated into the work of Kairos.

As with all contexts, the Canadian one is defined by the personal experiences of its members. But in this case, it is these personal experiences, which are uncommonly international, that make contextual adaptation all the more complex. Indeed, it was through overseas experiences that many first encountered the very liberationist message they seek to present to Canada. Joe Gunn discussed how his experience with the Jesuits and their "advocacy and solidarity work" in Central America served as his entry point into the work of the coalitions (2008). After his experiences in Central America and Mexico, he came back and worked with the Jesuits in Toronto. All of this was before he started with the Social Affairs Commission of the Canadian Conference of Catholic Bishops (CCCB). John Mihevc spoke about how his theology and understanding of the world was shaped by the "profound faith of many African women and men ... [and] the intimate connection to land, community, and culture" (2008). Paul Hansen recounted some of his work with the Maryknolls (a Catholic mission movement) in Venezuela in the 1980s. He

---

[9] Much of the theology Cormie (2004) details is not new. He argues that the movement did reaffirm the theory- and practice-oriented methods of reading the Bible and engaging in theological reflection. Although these may be theological in part, they are not a new or contextual theology but rather a more explicit incorporation of the liberationist theology.

recently learned that he had in fact first met his current coalition colleague, Jim Dekker of the Christian Reformed Church, back in 1984 at the Maryknoll house in Venezuela; often the personal histories of the staff are intertwined. These international experiences of members both have been prompted by faith and have propelled their subsequent work with the coalitions. In this way, experiences outside the Canadian context have helped to shape the coalitions into a unique context all their own.

Although a true contextual theology might still be lacking, the coalitions have, in other ways, embraced their Canadian identity. Their emphasis on liberation theology has contributed to self-reflection and coalition building, and this in many ways helped GATT-Fly to take on a Canadian identity, aware of their own global position. Kairos is an officially Canadian organization, and that linkage has perhaps become more important over time, influencing the values of the group. One of the most important ways this has played out is in their trade discourse; they believe their emphasis on human rights and state welfare separate them from the United States. As Howard-Hassmann and Welch (2006) have pointed out, although Canada and the United States are similar in many ways in how they enforce and act out human rights, there are some important differences in how the two countries *think* about human rights, with Canada taking more of an advocacy stance. Hildebrand (1987) argued that GATT-Fly emphasized this Canadian value on human rights and that ecumenical movements saw rights as part of their Canadian identity: "One can point to a socialist counter-culture ideology in Canada which has encouraged public participation in the economy, greater state intervention in the marketplace, the collective solidarity of workers, a broad range of social services and a more benign foreign policy" (98). Consequently, appeals to human rights have been used in attempts to get Canadians involved in the justice efforts of the coalitions.

Lipset's 1992 work on the differences between Canada and the United States of America are also relevant. He noted that Canada has had more debate over its identity and self-conception; citizens are more likely to recognize the existence of a national identity. He further suggested that the "presence of a larger, more powerful neighbor to the south has encouraged Canadians on the state to protect the nation's economic independence." There is an awareness that Canadians and those in the United States have a different cultural identities, and Canadians want to protect their identity and economic interests. This can be seen in the rhetoric of GATT-Fly, as they suggested that the Canadian identity of caring about rights was threatened through an FTA with the United States. In a 2006 statement against trade agreements, they acknowledged these values as national ones: "The glaring difference [between NAFTA and new FTAs] brings to light exactly what is at risk – Canadian democratic values of transparency and participation" (Kairos and APG 2006). The values that GATT-Fly promoted, according to Hildebrand (1987), were to contribute "to an understanding of what the Canadian social personality, identity, and culture ought to be" (100).

GRASSROOTS STRATEGIC ACTION

Organizational History and Church Affiliation

As explained in the early part of this chapter, GATT-Fly/ECEJ/Kairos has undergone significant restructuring since it started. A thorough explanation of its organizational history is in order here. GATT-Fly's initial creation cannot be understood outside the larger interchurch movement in Canada and the changes in the Catholic Church that took place in the 1970s. Hildebrand (1987) argued that the interchurch coalitions were a renewal of past concern for economic issues by earlier Canadian actors, such as the Canadian Social Gospel movement and Catholic Action. GATT-Fly was but one of several coalitions developed during that time.[10] Canada served as a unique place where ecumenical collaboration took off in the wake of Vatican II. Protestant churches had a history of ecumenical work dating back to the formation of the United Church in the early 1900s (Noll 1992). Paul Hansen noted that during his time in the Vatican working for the Redemptorists, Canada was seen as a model for ecumenical relations because of the work of its interchurch groups.

GATT-Fly (1973–1989) operated somewhat informally and separately from the churches. After the 1968 United Nations Conference on Trade and Development (UNCTAD), the major church traditions in Canada (Roman Catholic, United Church, Anglicans, Lutherans, and Presbyterians) formed the GATT-Fly coalition with a self-proclaimed focus on research, political action, and public education. Further, the vision behind their creation was "to represent the interest of the Third World countries on issues of international trade and monetary reform. GATT-Fly is a concrete expression of a growing interest in the churches with the problems of development and social justice" (GATT-Fly 1973a). Among members, this translated into a mandate to pursue alternative economic policies and present controversial ideas. Dillon explained this vision:

I think our self-image was that we wanted to be on the cutting edge of social change. And we weren't afraid to be out in front and to be maybe working on issues that others had not yet addressed. And so there was always the intent that our work would be taken very

---

[10] Some of the other coalitions were the Canada-China program (1972–1997); Ten Days for World Development (1972); PLURA – named after the Presbyterian, Lutheran, United, Roman Catholic, and Anglican churches that sponsored the group (1973) (although a predecessor group, Coalitions for Development, was formed in 1968); the Interchurch Fund for International Development (1974); Project North, which dealt with aboriginal rights (1975); the Taskforce on the Churches and Corporate Social Responsibility (1975); the Canada-Asia Working Group (1977); Interchurch Committee on Human Rights in Latin America (1977); Project Ploughshares (1977); Interchurch Committee for Refugees (1979); and the Interchurch Coalition on Africa (1982). All but Project Ploughshares (and the Canada-China program, which disbanded) eventually became part of Kairos. Most of these organizations also had a history several years before they were officially formed, when church leaders met together to discuss the issues that the coalitions eventually tackled.

seriously by the churches and eventually adopted in some way in policy or whatever. But there was never the sense that we have to wait for all of the denominations to catch up with us before we move ahead on a cutting-edge issue.   (2007)

Although some denominations did make use of GATT-Fly resources, the coalition itself did not focus their energy on the churches. Three other staff members eventually joined Dillon, and those on the administrative board – such as Tony Clarke with the Catholic Office of Social Affairs – also played an important role.

Thus, part of the coalitions' organizational identity has been not only a loose connection with churches but also a strong linkage with partners outside the Canadian religious community. Many of the staff members have worked with Catholic religious orders in Central America, and other civil-society and popular-movement actors are among the coalitions' partners. One of their central partner in Mexico, RMALC, is an alliance of civil society actors that works to resist current neoliberal trade policies and the WTO.

In 1990, ignited by recognition that their work no longer focused solely on trade and that the name did not represent their work to people outside the organization, GATT-Fly decided to undergo a remandating process. This decision by their board fit well with the organization's emphasis on thoughtful self-reflection. During this 1990 remandating process, the name was changed to Ecumenical Coalition for Economic Justice (ECEJ) to better reflect the organization's work. While issues of free trade were not erased from the agenda, concerns over the global financial crisis and international debt emerged. The issue of economic justice for women also became a focus of the organization; Lorraine Michael, who was previously involved with local Catholic social justice efforts, was hired to work with ECEJ on this topic. The name change also indicated plans to work more closely with churches. That is, although they retained their autonomy as an organization, they recognized the need to prioritize engaging churches in social concerns.

While the formation of ECEJ represented an internal reorganization, in 2001, a significant structural change took place. ECEJ joined forces with other ecumenical coalitions to become Kairos. This move, instigated by a funding crisis in the mainline and Protestant churches, both consolidated the coalitions into one organization and put the new coalition under the jurisdiction of the churches. GATT-Fly and ECEJ had been supported by member churches, both financially and intellectually, yet had been independent and autonomous. Kairos, in contrast, is expected to speak on behalf of the eleven churches that are part of its organization, even as their research need not be representative. A Kairos board with representatives from each member church must approve policies or major changes in the focus or activity of the organization. Unlike the Catholic bishops in Costa Rica (Chapter 4) or the General Assembly in the Presbyterian Church (USA) (PCUSA; Chapter 3), Kairos's research is not meant to officially represent a particular body, but rather to bring together those united over particular issues and provide ideas for congregations (and others) to consider.

Central Actors Involved in the Production of Discourse

Given the importance of policy research for members, and the volume of period-icals, the staff members who are creating the research have held most of the authority within the organization. The first hired member of GATT-Fly, John Dillon, was trained as an economist. John Mihevc, although not part of GATT-Fly, worked initially in the Economic Justice Division of the Inter-Church Coalition on Africa. A theologian, his dissertation, *So the Market Tells Them So: The World Bank and Economic Fundamentalism in Africa*, was published in 1995. Both still work with Kairos today and have been important for the intellectual and theological base of the organization. Dennis Howlett was another intellectual who served for a long time with GATT-Fly and ECEJ, starting only a few months after John Dillon and continuing until 1993. He is the author of GATT-Fly's history in the volume *Coalitions for Justice* (Lind and Mihevc 1994), a compilation of the histories of the interchurch movement in Canada. These staff members enjoyed a high degree of religious legitimation. Hildebrand noted the religious influences on these central actors in his research: "It is clear from the interviews conducted for this study that GATT-Fly staff are motivated in their work by a commitment of religious faith which incorporates political and social commitments and not vice versa" (1987, 122).

Because of their legitimacy and an informal organizational structure, such scholars were able to freely develop the cutting-edge and controversial research for which GATT-Fly became known. John Dillon specifically explained the significance and origin of the weasel clause, a statement on the back of the GATT-Fly and ECEJ periodicals (GATT-Fly 1980a, 4; ECEJ 1990a) that stated their research did "not necessarily represent the official policy of sponsoring churches":

The language of that clause was dictated almost verbatim by the former Primate of the Anglican Church, Archbishop Ted Scott.... He was getting all kinds of flak from business communities and others, about what church projects were saying. And he said, "I don't want to stifle you or stop your voice from speaking out on issues, but we've got to at some point make it clear when it's not actual church policy."   (2007)

Although staff members have definitely exercised autonomy from denomi-nations, their relationship with the Catholic Church in Canada has been complex. Tony Clarke is an example of one Catholic voice that has been important for GATT-Fly/ECEJ/Kairos. He had previously served as the direc-tor of the Catholic Social Affairs Commission and was involved with GATT-Fly in its beginning stages as the Catholic representative. He was still working with them when he took a leave of absence to co-chair the ACN in the late 1980s. Joe Gunn held a similar position to Tony Clarke within the Canadian Conference of Catholic Bishops (CCCB), and he later served as a co-chair of Kairos. Although no longer connected to the bishops' office, he continues to work with the Catholic religious community and Kairos. Both men have voiced their disappointment with the role of the CCCB in social justice efforts today.[11]

Even as the intent has been to create a collaborative process of producing research and policy, the reality is that, within the coalitions, staff members often have had more expertise and authority than volunteers and other activists. Most of the staff have reported either significant experience overseas working with religious and social justice partners and/or academic training in religion, theology, or the social sciences. Volunteers, though interested in serving on committees to help shape policies, generally have been less knowledgeable about any given issue. Rusa Jeremic noted that many on the program committees have not had the technical expertise to assist with research. So although volunteers have offered feedback or updates, staff members have remained the central authors.

In Kairos, there has been an addition of new voices to the discourse, even as those historically involved with the coalitions often continue to play an important role. Some religious activists of the past have become involved in non-religious sectors of civil society, and Hansen noted to me that some of this shift is due to disillusionment with the church. Whatever the reason, some newer voices consequently lack the religious foundations of earlier leaders. In acknowledging that some staff members have not been religious, Paul Hansen affirmed staff members need not personally identify as religious. Potential staff members are asked, "Can you live with the teaching of the churches in the membership of Kairos, religiously? And can you represent them?" Believing in these teachings is optional. As a result, some of the new staff share the political identity of the group but do not connect with any specific religious tradition.

Under the new oversight structure of Kairos, staff members admittedly do not have the same authority to develop new policy statements as they did in GATT-Fly or ECEJ, although they remain the central authors of research on economic alternatives. For example, Rusa Jeremic has been instrumental in developing the analysis on chapter 11, TNCs, and indigenous rights that is critical to Kairos's current trade strategies. She also served as the central author of the *Global Justice Report*, a periodical sent to interested members.

Strategies of Political Action

Kairos is a social movement organization, and its discourse is aimed specifically at social change. At the same time, it also serves as an ecumenical organization to help churches pursue justice in their local and global communities. Specifically, as a religious social movement, its goal is to speak in a prophetic voice, even

[11] Tony Clarke's book *Behind the Mitre: The Moral Leadership Crisis in the Canadian Catholic Church* (1995) documents the politics behind the Catholic Church's movement away from challenging the Canadian government over economic issues.

when that might limit their political impact. This is something not uncommon for progressive religious communities; Lichterman, in his study of progressive religious communities in the United States, discusses the costs of being "social critics." In describing the Justice Task Force, a faith-based activist group committed to raising awareness of poverty in the United States, he finds that the group "ended up marginalizing itself even as it tried to reach out. They assumed that marginality was the price for speaking truth to power" (2005, 101). Likewise, Wood (2002) has noted the power of religion in social activism, to empower groups in having a prophetic – and often confrontational – voice. The strategy of Kairos is not primarily to change politics, but rather to articulate a prophetic vision that can rally its members and change prevailing political ideas.

The goal of this strategic action in many ways seems to change the terms of the debate. Although Kairos, like its predecessors, clearly seeks concrete and practical political change, they know their power is not about their political authority. Like the case Lichterman studied, their power lies in the potential to change the political discussion. This potential to shape public discourse is important. Religious actors, Hofrenning (1995) has suggested, often have this power; although the positions articulated by religious activists are often outside the mainstream, those positions give people new language. Such discourse, then, may open new "cultural repertoires" (Lamont and Thévenot 2000), providing fresh tools for people to use in thinking about political and social concerns.

The discourse of Kairos in many ways is directed at two audiences: the Christian community in Canada, and the political bodies. With their discourse toward the church, they seek to rally members and to provide new discursive tools. Benford and Snow (2000) have noted the important role that calls to action, alongside diagnosing and interpreting problems, play within the framing process. For a group where many join because of a common diagnosis and prognosis of the system, calls for action are an important focus. Unlike the other two cases studied in the following chapters, the members of Kairos (and GATT-Fly and ECEJ) joined because they agreed with the political message or because they wanted to be involved in the work of social justice. (With Kairos, some may have joined without knowing the economic stance of the group, but such individuals would still have shared a commitment to ecumenical approaches to justice.) People are also free to join and leave the group if they disagree with its politics, as membership is defined by participation within the Kairos community, not by membership in their church denomination.

Kairos, like its predecessors, also pursues strategies of concrete political change. They do this in several ways. First, they include political bodies within their audience. Several times, people from Kairos have spoken before parliamentary gatherings. They have created a number of papers that outlined positions, and directed these at specific government officials who were involved in the decision-making process (for example, the letter to the Minister of Finance in 1997 by ECEJ, and the 2005 brief to the House of Commons Standing Committee on Foreign Affairs). In 2005, Rusa Jeremic, the coordinator of the

Global Economic Justice division, gave remarks before the subcommittee on trade, trade disputes, and investment.

The Importance of Alliances

Since their initial work in the 1970s, the coalitions' interactions with the government and international institutions – as well as the political content of their arguments – have changed. These changes were due to the changing environment in Canada as well as the organizational changes in their structure: both served to slow down efforts to promote an alternative economic order. A changed climate has meant changed models, as Rusa Jeremic has affirmed – "[s]trategies have changed a lot in different times and different moments" – yet the coalitions have consistently sought to "lift up alternative principles" in their action and research (2008).

The grassroots emphasis of the organization is driven by liberationist ideals. Empowering the poor through *communidades de base* was a central aspect of the liberationist movement in Latin America; for liberationists, typical hierarchies need to be replaced by flatter organizational structures. GATT-Fly tried to follow and promote such a model. *Ah-Hah: A New Approach to Popular Education* (1983) formalized such an approach to organizing communities around the globe so they could be more active in their own development.

The emphasis on alternatives was not just strategic, but prompted in part by a foundational mismatch of the coalitions' values with the existing order. The current order is in need of too many changes; the system has been broken beyond repair. The religious activists of the coalitions compared the current economic order to colonialism and slavery, noting how the economic globalization "is increasingly exploiting, excluding and marginalizing large numbers of people and regions of the world" (ECEJ 2000b, 1). They highlighted the exploitation and oppression under the hand of TNCs.

Alliance building has been critical for the organization. Ever since GATT-Fly joined and led the ACN in the 1980s, they secured their identity as a research engine within civil society. This identity was maintained by their continued economic research, participation in multiple alliances, and historical involvement in conferences and forums.

Strategically, their emphasis on alternative models has required alliances, especially those that transcend religious lines. The coalitions' lack of a clear theological foundation and lack of emphasis on religious doctrine mostly facilitated alliances across religious lines (even as some church bodies have rejected involvement in the coalitions because of this missing piece) (Lind and Mihevc 1994). Cormie (1994) also noted that this lack of clear theology at times hindered the connection of GATT-Fly and ECEJ with churches. In place of a set of standard doctrinal beliefs, their affiliation with other actors working for a new economic system has been critical to their identity. To that end, a number of staff have been involved in leadership of other alliances while working for the coalitions. Tony Clarke, for example, served with the CCCB when he advised GATT-Fly and headed the ACN, and Rusa Jeremic recently served as cochair of the Americas Policy Group while working on economic justice efforts at Kairos. Such dual alliances, however, have not been problematic; rather, they provide evidence of the coalitions' ideological solidarity with a broader movement.

Reception and Challenge of the Churches

How well have the coalitions represented the church in Canada? One of the coalitions' goals has been to challenge the entire church community, and not just those affiliated with the organization, to speak more prophetically regarding political issues. Unlike the other cases profiled in the following two chapters, church members are not under the authority of the coalitions. Have religious communities embraced their discourse? How representative *was* the discourse of the dialogue that has actually occurred in churches throughout Canada? GATT-Fly, ECEJ, and especially Kairos have had potential connections to a majority of people in Canada – with the official support they have received from numerous Protestant churches, the Catholic Church, and Catholic religious orders.

In a way, the coalitions' connection with the churches, though historically weak, has become stronger under Kairos, as it is more officially affiliated with the denominations. However, GATT-Fly and (to a lesser degree) ECEJ had more influence within the churches than Kairos does today because, at the time, the global religious climate was more conducive to their work, and Canadian churches were more interested in economic justice.[12] Many in the churches had not yet found a voice regarding international economics, and so people were open to investigating new ideas. When liberation theology was new, many found it energizing, not controversial; as Wuthnow (1987) and Swidler (1986) theorized, it is in such times of questioning that new ideologies have the most potential. Some of my interviewees spoke nostalgically of this earlier time, when churches were more invested and involved in justice issues.

The research and work of GATT-Fly was particularly important in the life of the Canadian Catholic Church, although it might be more accurate to claim a dialectical relationship was at work.[13] Tony Clarke, the head of social affairs for CCCB until the late 1980s and a central voice in GATT-Fly, argued that these two organizations influenced each other – and that the work of GATT-Fly was taken into account as the bishops' Social Affairs Committee produced their own statements. Howlett (1994) argued that the Catholic bishops implemented many of the themes of GATT-Fly. For example, during the recession in the 1980s in

---

[12] According to Cormie (2004), in the late 1980s and 1990s, progressive politics in Canada and the work of these coalitions were generally well received by the churches.

[13] Hildebrand (1987) claimed that a dialectical process developed between denominations and GATT-Fly, where the work of each influenced the other.

Canada, the bishops published *Ethical Reflections on the Economic Crisis* (1983), which politically challenged the economic system of the day. Although the bishops' theology was not shaped by GATT-Fly, the political challenges in their Catholic message were shaped by the coalition's analysis; many of the bishops' social messages called for the country to reorient their economic priorities and systems. As Tony Clarke stated, "I think it was pretty clear that we had an active, fairly active and dynamic Social Affairs Commission and Social Affairs or Social Action Office. . . . Pastoral letters on social justice issues coming out of diocese were not uncommon either" (2008).

Kairos has not enjoyed the same influence as GATT-Fly upon the Catholic Church. The CCCB, for example, recently eliminated their funding to the organization, attributing the lack of support to their financial inability to donate. Joe Gunn, another coalition activist formerly leading the Social Affairs Commission for CCCB, attributed this cut in funding to growing disinterest of the Catholic bishops with the movement. For the Catholic Church, the impact of ECEJ and the work of coalitions changed in the mid-1980s, around the time that FTAs were entering the political arena. Clarke suggests that after the bishops' 1983 letter *Ethical Reflections*, the Social Affairs Commission merited the attention of the Vatican, and by the mid-1980s, the CCCB understood that the global Catholic Church was "putting the brakes on liberation theology" (2008). The Canadian Catholic Church of the late 1980s was still invested in these issues but had more pressure from the Vatican to tone down their message than they had had in the 1970s. In the 1990s, there was another shift when the CCCB halted their discourse on the economy, in large part due to changes in leadership. In spite of this, Kairos has retained a strong Catholic contingent, although many are associated with Catholic religious orders or Development and Peace (a Catholic development organization created during the interchurch era of the 1970s).

Among Protestant churches, there also was initial strong support for GATT-Fly. A publication titled *Responding to Free Trade from a Christian Perspective* reveals the criticisms of free trade shared by Protestant churches, which universally shared strong critical views of the Canada–United States FTA. As that publication reported, "In general, the mainline Christian denominations in Canada have severe reservations about the Canada–U.S. Free Trade Agreement (FTA)" (United Church of Canada 1988, 13). The four founding Protestant members of GATT-Fly – the Lutheran, Presbyterian, Anglican, and United churches – expressed these concerns publicly, and these churches institutionalized stances against FTAs back in the 1980s (unlike their partner denominations in the United States). Yet, they did not reject free trade entirely, and today some of these same churches would not reject current FTAs. Dillon explained the current attitude of these churches:

On some issues like debt, the churches were so much on board with the Jubilee Debt Campaign that nobody ever questions if Kairos says something. . . . On trade, it's not quite as cut and dried and clear. But on the other hand, actually very few policy papers have ever really had to go through the Kairos board, because for the most part, there's a high level of trust. (2007)

The Protestant churches have largely decreased their support for the organization because of both organizational challenges and changing priorities and values. Hansen has explained: "The faith community right now is worried about the faith of the community" (2007). That is, they recently have been more focused on self-preservation and less concerned about participating in ecumenical efforts. Even as the churches have become less engaged with the trade battle during the era of Kairos, however, the coalition still has mattered for the life of the church. It has provided, and continues to provide, a space for justice-minded Christians to come together. It gives churches with limited resources political support for those trying to mobilize for justice.[14]

Although all the churches theoretically have never stopped supporting social justice, Hansen has noted that there has not been the sustained theological reflection occurring in any of the denominations or religious orders on par with the dialogue that occurred at the initial stages of interchurch efforts. With Kairos, there has been even less theological reflection on the ways that religious groups should respond to globalization. Hansen has argued that in his religious order, the Redemptorists, fewer religious leaders have been trained in theology and in how to think critically about their faith in dealing with social issues. Could this lack of religious involvement be a factor in why several of the recent staff members have not had strong personal religious identities? Whatever the cause, those drafting the policies of Kairos are not always guided by the same religious values or theological reasoning of the early activists.

New religious audiences, however, do exist for the coalition. At an international level, ECEJ and Kairos have produced documents for the Ecumenical Advocacy Alliance (in Geneva) and the World Council of Churches. As is the case of the Presbyterians in the United States (described in Chapter 3), the contributions of Kairos to the global ecumenical discourse have influenced the discourse of other churches and denominations outside their home country. Kairos may yet prove to be a leader in such international ecumenical dialogue, especially as more religious communities globally engage with issues of trade and globalization.

Ironically, conservative religious communities are becoming an audience of Kairos and may bring renewed theological reflection to the coalition. In the Atlantic region, for example, some Baptist churches are considering membership in the coalition for the first time. This has been facilitated by the more

---

[14] The Social Justice Institute, held in May 2007 in Edmonton, brought together a diverse religious group of ecumenically minded activists. One participant suggested that this served as a quasi–home church for some people, since it was one of the few places where they found others whose faith was centered in justice work. Many with a commitment to justice, she argued, felt like lone voices in their congregations.

mainstream identity of Kairos and by the growing concerns within the conservative Christian communities over issues of economic inequality.

CONCLUSION

The coalitions of GATT-Fly, ECEJ, and Kairos have been and still are an important part of the religious landscape in Canada. They were birthed by religious activists in Catholic and mainline Protestant communities in Canada, and a religious commitment to practicing justice has proven to be the foundation of the coalitions. GATT-Fly came into existence during a time when liberation theology was gaining popularity in Latin America, and this coalition adapted central liberationist principles into their own religious practices: solidarity, empowerment, and the protection of creation. These values of practice guided their initial critiques of neoliberalism, as they contested the reach of markets, the lack of democracy in international negotiations, and the weakening of states to manage their own economies. Such political positions became tied to the religious identity of the coalition, an identity defined by practice and their international perspective.

For GATT-Fly, an emphasis on liberation theology drove the organization to reject the status quo and struggle for an alternative economic structure. They encountered this theology through their work around the world, so liberation theology was both a product of their solidarity with others and a tool that reinforced the value of and practice of solidarity. This emphasis helped to shape the identity of GATT-Fly (and later ECEJ and Kairos) not only as a group in solidarity with the poor around the world, but also as one committed to strategies of grassroots involvement, research, and reflection. The commitment to solidarity explains their strong participation in civil society alliances and the movement against free trade. Although religiously shaped political values have continued to guide the organization, the work of Kairos has been influenced less directly by liberation theology and more directly by the practices adapted from it.

Many of those working out of the liberationist tradition have expressed disappointment at the changed times and the lack of energy within the Christian community at the turn of the century. Although Kairos has continued to work for justice, they are not charged with the same mission of pursuing controversial economic alternatives. Official linkages with the church have become more important for Kairos, and its religious identity is characterized more by its organizational affiliations. This changed identity has provided activists with a better platform for raising political concerns over free trade, but it also has made their work in favor of an alternative order more challenging. As Kairos enters into the future, questions remain about their audience, although they appear to have an important voice in global ecumenical justice efforts.

3

Covenants and Treaties: PCUSA's Evolving Trade Policy

In 2003, the Presbyterian Church (USA), or PCUSA, approved a social policy that rejected the Free Trade Area of the Americas (FTAA). It called upon its members to learn about trade agreements and the "role of the International Monetary Fund (IMF), World Bank, World Trade Organization (WTO) and other multinational organizations in creating and enforcing globalization policies that are unsustainable and unjust" (General Assembly [PCUSA] 2003, "On Opposing the FTAA"). Attention to free trade agreements (FTAs) in the early twenty-first century was not unique to the PCUSA. In the 2008 presidential election, candidates offered valuable airtime to the topic of free trade. They discussed their positions on whether and under what conditions NAFTA should be continued and how other FTAs should be implemented. Central to most of these conversations was the plight of displaced American workers. This stands in contrast to twenty years earlier, when most of the U.S. population was unaware of the Canada–United States FTA.

Like the United States at large, many people in religious communities are more concerned about and aware of FTAs today than they were twenty years ago. The PCUSA is a prime example, as its 2003 statement was its first social policy to reject a specific FTA. In the middle of the century, the church had encouraged the United States to strengthen its trade relationships with other countries. Then when FTAs first appeared on the scene, the PCUSA was silent; it did not address the Canada–United States FTA of the 1980s in its social policies. In 1993, however, there was a shift as PCUSA leaders called for their members to become educated on the policies of NAFTA, and they called for fast-track procedures to be repealed so more deliberation on the FTA could occur. By 2003, their social policy against the FTAA was adopted, and in 2004, they also rejected the Central America–United States Free Trade Agreement, or CAFTA (which later became the Central America–Dominican Republic–United States Free Trade Agreement, or CAFTA-DR). Unlike the general debate in the public sphere, however, the analysis did not draw centrally upon the fate of displaced American workers but instead took a more global perspective. The PCUSA charged that the market has too much power, rights are not protected, and businesses and single states have too much control in the current system. None of these values makes the PCUSA stand out in significant ways from the two other case studies in this text, but their endorsement of global governance as a solution was unique.

Since 1967, when the most recent confessional doctrinal statement for the church was accepted, the PCUSA has held a consistent set of theological values and understandings of religion's role in public life. Religious and moral values have been authoritative in developing their policies. Claims of God's sovereignty, the responsibility of being in a covenant with a global community, and an attitude of hope for change have pervaded the discourse found in research reports, policy statements, and calls for actions. Influenced by the Reformed tradition and its emphasis on covenant theology, their concept of justice is consistently framed in terms of right relationships, which they have found lacking in current trade agreements.

Why did the PCUSA change their stance on free trade and free trade policies, from virtually ignoring the Canada–United States FTA to actively lobbying against FTAs at the beginning of the twenty-first century? Their values and creeds did not change, but increased U.S. public attention to the issue of trade and more personal experiences of Presbyterians with international network partners put the issue of free trade policies under the lens of the PCUSA and demanded its theological attention. Empirically based, democratically developed research played a central role for the church in its reflection. Given that policies garnered authority through consensus, representativeness of discourse was especially important for the PCUSA.

In this chapter, I begin by explaining in more detail how the PCUSA's political stance on trade changed over the years, up to its current stance of finally spurning several FTAs. To assess their stance, I rely mainly on policy statements and publications from several different PCUSA ministry divisions and advisory councils. They have called for limits on the market, economic rights for all people, and improved global governance to ameliorate market inequalities and abuses. I then highlight the role that Reformed theology – and specifically values of sovereignty, covenant, community, and hope – has had in influencing the political stances of the group. I go on to explain the roles of research, policy, and activism in creating the church's political identity. Finally, I examine the question of which voices have contributed to the discourse, probing the importance of democracy and dialogue to the church's perspective. Although I find that members have underutilized the research reports and policies developed, analysis of panel data suggests the discourse has resonated with members. Further, the church's discourse over trade has served as a valuable resource for those members wanting to be involved in economic social change.

POLICIES ON TRADE AND GLOBALIZATION

Three Stages of Trade Policy in the PCUSA

The Presbyterian Church[1] first spoke about international trade in the middle of the century, with initial policy directed at increasing U.S. involvement in the global community. In a time when it was feared that protectionist sentiments would hurt the economic restructuring of war-torn nations, such policies were a way for the United States to engage internationally in the development process. Over time, a more international perspective of the PCUSA has been reflected in increased research on the impacts of certain terms of trade, often with a focus on the detrimental impacts to poorer and more vulnerable populations. Through its social policy-making body – the General Assembly (GA), a representative group of laity and clergy – the church has actively called for more research on the North American Free Trade Agreement (NAFTA) and subsequent FTAs; and its most recent policies have rejected current agreements and facilitated lobbying in Washington, DC, against such FTAs.

National Engagement. After the Second World War, the GA of the church issued one of its first statements on trade and globalization:

> We look with alarm upon the attempts of certain groups to modify the Reciprocal Trade Agreements so as to nullify future steps toward freeing international trade.... The denial of trade with any country will imperil mutual understanding and good human relations, and will not promote peace, world order and Christian fellowship.
>
> (General Assembly [PCUS] 1948, "On Trade")

Six years later, the GA issued a similar statement: "We reaffirm our conviction that our nation has a large measure of responsibility for the economic well-being of the free world of which it is a part. We encourage the development of policies which contribute to the expansion of world trade" (General Assembly [PCUS] 1954, "On Trade"). A United States–centric focus toward development was rejected, and the church maintained that the nation had a responsibility to act for the welfare of other nations. They proposed U.S. engagement in trade as a benefit to other countries, though they provided little explanation as to their reasoning.

The Confession of 1967, as introduced in Chapter 1, is the most recent theological treatise of the organization. Although not a policy statement, it prioritized international issues for the church and called for more critical analysis of such issues. The Confession named racism, international relations, poverty, and sexism as four central areas of concern for the church. The creed

---

[1] The mid-century Presbyterian Church looked different from the church today. In 1958, the small United Presbyterian Church merged with the Presbyterian Church's northern branch. Then in 1973, the southern branch split into Presbyterian Church U.S. and the more conservative Presbyterian Church in America (PCA). Finally, in 1983, Presbyterian Church U.S. merged with its northern counterpart to form the PCUSA.

defined a new path for the church, along with the subsequent mergers and divisions, largely prompting members' attention to questions of international economics.

For example, a study of transnational organizations was commissioned by Presbyterians in the late 1970s. In the report on transnational corporations (TNCs) eventually submitted to the GA, the advisory committee discussed the past reluctance of the church to consider problems of structures and institutions. They attributed a past unwillingness to examine structural complexities or challenge governing structures and systems in part to the number of Presbyterians serving as members or leaders of TNCs. As noted previously, strong opinions and perspectives often prohibit critical attention to issues of poverty and inequality.

> The task force has documented and described some powerful feelings and strong differences of opinion among Presbyterians on issues related to economics and corporations. We are not facing these differences openly or exploring together the requirements of Christian witness in the midst of these complex and challenging issues.... Our life and work together are a model of what we earnestly wish for the whole church, within which we believe the serious and sustained engagement with the intersection of faith and economic institutions is long overdue and urgently needed.
>
> (General Assembly Mission Council [PCUSA] 1984, 7)

Another report from 1984, *Christian Faith and Economic Justice*, also analyzed critical economic concerns, ultimately declaring both capitalism and socialism as flawed systems. In this extensive report, the church approached questions of the role of the United States more critically than in the past: "[We] benefit from economic structures that have very negative consequences for so many so-called 'developing' nations." The report called for Presbyterians to work toward a more just economic order: "We have got to take sides – and for many of us, that means we must change sides" (General Assembly [PCUSA] 1984, section 29.339).

Although both *Christian Faith and Economic Justice* and the TNC report (in part guided by the mandates of the Confession of 1967) drew new critical attention to economic structures, there was still an overwhelming focus on the United States. Global poverty was discussed, but at an abstract level: "The gap between rich and poor countries continues to grow. In 1982, in the United States, there were 34.4 million persons (15 percent of the population) who were officially poor.... In Third World nations it is even worse. Poverty is a way of life for the bulk of their populations" (General Assembly [PCUSA] 1984, section 29.149). Attention to international social issues was still connected with the concerns of economic challenges faced by those in North America. Yet another example from *Christian Faith and Economic Justice* reveals how even amid concern for poverty in developing countries, the PCUSA directed attention to the possible negative impacts that helping such economies would have on the United States:

It is imperative that global justice is not achieved at the expense of the displaced American workers, but neither should we ignore the benefits the poorer nations can receive via increased manufacturing.... In general, this committee favors free trade when all competitors play by the same rules and views with concern the rise in protectionism around the world. (General Assembly [PCUSA], 1984)

In addition to *Christian Faith and Economic Justice*, another report, *Toward a Just, Caring and Dynamic Political Economy* (1985), addressed the domestic economic policies of the United States. Together, these reports from the 1980s represent the church's shift toward a more critical and structural analysis of the economy.

Such trends fit with what Steensland (2002) finds in his study of mainline Protestant advocacy in the United States on domestic poverty. He finds that starting in the 1960s, mainline advocates began calling for significant reforms and joining in broader coalitions. During the 1980s, when the PCUSA was producing the documents noted previously, others in the mainline Protestant community were also involved in critical analysis of economic systems.

Global Solidarity. A second shift in trade policy emerged when discussions over NAFTA entered the political horizon in the late 1980s. As the age of bilateral trade agreements began, church leaders lacked clarity about how to process this new era of globalization. Even with the recognition of a flawed and unjust international economic order, there was uncertainty over how to think about FTAs. Negotiations over the Canada–United States FTA were not a focus of PCUSA social policies. Just a few years later, however, NAFTA piqued their attention as social policy rejected the fast-track procedures to ensure more discussion over the treaty. And in discussions over NAFTA, the church showed an increased awareness of international conditions that was not present in some of their other studies of international economic systems. Their GA policy on NAFTA proclaimed these concerns:

The comprehensive Free Trade Agreement is a free trade issue for all persons living in the United States, Canada, and Mexico, with particular devastating impact on women workers and their families living along the U.S.-Mexico border.... The Free Trade Agreement will have a domino effect on employment and other economic factors on persons living in the U.S. and the American continents.

(General Assembly [PCUSA] 1992, "Free Trade Agreement")

At the same time that the GA was speaking about NAFTA, *Hope for a Global Future* was in its beginning stages. This report was commissioned in 1991 to provide an in-depth analysis of and theological reflection on globalization. *Hope for a Global Future*, completed in 1996, was part of a larger corpus of research; out of the document, the GA commissioned four research reports on globalization. Policies approved from *Hope for a Global Future* included recommendations for the U.S. government to more carefully consider the impact of new trade policies on the poor and the environment, to more critically hold their own power in negotiations, and to practically incorporate sustainability criteria into trade agreements.

As the PCUSA continued to evaluate the changes wrought by globalization, the GA accepted a second report. *Just Globalization* (2006) largely echoed many of the stances in *Hope for a Global Future*. But it extended the PCUSA's position in light of more empirical evidence on the impacts of trade: it declared their solidarity with the global community, affirming the church's support of the United Nations (UN) and the rule of international law. Presbyterians were encouraged to support fair trade initiatives, as the report called for "guidelines and mechanisms to help balance appropriately the interests of transnational corporations and of host or trading nations with weakened internal governance structures" (Advisory Committee on Social Witness Policy [ACSWP] 2006, 2). Ultimately, the church declared in *Just Globalization* that "*Hope for a Global Future* was and still is right in its conclusions, 'Trade rules that enable affluent nations to profit at the expense of poor nations or that do not contribute substantially to the reduction of poverty in all nations cannot be accepted ethically'" (ACSWP 2006, 19).

Evaluating Empirical Realities. Although the research in 2006 looked similar to the research from 1996, GA policy toward trade changed more significantly during this same time span. Whereas policy in the early 1990s took a cautious stance toward NAFTA, GA policy in 2003 officially denounced the FTAA, calling on the church to "oppose multinational actions and trade agreements that elevate rights of corporations over the right of governments and indigenous peoples to pass and enforce laws that preserve the public good and protect their citizens, economies, and environments" (General Assembly [PCUSA] 2003, "Opposition to FTAA").

Such a position was based in part on economic analysis of NAFTA's impact. This rejection of FTAs prompted the PCUSA's Washington, DC, office to lobby against CAFTA, the FTAA, and the more recent United States–Peru and United States–Columbia agreements: "[We direct] representatives of PCUSA programs dealing with economic justice, hunger, and advocacy, to promptly communicate the General Assembly position to the U.S. trade representative, U.S. senators and representatives, congressional committees with trade jurisdiction, and state legislators " (General Assembly [PCUSA] 2003, "Opposition to FTAA").

Although rejection of most FTAs is recent, the concerns over such policies are consistent with the historical approach of the Presbyterian Church towards economic markets. The PCUSA has called for more limits to be placed on the market in order to restrict those who would try to expand the reach of the market or exploit it for their own gain. Arguing from a perspective that human rights must include economic rights, redistribution has been offered as a concrete example of how the market could deliver such economic rights. Finally, they have advocated that global governance is central to accomplishing these changes in the market, expressing their faith in current global bodies such as the UN to regulate market life.

Limit the Market and Protect the Poor

After World War II, GA policy encouraged the United States to engage in free trade with all nations with the goal of economic development and rebuilding. To this end, the PCUSA accepted the liberalization of international economic markets. Yet their research in the 1980s reveals their reluctance to fully endorse the free trade, free market model. In debates over capitalism and socialism as systems, the PCUSA highlighted problems and benefits within each.

A key goal of the PCUSA, much like that of the Costa Rican Catholic Church, has been to establish ethical development guidelines within capitalist markets. In one of the four academic reports resulting from *Hope for a Global Future*, Gordon Douglass, a Presbyterian, economist, and member of the *Hope for a Global Future* task force, brought up the idea of how religious values should guide market behavior:

This insistence on social and moral autonomy has caused critics in the church to denounce "the market society in whose logic God's grace and God's justice cannot appear." To acknowledge a sphere of life from which moral scrutiny is excluded is to abridge God's sovereignty and create an absolute that rivals God. Biblical faith acknowledges no such rival. An unfettered world market is not a biblical vision. The biblical goal is not maximization of the freedom to seek individual benefits, corporate profit, or national advantage in the international market.   (Douglass 2001, 2)

The church supported trade when such trade was evaluated as just. But the justice of market activity and trade were predicated on whether certain regulations were followed and whether the end results were sustainable and beneficial to the community.

Checks and balances on the market, then, are essential. This includes guaranteeing that the poor are not hurt by the system, that human rights are not violated, and that those in power do not abuse their position. Critiques on the market, however, have revealed an assumption that free markets are generally good and useful. The church has thought about the positive ways to use free markets. Reports on TNCs, both in the 1980s and more recently in 2006, have been indicative of this support, with restrictions, for free markets. Task force participants rarely have barraged TNCs for being evil but have looked instead at how to make corporations part of a positive story for the economically disadvantaged.

The emphasis on protection of the poor has been tied to the assumption that free markets often largely benefit companies and businesses and that guidelines should be directed at changing this dynamic. This attitude has evolved over time in the denomination, and when the report on TNCs came out in the mid-1980s, it reflected the mixed opinion on corporations. By the turn of the century, there was a stronger critique of the power such corporations wield and a stronger push for ethical governance of these corporations. Empirically, the power of corporations also has increased since the mid-1980s, as has international awareness of corporations and their impacts. GA policy against current bilateral agreements has discussed the violations of such companies. The policy on *maquilas* stated that "many of the mostly U.S.-owned maquiladoras along the Mexico-U.S. border are in violations of principles of justice toward both the human community and the environment" (General Assembly [PCUSA] 1992, "Maquiladoras along the U.S.–Mexico Border"). As a result, the church has promoted stricter regulations for these businesses.

Standards to protect laborers have been one regulation the GA has encouraged. After referring to the clause in CAFTA that each party must "enforce its labor laws," the GA declared its skepticism:

> For countries where labor violations are egregious and systemic, this clause is insufficient to guarantee protection of worker's rights ... The labor provision in CAFTA will also replace the Generalized System of Preferences (GSP), which includes a petition process, leading to the loss of a useful, if modest, enforcement mechanism. Finally, no protection systems are established for rural or urban workers adversely affected by the trade agreements.
> (General Assembly [PCUSA] 2004, "Opposition to CAFTA")

Although the church called for concrete standards, its willingness to endorse and support capitalism distinguished the PCUSA from some other groups within the larger international Reformed community, as described later in the chapter.

In contrast to Kairos, there has been less attention within the PCUSA toward the problems faced by indigenous communities or ethnic minorities and women. *We Are What We Eat*, a report from 2002, is a notable exception, as it asserts concern that women are disproportionately represented among the poor. But there has been little attention to the unique challenges faced by poor women. Lois Livezey, a professor at New York Theological Seminary and former head of the theological educators task force of the PCUSA, noted the inadequate attention that women received in Presbyterian research on globalization; even though she had been consulted about the topic, little flowed from that effort in terms of written research. That is, although the church has addressed systemic problems of poverty arising from the construction of the market, they have been less attentive to analyzing how different groups are unequally situated within such systems.

Expand Human Rights

The PCUSA demanded that protection of human rights had to be central in trade agreements; further, they expanded the basic definition of rights to include economic rights. Redistribution, alongside the promotion of the democratic governance, was supported to advance such rights and enforce the political and economic welfare of all people.

The emphasis on the protection of the poor and their welfare may have been strategic due to political division in the church. That is, even though politics are dicey, there is a shared value of caring about the poor. Mark Adams and his work with Presbyterian Border Ministries are a good example of shared concern for the poor in the midst of political disagreement. He worked with both liberal and conservative churches in Arizona but noted that all churches shared some common ground: concern for the Central American and Mexican migrants, especially those illegally crossing the border. Stuart Taylor, pastor at St. Mark's Presbyterian Church in Tucson, mentioned that even those endorsing the restrictive U.S. policy on immigration do provide humanitarian aid to migrants and see a need to care for their human rights.

PCUSA statements against the FTAA and CAFTA referenced the violation of rights as the primary cause for their lack of approval, and their understandings of these rights is expansive: "We declare our opposition to the Central American Free Trade Agreement (CAFTA) in its current form as it fails to adequately protect workers' rights, human rights, food security, and environmental standards" (General Assembly [PCUSA] 2004, "Opposition to CAFTA"). These rights follow with the concept of dignity also promoted by the Catholic Church in Costa Rica, the right to work to provide for oneself. As reflected in a 2004 policy statement, "As Presbyterians, we affirm the right of all people to meet their basic needs ... all of which presuppose a living wage. We affirm the right of farmers to make an adequate living on their lands" (General Assembly [PCUSA] 2004, "Opposition to CAFTA"). The church had previously defined rights as covering not only basic needs but also the ability to participate fully in political and economic life:

All humans are entitled to the essential conditions for expressing their human dignity and for participation in defining and shaping the common good. These rights include satisfaction of basic biophysical needs (e.g., adequate nutrition, shelter, and health care), environmental safety, full participation in political and economic life, and the assurance of fair treatment and equal protection of the laws.   (ACSWP 1996, 62)

Practically, redistribution was endorsed as a way to uphold rights in trade agreements. The church argued that within free trade, there were winners and losers and that states should be involved in compensating those who are harmed. That is, the church recognized the benefits that free markets could produce but demanded that states deal with the negative aspects of such markets. In *Resolution on Just Globalization*, the church specifically critiqued current ideas about property and the market: "The values of sharing, sufficiency, and sustainability make for a stewardship society more than an ownership society" (ACSWP 2006, 6). How to share resources takes priority over protecting individual rights to private property.

Part of the redistribution they called for was between nations; this has been encouraged since the PCUSA began talking about trade. In one of their earliest social policies on trade, the GA encouraged the United States to engage in trade in part because of its redistributive nature. It called the nation to "support appropriate mechanisms that will automatically transfer some resources from the rich to the poor nations" (General Assembly [PCUS] 1977, "On Lowering Trade Barriers"). The PCUSA supported debt relief for some of these same reasons. In *Voices from Korea, U.S.A., and Brazil* (a report that brought together five denominations from three different countries to discuss economic issues[2]), the church made the argument that rich countries must bear the costs for poorer nations to participate as "the price of doing business in a global economy" (Office of Ecumenical Affairs 2001, 16). Such redistribution promotes stronger relationships and community, according to the task force of *Resolution on Just Globalization*: "optimal exchange occurs between societies that share similar social and economic goals and institutions," which is more likely to exist when economic redistribution occurs (ACSWP 2006, 21). Taxing international businesses was supported as a "major source of revenues to be used mainly if not exclusively in poor countries for ending poverty, preserving life, strengthening social safety nets, and protecting the environment" (ACSWP 2006, 46).

Presbyterian history also reveals calls for redistribution among individuals. In *Economic Justice Within Environmental Limits*, the church asserted that redistributional efforts must accompany trade within a country: "If trade is liberalized to allow more foreign goods to enter the United States, we should not ask those individuals adversely affected to bear the brunt of those policies. The public at large should pay the costs of developing new employment opportunities and retraining and relocating workers" (Advisory Council on Church and Society [ACCS] 1976, 44). Douglass (2001) affirmed in *The Globalization of Economic Life*, "Any movement towards free trade should be accompanied by more generous adjustment assistance policies, including unemployment benefits and retraining and relocational subsidies" (12). *Just Globalization* echoed this call:

Labor, corporate America, and government must leave behind the old model of assuming that a fair sharing of economic benefits will emerge most efficiently from an unending struggle among them . . . [They] must think together about how to best shape a future that will bring a more just distribution of benefits to our society.   (ACSWP 2006, 29)

Clearly, the church has supported some level of redistribution, both between and within states, to promote human and economic rights, including more equitable (and so, more just) economic relationships.

Increase Global Governance

Although God, to the PCUSA, reigns over the market, it is a global civil society that must govern it. While both of the other cases in this book also have supported international governance, the PCUSA has been the most supportive

---

[2] In addition to the PCUSA from the United States, this dialogue included the Ingreja Presbiteriana Independente do Brasil, the Ingreja Presbiteriana Unida do Brasil, the Presbyterian Church in Korea, and the Presbyterian Church in the Republic of Korea.

of the UN and other global institutions. International organizations often have been referenced as potential avenues through which to confront unequal relationships between states, and Presbyterian social policy in the last thirty years frequently has used UN documents authoritatively. Recent discussion about international organizations overwhelmingly has lent support to the UN, often adopting their guidelines and frequently calling on the United States to give more support to this international organization. The UN Declaration of the Rights of the Child, the UN Millennium Development Goals, and the Earth Charter Initiative were listed within PCUSA documents as sources of productive guidelines for society.

As described earlier, the postwar PCUSA church actively urged the United States not to withdraw from global society but to increase their economic and political transactions with other countries. As the United States accepted its role in a global community and tried to lead, the emphasis within the church shifted to the need for the United States to become more of a team player. For this to happen, the nation had to give up some of its power. *Economic Justice Within Environmental Limits* emphasized this imperative:

It might come as a surprise to many Americans to hear that they have been the beneficiaries of practices that others have termed "exploitative" and "imperialistic." Correcting global inequalities is a necessary but painful process for those of us who have benefitted from present structures. The New International Economic Order (NIEO) championed by Third World countries in the United Nations demands a fair price for raw materials. That will likely result in higher prices for consumers in industrial countries.   (ACCS 1976, 44)

Although the acknowledgment of U.S. power often has been critical, it has not been viewed solely as negative. In *Hope for a Global Future*, for example, one of the important changes made during the synod consultation process was recognizing the power the United States had yielded in trade negotiations. The committee added the line, "Given the unequal bargaining position of various nations" (ACSWP 1996, 135), before listing some of the problems with current trade policy. In *Resolution on Just Globalization*, the authors noted that "the United States government can play a huge role in moving the world towards the positive vision," if they work with others to pursue policies toward globalization that benefit the community (ACSWP 2006, 49). The PCUSA has encouraged more reflection on the part of the United States toward its power and has advocated for more control by international institutions as a way to monitor the power of individual states.

Concretely, the PCUSA views global institutions as providing an alternative to the current trade situation. The GA called for the following:

a multinational effort to transform the GATT into the GATE, the General Agreement on Trade and the Environment. Primarily still a trade agreement, GATE nonetheless would recognize the importance of sustainable resource consumption and ecosystems preservation as part of a strategy for assuring long-term efficiencies in the production of wealth and trade.   (General Assembly [PCUSA] 1996, "Hope for a Global Future")

Although many groups have emphasized global governance to restrain the market and key market actors, such as the United States, the PCUSA is unique in their hope that current international institutions will govern justly and their belief that power can be used to benefit everyone.

RELIGIOUS TRADITION IN THE PCUSA

There are no authoritative doctrinal documents that bind the PCUSA to the global Reformed community, and the PCUSA experiences the Reformed tradition from a U.S. perspective. That said, such a Reformed theology is at the core of their market critiques. In speaking about their role in trade and globalization, three values have been central: the sovereignty of God, covenant and community, and hope. A sense of God's sovereignty squarely places the market in the realm of church concern, covenant mandates how relationships in the market should be structured, and a sense of hope prompts the church to participate in individual and corporate action.

The Importance of Scripture

Due to a decentralized and democratic structure, the international Reformed community is united mostly by a shared identity based on Reformed principles, as previously mentioned in Chapter 1. Such Calvinist principles include an emphasis on the sovereignty of God, the doctrine of the Trinity, and the doctrine of election. Reformed communities also give a great deal of authority to scripture, which was one of the principles behind the Reformation itself.

Scripture has been consistently affirmed as an important basis for authority, even as understandings over hermeneutics have changed.[3] In a document adopted by the PCUSA, *Why and How the Church Makes a Social Witness Policy*, the task force stated, "We affirm the authority of Scripture for our faith and life, not only as individuals but also as a witnessing community in the world" (ACSWP 1994, 13). Although texts throughout the Bible are used to support action and certain ways of viewing the world, there is a tendency to evoke a biblical *framework* rather than specific biblical analysis or exegesis. For example, in their social policy statement on *maquilas*, the GA asserted that "the Presbyterian Church (U.S.A.) has historically supported justice for all people in all areas of life, including the economic, basing its stand on biblical study of both the Old and New Testaments" (General Assembly [PCUSA] 1992, "Maquiladoras along the U.S.–Mexico Border"). There is no further explanation on how the Old and New Testaments support such points, but the act of referencing scripture

---

[3] As noted in Chapter 1, the Confession of 1967 was instrumental within the Reformed community. It moved the church from a literal reading of scripture to a more critical reading and the "historical peculiarity of all creeds" (Coalter 1999, 65).

provides legitimation. Other examples of this tendency can be found, as demonstrated by the beginning of *Hope for a Global Future*: "this policy statement addresses international issues in the economic structure. It is based on a biblical theology and Christian assumption of the mutual responsibility and equality of human beings in God's sight" (ACSWP 1996, 1). The lack of biblical analysis here was due in part to the purpose of policy statements: to simply declare the position of the GA. In *Hope for a Global Future*, an early chapter developed a theological framework to understand and analyze globalization, and much of the work produced by the ACSWP followed this template:

> The commitment to justice also is clearly visible in the New Testament. Jesus was certainly in the prophetic tradition of Isaiah, Amos, and Hosea when he denounced those who 'tithe mint, dill, and cummin, and have neglected the weightier matters of the law: justice and mercy and faith. It is these you ought to have practiced without neglecting the others' (Matt. 23:23, NRSV; cf. Luke 11:42). Similarly, Matthew's gospel recalls the prophets in its description of divine judgment. Christ comes to us in the form of people suffering from deprivation and oppression, soliciting just and compassionate responses. Individuals and nations will be judged on the basis of their care for the 'have nots' (Matt. 25:31–46).
>
> (ACSWP 1996, 65)

Presbyterian Jack Stotts, a past professor of Protestant ethics and former president of both McCormick Theological Seminary and Austin Presbyterian Theological Seminary, argued that attention to biblical themes, rather of biblical exegesis, was more likely. He explained why in a chapter he wrote for the PCUSA-produced book *Reformed Faith and Economic Justice*:

> Since economics is a more pervasive issue in the Biblical Story than a more circumscribed topic such as homosexuality, those of us in the Reformed tradition believe it is appropriate in dealing with economics not to exegete specific passages. . . . Whatever the case, we tend to speak and to write more in terms of biblical understandings, biblical themes, and biblical perspectives, more than being engaged with specific passages. (1989, 9)

For the PCUSA, the Bible is authoritative when it takes social context into account. And interpreting the Bible is not the job of a particular leader or group of leaders; it is, rather, a corporate process.

Sovereignty

God's sovereignty was the most frequently cited theological value in interviews with PCUSA leaders. Former clerk Clifton Kirkpatrick attested to its significance:

> We are saved because God's mercy is shared with us in order that we can be a part of God's plan to transform the world. Reformed Christians have always had a sense of the sovereignty of God for the world. That's an understanding from the Bible, it's written, and it begins with God's good creation. It moves to the Exodus, to the Prophets, to Jesus's liberation, and to the vision in Revelation of a new heaven and new earth filled with justice and peace. (2007)

Likewise, in *Hope for a Global Future*, the church declared sovereignty as central: "The first statement of the classical creeds is that God is the maker of heaven and earth. This is an affirmation of divine sovereignty, universal providence, creaturely dependence and human responsibility" (ACSWP 1996, 59). Lois Livezey translates sovereignty as "God holds the whole world in His hands." Seeing spheres as interconnected means that the economy cannot be considered outside the realm and power and authority of God. As Livezey continued, "There really isn't debate on whether it's all right to be concerned about the magistrate."

In one of their early forays into international economics, a 1980 policy resolution on the United States and international economic justice, the church asserted God's sovereignty by declaring, "The Presbyterian Church in the United States exists to proclaim the Lordship of Christ and to promote its practice (God's rule) in every sphere" (General Assembly [PCUSA] 1980, "The Presbyterian Church in the United States and America's Role in International Economic Justice"). Such sovereignty transcends time. *Hope for a Global Future* declared, "Because God's ministry is universal, the church's concern must be global as well as local (Isaiah 42:6, 49:6). Because our God is the Sovereign for all time, the church must commit to a sustainable future for all generations" (ACSWP 1996, 70).

A Presbyterian understanding of God's sovereignty rejects people asserting their own dominion. The theological exposition in *Hope for a Global Future* established this before its diagnosis of globalization. "Nothing in creation is independent of God. . . . Thus, no part of the creation – whether other humans, other species, even the elements of soil or water is our property to use as we wish. They are to be treated in accord with the values and ground rules of God, the ultimate owner" (ACSWP 1996, 59).

This idea of sovereignty also means that no sphere of life can take dominion over people. Rather, institutions in society should honor God and community. In *Voices from Korea, U.S.A., and Brazil*, the authors used this argument to place the market in the appropriate context:

The sovereignty of God – the historic core of our shared Reformed faith – calls us to be responsible stewards for all aspects of life in this world and, at the same time, to deny any attempt to establish an alternative center that would compete with faithful worship and service to Jesus Christ. Our Reformed tradition affirms that the purpose of the economic order is to sustain life in community. The body of Christ thus witnesses to a just and sustainable human community.   (Office of Ecumenical Affairs 2001, 18)

Covenant and Community

A second theological theme that impacts trade attitudes in the PCUSA is the notion that people enter into a covenant with a creator God. Covenant theology also mandates commitment to the neighbor. *Hope for a Global Future* characterized the Christian idea of covenant as one of responsibility to God and all people:

The covenants between God and the liberated people were understood largely as God's laws for right relationships. They established a moral responsibility on the part of the society and its members to deal fairly with participants in the covenant and provide for the basic needs of all.... Faithfulness to covenant relationships demands a justice that recognizes special obligations, "a preferential option" to widows, orphans, the poor, and aliens – in other words, the economically vulnerable and politically oppressed (Ex. 23:6–9; Deut. 15:4–11; 24:14–22; Jer. 22:16; Amos 2:6–7; 5:10–12).

(ACSWP 1996, 64–65)

Clear ties are made between a covenant with God and the responsibility one has toward what and whom God has created. Supporting covenant theology translates to promoting equitable and just relationships among people. The GA stated that "God is the Judge and Redeemer of all nations.... The world has become a neighborhood" (General Assembly [PCUSA] 1984, "Addressing International Concerns Beyond the U.S."). Such a policy suggests that people are in a covenant with the whole of global society and not just those immediately around them. This global covenant legitimated the PCUSA's impelling of members to care and act more on behalf of the global community.

Beyond trade documents, those on immigration and migration also highlighted the inclusive value of covenant. In *Resolution on Just Globalization*, the idea of covenant was supported with relation to Genesis:

Whether between God and humankind or between family members or near strangers, a covenant involved mutual promises, responsibilities, and commitments. God's covenant with Abraham was not to show favoritism for one person, family, or nation; it embodies a promise for all people.... Christians see in Jesus the personification of God's intent to break the bounds of nationality, race, ethnicity, and geography, to include all peoples and nations in the covenant of justice. Covenant theology reminds us that while faith is personal it is never merely individual. We are called to the community of faithfulness that is engaged in doing justice and in seeing that justice is done.   (ACSWP 2006, 8)

Covenant requires a certain depth of relationship as well. Gordon Douglass (2001) wrote in his report on globalization what covenant entails: "A global economy of biblical dimensions seeks a community of shared values and commitments that transcends geographic, political, ethnic, and cultural divisions. Community involves covenant, not merely contact" (2). The basis of such a community is God, as *Hope for a Global Future* attested: "Communal identity is found not in bloodlines nor culture, but rather through Jesus Christ, in whom is the dignity and equality that unites humanity in a covenant of rights and responsibilities" (ACSWP 1996, 66). An obligation to community prompted the involvement that Presbyterians now have in the world.

Covenant and community also have been central to the experience of worship for the PCUSA, and communal confessions serve a central role. Although in part an aspect of the confessional nature of the PCUSA, this role also reflects its emphasis on community.

Covenant, although primarily about one's relationship with God and community, also requires attention to the relationship between individuals and the earth. Two reports that especially expressed this were *Restoring Creation for Ecology and Justice* (Committee on Social Witness Policy of PCUSA [CSWP] 1990) and the globalization paper on the environment by Stivers (2003). Theologically, the responsibility of people toward the environment is based on the fact that creation is God's product, an argument put forth by *Restoring Creation for Ecology and Justice*, which stated that "the biblical-theological basis for restoring creation is very simple: The Creator is always the Redeemer, and the Redeemer is always also the Creator.... Because God the Creator loves the whole creation, God the Redeemer acts to save creation when it is bound down and cries out" (CSWP 1990, 19). The life inherent in creation, if not human, is still life that people must respect. As Robert Stivers (2003), a Presbyterian and religion professor, wrote in research on the environment stemming from *Hope for a Global Future*, "Voices should be heard, and if not able to speak, which is the case for other species, then humans will have to represent their interests" (17).

Important for the concept of covenant, care for the environment was often framed as caring for people impacted by it and with whom we share a covenant bond. This especially includes the poor, given their vulnerability and increased need for protection. Promoting sufficiency and protecting resources is important, as such resources mean that society, as Stivers (2003) argued, can "meet basic human needs.... It expresses a concern for future generations and the planet as a whole" (15).

Hope

Hope was a third theological theme emerging in the documents. Although not identified by name from interviewees as a central value, it emerged in almost all the documents, especially in discourse over action and change. Much of the policy and research on trade and development placed an emphasis on structural solutions. Yet there was always a notion that change was possible and that individual actions mattered. Hope was integrally connected to the concept of redemption. There is always hope that with God, the individual can be redeemed from sin and can be involved in broader societal redemption.

In a statement addressing the issue of global hunger, the GA declared this hope that prompted their action and attention: "However, we believe that, massive and complex as these problems are, there is yet hope. Given the will and commitment, it is possible to redress injustices and overcome the worst aspects of widespread hunger and malnutrition" (General Assembly [PCUSA] 1987, "Affirmation on Global Hunger"). This policy also addressed the need for such hope in light of what might seem a practical inability to influence and promote change: "We recognize the enormity of the task to which we are committing ourselves as well as the risk of much that we shall seek to do. We have no illusion of easy success in this undertaking. Yet we dare to act because we dare to hope."

Such hope is rooted in seeing oneself as God's partner; people's actions in the world are connected to God's action in the world. This prompts the church to work for change in obedience to God and to actively hope for change because of God's power. The *Sustainable Development* study guide states, "Presbyterians believe that God is present and active in our world as creator, sustainer, redeemer, liberator, and judge. We confess that 'in Christ God was reconciling the world to himself' (2 Corin 5:19). We talk about Jesus Christ as Lord and Savior, the 'only Mediator between God and man [*sic*]'" (ACSWP 1994, 15). This statement supports a notion that the church must work for *and* hope for change in the world.

This partnership with God is based in a theological understanding of people as created in the image of God. The theological reflection found in *Hope for a Global Future* asserts:

The concept of the image of God provides a basis for Christian affirmations of the dignity of individuals, human rights, and democratic procedures. It suggests that human beings have a God-given dignity and worth. . . . To be in the image of God is a vocation or calling, based on the biological fact that humans alone have evolved the peculiar capacity to represent, in modest caring ways, God's care for the Creation."   (ACSWP 1996, 63)

The document continues to explain how hope sustains the PCUSA's work in the world:

There are good reasons for persistence in the struggle despite demoralizing defeats. Evil is not the whole story. Forces of good are also present. Positive though limited changes can and do occur with persistence. The Resurrection of Christ is a constant reminder that pessimism is premature! Hope is always warranted. New possibilities are always emerging on the socioeconomic scene. . . . Our God is always present, active, and creating new possibilities for expressing the covenant of justice. . . . Our power is in the confidence that God is empowering us for God's cause.   (ACSWP 1996, 71)

Sovereignty, covenant, and hope are interconnected themes dealing with the relationships between God, people, and society. Rooted in Reformed theology, such values were found throughout the PCUSA's research and policies on development and trade. Although these values have had a long history in the religious tradition of the church, it has been in more recent history that they were connected to issues of trade policy as the Reformed emphasis on social ethics increased.

Nationalist Ideals

As the previous and following chapters discuss, religious actors in Canada and Costa Rica were more likely to name important positive national values and practices that were guiding their behavior, and to explicitly reference such national rhetoric to increase the appeal of their message to other citizens. Given that trade debates were often about the relationship of Canada or Costa Rica with the United States, such values often implied a contrast to the United States. Among the PCUSA, rhetoric was more likely to talk about global/human values, and to make connections across nationalistic boundaries.

This does not mean, however, that those in the United States were less influenced by their national location; rather, it speaks to the fact that these religious actors were perhaps less aware of the impact of nationality. As is the case in other instances of privilege, nationality may serve as a taken-for-granted aspect of identity. The idea of not recognizing national context is, in itself, associated with American exceptionalism (McCloskey and Zaller 1994).

Lamont and Thévenot (2000), in their comparison of the United States and France, highlighted that market-based repertoires are more easily accessible within the United States context; likewise, equality of opportunity is more likely to be stressed in the United States than elsewhere (McCloskey and Zaller 1984). I would argue that those in the United States have a less critical approach to dominant institutions, whether economic or political, than other actors. Earlier in the chapter I noted that the PCUSA had a positive view of global governance and global institutions, and the hope that these could and would be just. A hope in governance and institutions is predicated, by nature, on an emphasis on process. The fact that Americans are more likely to emphasize the equality of process (versus outcomes) seems relevant, paired with positive experiences of the global capitalist system when compared with other national contexts.

PCUSA policies and research that rejected FTAs lacked the biting critiques of capitalism voiced by many other members of the World Alliance of Reformed Churches (WARC).[4] In contrast to the previously mentioned positions of the PCUSA, consider the following statement from WARC's ACCRA confession, *Covenanting for Justice in the Economy and Earth*:

This [neoliberalism] is an ideology that claims to be without alternative, demanding an endless flow of sacrifices from the poor and creation. It makes the false promise that it can save the world through the creation of wealth and prosperity, claiming sovereignty over life and demanding total allegiance, which amounts to idolatry ... We see the dramatic convergence of the economic crisis with the integration of economic globalization and geopolitics backed by neoliberal ideology. This is a global system that defends and protects the interests of the powerful. It affects and captivates us all.   (2004, 3)

WARC went on to indict the United States and call for a change in the current order:

As markets have become global, so have the political and legal institutions which protect them. The government of the United States of America and its allies, together with international finance and trade institutions (International Monetary Fund, World Bank, World Trade Organization) use political, economic, or military alliances to protect and

---

[4] In 2010, WARC merged with the Reformed Ecumenical Council to become the World Communion of Reformed Churches.

advance the interest of capital owners. . . . *Therefore, we reject* the current world economic order imposed by global neoliberal capitalism and any other economic system, including absolute planned economies, which defy God's covenant by excluding the poor, the vulnerable and the whole of creation from the fullness of life.   (2004, 3; italics added)

Although the PCUSA has criticized most economic systems over time, they have stopped short of rejecting the current system and the naming the United States as a central villain.

POLICIES, RESEARCH, AND ACTIVISM

Democratic Process

The PCUSA is a large and decentralized mainline Protestant denomination, producing a myriad of resources from its various offices. Rick Ufford-Chase, a former moderator of the church and current director of the Presbyterian Peace Fellowship, explained its governance structure as: "Presbyterian polity, it pretty much mirrors U.S. governance. . . . In fact, some people say, and I think it's probably true, that much of how our Congress works was designed by Presbyterians and it came directly out of their experiences with Presbyterian governance, now 250 years old" (2007). Although the PCUSA is part of ecumenical international communities such as WARC (lated the World Communion of Reformed Churches) and the World Council of Churches, they retain their autonomy as a democratically run organization.

Policy statements approved by the GA represent the official position of the church, which is meant to be representative of the church at large. PCUSA discourse over trade (as with other topics) also includes research reports from committees and actions by ministry programs within the denomination. The ACSWP develops most of the research of the PCUSA. An official task force, they are charged with researching social, political, and economic issues at the GA's request. Then the DC office and ministries like the Hunger Program carry out advocacy programs based on the GA's resulting policies.

As the church's primary source of discourse, GA policy speaks for the church at a specific moment in time. The GA met annually until 2006 and now meets every two years. Composed of half clergy and half laity, participants in the week-long gathering vote on policy statements, and attendees are randomly assigned to committees to discuss resolutions. If such resolutions become policies, they are authoritative for the work of the denomination and represent the official position of the church at a given period. A clerk serves over the GA, acting as a spokesperson for the church and the assembly. Clifton Kirkpatrick had held this position since 1996 at the time of this research.[5]

---

[5] He has recently stepped down but continues to serve with the World Communion of Reformed Churches. Kirkpatrick, in his role as clerk, also personally voiced criticism about the role of free trade, in line with GA policy.

The Role of Research

Research both is commissioned through and informs GA policy. When the GA decides more study is needed on a topic, it refers the issue to a task force for analysis. The task force develops and oversees research that will later shape GA policy. Christopher Iosso, an ordained and practicing Presbyterian pastor, has served as the GA liaison and coordinator for the ACSWP since 2005. He worked with the PCUSA in the 1980s on social responsibility and investing. Ron Kernaghan, a professor of theology and Presbyterian ministries at Fuller Seminary, is a member of ACSWP. Although such members give oversight to research projects, subject-matter experts also are accorded a special role. Economists, ethicists, and those involved with business and international institutions often are represented on the various task forces. Most task force members have advanced educational training or extensive business experience. The task force for *Hope for a Global Future* included a number of academics, most of whom also served as elders,[6] and produced the most extensive research to date from the PCUSA on globalization.

Other publications also have spun out of this research. The volumes on the economy by Douglass and on the environment by Stivers, already introduced, were two of these. In addition, Pharis Harvey, a Methodist minister and director of the International Labor Rights Fund, wrote a report on employment, and Ruy Costa, a former ACSWP coordinator, penned one on globalization and culture. In 2006, when the ACSWP produced *Resolution on Just Globalization* to tackle similar issues, the task force was informed by experiences of that globalization and a body of empirical research on its impact. The newer task force included more business leaders and economists, bringing together more diverse points of view.[7]

---

[6] The full membership of the task force included many Presbyterians: William Bracket (elder and CEO of World Neighbors), Gordon Douglass, Alice Frazer Evans (elder and director at Plowshares Institute), William Gibson (minister and former associate of the Eco-Justice Project at Cornell University), Heidi Hadsell do Nascimento (social ethicist and dean of faculty at McCormick Theological Seminary), James Kuhn (elder and emeritus professor at Columbia Graduate School of Business), Charles McLure, Jr (elder and senior economic fellow at Stanford University), Mary McQuillen (elder and instructor in Native American Oral History), Robert Patterson (elder and professor of agricultural science at North Carolina State), and Sarah Blythe Taylor (pastor and former vice president of Citibank). Additionally, Edna Ortiz (elder in the United Church of Christ) and Louise Tappa (Baptist minister in Cameroon) served as WARC representatives. Affiliations listed are from 1996.

[7] The "resolution" team for the 2006 report included Kim Bobo (executive director of the Interfaith Committee for Worker Justice), Ruy Costa, Clifford Grum (retired president and CEO of Temple-Inland and former director of Texas Association of Business and Chambers of Commerce), Ayn Lavagnino (manager of church development program), Lewis Mudge (retired professor of ethics), Rebecca Peters (professor of religious studies), William Saint (senior development specialist for the World Bank), Ronald Stone (retired professor of Christian ethics and former ACSWP chair), and Walter Owensby (former associate with PCUSA DC office). Affiliations listed are from 2006.

In true PCUSA form, it is research that is highlighted in determining the best course of policy action. The Reformed tradition in the United States is shaped by an emphasis on rationalism and intellectualism, evidenced especially by the central place research holds for the PCUSA; it would be hard to find another church where research is so central. The PCUSA houses a number of the intellectual elite, and they have been involved in efforts to produce research in line with their theology. A PCUSA document on social witness policy expanded on this priority:

> A social policy development employs the full range of expertise available to the church. Biblical, theological, and ethical scholarship is sought.... We also seek the insights of other faith and ideological traditions, and secular disciplines.... The formation of a social witness policy includes understanding past policy ... and discussion of the current factors, circumstances, or situations that support the need for the policy's formation or reformulation.
>
> (CSWP 1994, 25)

This emphasis on research, however, is not just an aspect of the Reformed community; Steensland (2002) has noted the importance of research among the broader mainline Protestant community. During the twentieth century, mainline Protestants moved toward more research and policy activism. As a primary focus on institutional reform in the 1960s and 1970s was replaced with an emphasis on assisting the most vulnerable in the late 1980s, research became critical. In their practical calls for action, mainline communities relied on research for their specific policy positions (Steensland 2002).

From Research to Policy and Activism

Policy has been crucial for the work of the staff offices and ministries of the church, such as the Presbyterian Hunger Program and the Washington, DC, office. Andrew Kang Bartlett, the director of the Presbyterian Hunger Program and the staff member behind the PCUSA's "just trade" web site (a compilation of church resources dealing with trade that promotes more just relationships), noted that the staff works directly from policy mandates. In discussing the GA policies on FTAA and CAFTA, he stressed that he was not a part of developing final policy resolutions. Even as a Presbytery may submit policy recommendations, for example, that policy is reviewed within a committee at the GA before being submitted to the entire assembly. He did admit, however, that these committees sometimes consider staff as resources as they develop final policy recommendations. "They [the committee] say, 'Well, as staff, what's going to be helpful to you all? Because you guys have to be the ones kind of initiating some of this work.' So that gives us the chance to work with them and modify the recommendations so it makes sense to the [people and] programs that are already interested [in a particular issue] and going to be doing the work on this" (2007). Catherine Gordon, who works with the DC office on international issues, also confirmed that their policies and work follow from the policy of the

GA. Policy, research, and the work of denominational program offices are all part of the church's discourse and action, which mirrors Steensland's (2002) assessment of how the mainline Protestant community began to engage in the 1980s in more of the "technical language of policy evaluation" (214).

Unfortunately, the high priority that the GA places on research has not translated into motivation of members. Congregations are likely to request information on issues they are already interested in investigating; policies rarely bring new issues to the attention of a congregation. The largest PCUSA church in the country at the time of this research, Peachtree Presbyterian in Atlanta, has a very active ministry focused on international issues. Yet, their director, Marilyn Borst, has suggested that most members know little about trade issues. Mark Adams, a leader of Presbyterian Border Ministries, has admitted that although they deal with border issues and immigration, they do not make use of much research from the GA. He argued, "I don't think we need more statements. I think we've got pretty much everything we need. And the only question is: 'How are we going to help it get embraced?'" (2007).

In light of the limited impact of research reports, more interactive strategies have taken hold. The church, for example, has developed a number of programs to promote fairer trade within the current system, and these appear to have attracted wide support. One example is the alternative trade movement, in which the PCUSA encourages churches to participate corporately by promoting "fairer trade" items, such as palm branches on Palm Sunday. Other examples include the Joining Hands program abroad, the Presbyterian Coffee Project, and the Sweat-Free Ts program for clothing. One of the more recent GA policies encouraged people to "become actively engaged in learning about and support-ing fair trade and sweat-free products" (General Assembly [PCUSA] 2006, "Just Globalization").

In discussing his work with the Presbyterian Border Ministries, Mark Adams talked about the appeal of such programs. His group is an example of a ministry involved in fair trade without being politically active on trade policy. They work with Café Justo, a coffee initiative to help Mexican farmers sell their coffee directly to U.S. markets, allowing farmers to retain a larger percentage of the profits and avoid the need for migration. At the time of our interview in May 2008, Café Justo was not supported by the PCUSA as a whole, but rather partnered with Catholic Relief Services. As Adams explained, the PCUSA "has had a coffee program for some years and they partner with Equal Exchange in what they do." Later, however, their relationship with Café Justo was strengthened, according to Adams in October 2009, and there was more willingness to work together. This example reveals both the challenges of bringing new ministries on board and the commitment and flexibility of the church in working with new initiatives that have indigenous support. The PCUSA – at the policy level, within its ministries, and within specific programs – has been united in working to create alternative relationships where just trade can occur.

Fair trade is only one example of how Presbyterian efforts have been directed at improving economic situations. Responsible investing in companies, along with strategic use of shareholder power to influence corporations, were strategies the church employed back in the 1980s. They also have wielded economic power through the use of boycotts, as was the case with Taco Bell in 2002. The PCUSA encouraged Presbyterians to boycott the restaurant chain (owned by Yum!) because of the low prices paid to Immokalee tomato farmers in Florida. The church also helped organize a march to the Yum! headquarters in Louisville, just blocks from the PCUSA office, and subsequently helped broker a deal between the company and the tomato farmers for higher wages. Although some of these actions may not have received universal support, congregations often have supported programs that center on influencing change in personal ways; fair trade, in creating alternatives but not changing the larger system, has received the most support.

The focus of several ministries in the church on more personalized actions, however, does not negate the central purpose of PCUSA research: to bring about change within the economic system. The office in Washington, DC, is integral to this effort, and has been tasked with lobbying the federal government based on the policy positions approved by the GA. Almost all of the church's social policies dealing with trade have included this mandate to advocate for policy change. For example, the 2003 statement against the FTAA clearly mandated:

Direct the Stated Clerk of the General Assembly, as well as representatives of PCUSA programs dealing with economic justice, hunger, and advocacy, to promptly communicate the General Assembly position to the U.S. trade representative, U.S. senators and representatives, congressional committees with trade jurisdiction, and state legislators.
(General Assembly [PCUSA] 2003, "Opposition to the FTAA")

Those working in the DC office work with other faith-based offices in Washington, DC, to make lawmakers aware of the different PCUSA policy efforts. But, as Hofrenning (1995) found, mainline Protestant lobbyists (as well as those from some other religious traditions) are less likely to petition lawmakers for change using an insider approach than they are to propose new agendas and have a prophetic voice: they "want to preach as much as they seek to lobby" (117). For those in the pews, however, it is on-the-ground action rather than political efforts that often appeals to them (Steensland 2002).

PARTICIPANTS IN POLICY DIALOGUE

Texts of the church often speak to specific issues and experiences. The specific contexts of participants in PCUSA discourse – and their perspectives on those contexts – determine which issues receive theological reflection and how they are interpreted. Even as PCUSA discourse has retained a U.S.-based perspective, its trade discourse has increasingly incorporated international experiences and realities. This discourse has been shaped by both those with experience near the border and/or relationships with Latin Americans and those who were part of institutional linkages with international partners.

At one level, the national location of the church in the United States has given the PCUSA a particular perspective on trade agreements that differs from the other cases under investigation. The PCUSA is located in a country with a high level of economic power that is often setting the terms for FTAs. Just as trade was not a central topic of discussion in the United States at large until NAFTA was being debated, the PCUSA did not speak out against specific FTAs until after NAFTA emerged in the early 1990s. Trade policy failed to merit attention as a social problem (for example, under GATT) because most Presbyterian members had not felt the social ills from new trade policies and were not convinced of the need to evaluate them from a theological angle.

Within the United States, the PCUSA also occupies a privileged position. The authors of the *Resolution on Just Globalization* report from 2006, for example, included a senior officer at the World Bank and another retired CEO of a large company. These are not the people losing jobs when a steel factory moves overseas. Yet, even as many of the members and dominant voices occupy high-status positions, there have been intentional efforts to broaden the PCUSA's perspective, along with increasing recognition of the limits of their perspective.

Beyond U.S. Borders

Although the personal experiences of members of the PCUSA have not been monolithic, they often are a motivating force for action, reflection, and study regarding economic forces. Several members who have raised concerns over trade and economic globalization have had experiences with people impacted negatively by international trade, especially those living on or outside of the U.S. border. Since the Sanctuary movement of the 1980s, when the PCUSA housed Central American immigrants in many of their churches,[8] such relationships have been in existence and held importance for the PCUSA. The church also has protested the involvement of the U.S. military in Central American conflicts. Many of the same actors who were involved in the Sanctuary movement also are involved in current immigration issues, some shaping the discourse of the PCUSA on trade-related issues.

Southside Presbyterian in Tucson, Arizona, was instrumental in the Sanctuary movement and the first church to become involved nationally in such a cause. Southside became invested in immigration debates as a result. But what drew their attention to immigrants coming to the United States as a result of civil wars was not ideology. It was their experiences with the immigrants and later fact-finding missions to Central America. Reverend John Fife,

---

[8] Smith (1996) demonstrates the central role that various religious institutions, particularly mainline Protestants, and religious ideas played in the U.S. Central America peace movement of the 1980s.

one of the key leaders of the Sanctuary movement and former pastor at Southside, is a current political activist in the immigration crisis. He commented on how he originally became concerned about immigrants while he was in seminary:

This guy calls me from Tucson. . . . We talked for a little while, and he said, "Well, do you have any questions?" And I said, "Yeah, what's an Indian and what's a Reservation?" And he said, "Oh." And I said, "Well, you need to know, I'm from Pennsylvania and I've never been in the Southwest. I don't know anything about Native American culture." And he said, "Well." After a long silence, he said, "The church has done a considerable amount of damage to Native Americans over the years; you probably can't do much more in three months. Why don't you come out?" So I did. And I just fell in love, with the desert, with the proximity to the border, and the people, and everything. I decided that I wanted to come to the Southwest. (2008)

As the example of Tucson churches reveals, attention within the PCUSA has been focused on issues not only when they are of national concern, but also when particular segments of the church in America have personal experiences with certain communities. For those active in the issues of immigration related to economic restructuring in North America, it was the increased immigration that occurred after NAFTA's implementation that jump-started involvement as PCUSA members learned firsthand of both the reasons that people were immigrating and the dangers involved in such a process.

I do not want to suggest that the perspective of the PCUSA has merely echoed national realities or followed from individuals' personal experiences. It is true that the experiences of those in the church have influenced what issues have been identified as subjects of concern. Yet, within this analysis, the PCUSA often intentionally sought an international perspective, just as Kairos was intentional in its perspective. The church's rejections of FTAs, though not as oppositional to the economic order as WARC's, were more expansive and critical than most from the United States. In fact, many of the concerns raised by the PCUSA had little traction with the public concerns over NAFTA and new FTAs; in place of more domestic outrage over outsourcing U.S. jobs, the PCUSA addressed issues important to people in other countries as well.

International Voices

Improvements in communication have allowed for increased networking within the global community, and this has had implications for the PCUSA and their policy. Kirkpatrick, who headed the worldwide ministries division before serving as clerk, noted the impact of these networks for the church, especially as they changed during his time of service: "The direct connections between people became far more possible, and so we started these Presbytery partnerships. So all of the sudden, folks who had only listened to missionaries from the Congo that came home every seven years were in direct conversation with Congolese

Christians and their churches" (2007). Partnerships, especially with other Presbyterian and Reformed churches, have been vital, then, to how the PCUSA has thought about involvement in their world.

The church's discourse on globalization reveals not only the ways in which it has tried to promote an international perspective among members, but also the ways in which new voices have been brought into the dialogue. Ruy Costa's perspective on globalization (2003), for instance, was that of an elder from Brazil. *Voices from Korea, U.S.A. and Brazil* (Office of Ecumenical Affairs, 2001) is another example of an endeavor in which international perspective was central. The GA policy that prompted this report and dialogue did so to help the church in three ways:

a) understanding the social, political, and economic forces that are driving the global economy; b) seeing how these forces are affecting people at the grassroots level in those three countries; and c) exploring what can be done within the church to promote changes that will make the global economy better serve the needs of the people and especially those whom the Lord Jesus called "the least of these."

(General Assembly [PCUSA] 1997, "Global Economy: Brazil and South Korea")

Such international voices not only have shaped research, but also have had an influence on the resulting policies of the PCUSA. In fact, it was those linked with the Presbyterian partner UMAVIDA (Joining Hands for Life) in Bolivia who originally submitted the 2003 statement against FTAA. UMAVIDA is a local Bolivian organization that works with the PCUSA through Joining Hands (an international approach of the Presbyterian Hunger Program). Although such partner organizations cannot submit policy, they often enjoy especially strong links with a particular synod or Presbytery. Andrew Kang Bartlett gave some background on how such partnerships have shaped the GA policy on FTAA:

One thing that you may not know about is that the origin of the overture was partly, if not primarily, due to the Joining Hands Program.... He [Stephen Bartlett, a facilitator] did a talk with folks related to the Joining Hands Program ... [This developed] their interest in how trade was impacting the country ... They developed an overture, the first overture.

(2007)

Even the text of the policy against FTAA made clear its connection with Joining Hands: "Bolivia, the Joining Hands Against Hunger partner of the Presbytery of San Francisco, is currently the poorest nation in the Western Hemisphere." The GA went on to note the negative impacts of free trade occurring for their partners:

Our Joining Hands partner network in Bolivia, UMAVIDA (Joining Hands for Life), is asking for help from the Presbytery of San Francisco in opposing trade agreements and other multinational actions that deepen their poverty and negate their ability for self-determination. In heeding their call for solidarity and accompaniment, we may also be defending our right to democratic government.

(General Assembly [PCUSA] 2003, "Opposition to FTAA")

The shift in GA policy in the last decade to more clearly denounce current FTAs was a shift prompted and instigated by stronger connections with global network partners of the PCUSA.

Connection with the Church Members

Policies are developed in part to educate members; as Ammerman (2005) noted, education of members is a central task of many religious traditions. And this is a task the PCUSA has taken seriously in developing research. The social policies of the GA on NAFTA and CAFTA recommended that people learn about globalization and its impacts. There were repeated calls to distribute research among churches. In the first FTA-related policy, only two motions were listed, and the first called for Presbyterians to become intellectually engaged on the trade issue, as it asked "Presbyterians to engage in studies of the impact of the Free Trade Agreement upon the economic life of persons in the Americas" (General Assembly [PCUSA] 1992, "Free Trade Agreement").

Unfortunately, church members often have been uniformed about policy, due to the sheer volume of it. Further, some Presbyterians have vocally opposed GA policies. For those who have voiced skepticism about social policies in general, two concerns have emerged: a procedural concern that the process has not been truly democratic, and a substantive concern that policies have been too political or ideological (a concern found especially among those favoring a more personal approach). Those working on policy would acquiesce that both charges have some validity. Nevertheless, I argue that congregations are mostly in agreement with the GA trade policy, even as many are not aware of its specifics. Nonetheless, nationalistic values, such as a strong belief in capitalism and the free hand of the market, are often held concurrently with a Presbyterian emphasis on more just economic markets.

One former commissioner from a large, theologically conservative PCUSA church voiced her concern about the process of policy construction and the role staff plays in creating GA policy: "There's some question about whether they support it, whether they direct it, whether they subvert it, circumvent it, or ignore it." This individual suggested that policy is not always democratically produced; many proposed policies have come from staff and the Louisville offices, and not congregations, as intended. Additionally, the former commissioner suggested that the staff in the Louisville GA office has played too large a role in the final policies it has approved: "It's pretty intimidating. So these folks wield an awful lot of power, because they sit in on all the committee work. They serve as experts; they give extensive testimony, and make recommendations. And people are overwhelmed with [all the policies], and just tend to think they're experts and we have to rely on them" (Former GA commissioner, 2007). Recall that Bartlett, with the Presbyterian Hunger Program, acknowledged that committees do interact with staff and ask them what they need. Given that policy guides the work of the staff, the staff members have a large stake in what is produced. But even as staff members have played a larger role than a purely democratic process would dictate, they have not orchestrated the policies. Committees ultimately have had to both ask for and accept their recommendations. Much like with Kairos, one would suspect their authority would hold more weight in more technical areas. However, unlike Kairos, the technical experts are merely consulted; they are not the ones creating policy.

There also has been a concern that policy and research emanating from the GA is in opposition to the beliefs of most in PCUSA congregations. The research mandated by policy and produced by the GA has not been the result of a fully democratic selection process but rather a representative one that is flawed. The former commissioner mentioned earlier argued that often in selecting these experts, there has not been enough diversity of thought:

It is typically very one-sided, weighted toward the ideological bent of the Louisville offices.... And there's a vast difference between how they feel and how the individuals in the pew feel. So what's happening in the Louisville offices is often almost in direct contradiction or certainly deviates significantly from what the congregational level would signify.... Evangelical congregations are very likely – and not just evangelical, I think all the way over to the moderate center – are more likely to look with suspicion on many of the directives that come out of the General Assembly.   (2007)

Although I found in my interviews that the staff members in Louisville were ideologically more liberal than the average Presbyterian, I did not find that the task forces on globalization were one-sided. In contrast, for example, to the Kairos economic justice team, those working on *Hope for a Global Future* (ACSWP 1996) and *Resolution on Just Globalization* (ACSWP 2006) had diverse expertise and ideological assumptions. There were academics in agricultural science, economics, and business, along with ethicists and pastors. *Resolution on Just Globalization* even included a senior associate with the World Bank. While I am not arguing that every view has been represented, I did find the PCUSA to be unique from the other two cases in the diversity of thought represented among individuals involved in producing the discourse.

Further, I did not find strong opposition within the church toward the trade policies endorsed. One of the strongest voices against certain social actions of the PCUSA has been *The Layman*, a publication of the Presbyterian Lay Committee that is committed to "restoring our historic witness to Biblical faith" (Presbyterian Lay Committee 2007). They formed in 1965 and protested the church's acceptance of the Confession of 1967. According to *The Layman*, 450,000 Presbyterians (or about a quarter of PCUSA members) receive the publication. One of the Lay Committee's four stated objectives touched on economic issues: "To inform and equip individual Christians in the PCUSA and other denominations to engage the ethical and moral issues in cultural, economic and political affairs as Christ's active disciples" (Presbyterian Lay Committee 2007). Such an objective notes the individual nature of political action endorsed by the organization. As one peruses their stances, however, it is evident that trade policy has received little attention.[9]

In addition to the fact that trade policy has been a less contentious issue than have other social issues within the church, the disagreement that has existed over economic policy has not been an issue of theological division. And, even as *The Layman* and its supporters promoted a more individualized concern and response toward economic problems, they did not represent all those with a conservative theology. Ron Kernaghan noted that opposition to PCUSA economic or political policies is not about theology and a liberal/conservative divide. Rather, the work of ACSWP has continually been based on a structural rather than a more personal understanding of social problems. As historical work would affirm, this tension over structural responses has existed within the church for a long time; in the Confession of 1967, the church clearly made a choice to identify itself with a more politically engaged and structurally focused social ethic.

Thus, even when considering some polarized views, the reality is that many in the church have not paid attention to the trade policies of the GA, and others have simply avoided involvement in political issues. Still others have disagreed with the GA's stance on CAFTA. Overall, trade policy has failed to attract significant attention within the PCUSA, especially compared with other economic issues like debt relief (in the Jubilee Movement). Wuthnow and Evans (2002) argued that within mainline Protestant churches more generally, members are often unaware of what is happening politically within the denomination. Within the PCUSA, it appears that members are often similarly uninterested in the social policies of the church. Taylor, in discussing why his Tucson-based Presbyterian church has not engaged the trade issue, attributed it to the polarization surrounding political issues in the public arena. He mentioned that "it's always a minority that are willing to do the grunt work of policy advocacy" (2008).

Given that GA trade policy has been underutilized and ignored, I analyzed Presbyterian Panel Data (PCUSA 2006b) to assess whether the concerns against the market found in PCUSA policy were concerns shared by most Presbyterians. Presbyterians largely supported a pro-market ideology, but they also supported restrictions and restraints on the market in line with PCUSA policy. True to concerns by conservative members, one's theology *does* influence the likelihood of supporting many of the economic claims made by the church related to markets and trade.

Only a small minority of members (13 percent) and elders (16 percent), and a somewhat larger minority of pastors (35 percent), believed that Presbyterian teaching suggests redistribution is required in free markets. By contrast, 66 percent

---

[9] There also has been opposition to some policies of the church from the left; more often, however, the left has supported policies for change in the church that have been rejected by the GA. Policy approved by the GA of the church consistently has the support of at least leaders within the large moderate population of the PCUSA.

of members, 68 percent of elders, and 58 percent of pastors believed that free trade should be allowed without government appearance. At first glance, such statistics suggest that attitudes of most Presbyterians are at odds with the official teachings of the church on economic globalization. Furthermore, those identifying as conservative are both more likely to support free markets and less likely to support redistribution.[10]

Yet, even as Presbyterians support the free market, many support standards that would restrict that same market. For example, over three-quarters of members, elders, and pastors thought that international environmental, labor, health, and safety standards should be both strengthened and enforced. Over 70 percent of members and over 90 percent of pastors thought substandard salaries paid to low-skilled workers are an ethical issue. Finally, when it comes to the issue of global governance, Presbyterians seemed to be on the same page as the official stance of the church, with two-thirds of members supporting a stronger role of the UN for the purpose of alleviating poverty.[11]

In sum, even though a majority of Presbyterians support "free trade" and reject "redistribution," they actually support limits on the market, argue that people have economic rights, and support global governance. Theology appears to play a role in such attitudes, even though it explains only a little of the variation in attitudes. There is more resistance from theological conservatives to calls for redistribution and market restraint than among those who are more theologically liberal. Nevertheless, a majority of those in the church still accept the basic concerns voiced by the PCUSA.

Those who have become engaged in the discourse over the political economy often have relied on the resources of the PCUSA and used them to shape their analyses. Taylor noted this to be true: "our social teachings are very progressive and are an incredible treasure, I think, and support this kind of progressive work. The general temper of the larger church, in terms of at the congregational level, it's not necessarily here." Ufford-Chase also commented on the rich resources available to churches:

A church that is already invested in this set of questions or becomes interested in this set of questions will call the denomination offices and say, "What's out there that we ought to know about?" And they might pick this book [*Hope for a Global Future*] up. Actually, environmental stuff is a really good example, right? We've got some really amazing documents that the church has produced in the last fifteen years on the environment. And more and more churches are getting involved in environmental work and creation. And when they do, some of them will turn to the denomination and say, "What do we have?" And they find really, really powerful documents when they do it.   (2007)

---

[10] Based on a series of logistical regression models, I found that conservatives have twice the odds of supporting free markets as theological liberals, and liberals have odds almost five times higher than conservatives for supporting redistribution.

[11] I also found that theological liberals had odds six times the odds of conservatives for supporting the UN.

CONCLUSION

Based on a view that religion should be used to analyze policy, the PCUSA has chosen to be involved in debates about trade policy. Over time, they have moved from being concerned about the U.S. involvement in the world to actively critiquing specific FTA policies. Three key theological ideas – sovereignty, covenant, and community – especially emerge in their policies, research, programs, and personal views (assessed by interviews). Although these values are critical to understanding the church's trade policy, recent years have witnessed a change in trade policy not brought about by a change in underlying theological values. I suggest that even as the church has been guided by religious and moral values, such values have had to be applied to concrete circumstances to be truly author-itative in public life. Personal experiences, changes in the political economy, and global connections with partners have all been important in shaping the per-spective of the PCUSA on issues of globalization and trade policy.

Research is where the theological values of the PCUSA have been translated into political policies based on the perspectives of involved members, which have been informed by economic and religious experts, as well as international partners. The central PCUSA document on globalization, *Hope for a Global Future* (1996), was the result of a five-year creation process and was mandated as the United States started looking toward extending the Canada–United States FTA to include Mexico. In this report, as well as in others that followed, the PCUSA sought to broaden its perspective of globalization and its effects beyond the United States. Yet even as the church has produced numerous reports and policies on trade issues, its impact on members is underwhelming. The research of the PCUSA has not been effectively utilized within the larger Presbyterian community; members often have accessed such resources only after they have already become interested in a social issue. However, research has successfully contributed to an environment in the PCUSA where structural accounts matter, FTAs are understood as flawed in their current state, and activism on economic and justice issues is common. This is an environment to which most Presbyterians have been exposed.

4

Dialogue and Development: The Costa Rican Catholic Response to CAFTA-DR

The day of the Virgin of Los Angeles is commemorated in Costa Rica by a pilgrimage to Cartago on August 2nd every year. Thousands of *peregrinos* (pilgrims) – adults and children alike – begin their journey from the capital city about 23 kilometers away. Costa Rica's president and other public officials attend the event, arguably the nation's most important public holiday. For a week beforehand, bishops deliver homilies in the public square, street vendors fill the city, banners fly overhead, and many of the faithful enter the church on their knees to pay tribute to Mary. It is a holy event.

Bishop San Casimiro of Alajuela, Costa Rica, delivered the keynote homily in 2007 to honor the Virgin. Notable were his political statements referencing the heated debates over the Central America–Dominican Republic–United States Free Trade Agreement (CAFTA-DR).[1] He called for people to show the "strength to construct a type of more inclusive country ... based on pillars of justice, solidarity, truth, and respect."[2] As the nation prepared for a public vote over the trade agreement, the future of CAFTA-DR – or the TLC as it was called in Costa Rica – was the prominent issue on the minds of many, even in the midst of a traditional religious festival.

Costa Rica officially entered the Central America–United States Free Trade Agreement (CAFTA) negotiations at the start of 2003, and the official national debate over whether Costa Rica would ratify CAFTA began in January of 2004. Later in 2004, CAFTA changed into the Central America–Dominican Republic–United States Free Trade Agreement (CAFTA-DR). Oscar Arias won the presidential election by less than 1 percent of the vote in 2006, after running primarily on a pro–CAFTA-DR agenda. When the country eventually voted to implement

---

[1] In some of the references to CAFTA-DR, however, even after 2004, discussion in Costa Rica often referenced CAFTA rather than CAFTA-DR, most likely because the United States was the foreign country that usually received attention in such discussions.

[2] All documents and interviews originally recorded in Spanish were translated by the author.

CAFTA-DR in an October 2007 referendum, it was a narrow victory (51 percent to 48 percent). Costa Rica was the only country in Central America where the agreement was so hotly contested in the public square before it ultimately came into force in 2009.

To be sure, some in the global Catholic Church have expressed concern and dissatisfaction over trade agreements. For example, in all three of the countries participating in the North American Free Trade Agreement (NAFTA),[3] multiple bishops spoke out against the treaty's negative impacts on the poor. In other regions of Central America, national bishops similarly voiced concerns about CAFTA policy. However, Costa Rica stands out in its bishops having issued a significant proportion of official Church statements on free trade agreements (FTAs); it is also one a few places where Catholic bishops have spoken in a unified voice on the matter. How did the Church enter such a contentious political debate, and how did it legitimate its political claims?

Costa Rica has eight bishops (priests serving in authority over a diocese) who make up the Episcopal Conference of Costa Rica (CECOR). They serve as official representatives of the Catholic Church. Appointed by the Vatican, a bishop usually serves until his 80th birthday, when he is informally expected to retire. Not all bishops are from Costa Rica; several are from Spain. The archbishop of Costa Rica resides in the capital, San José,[4] and serves as the figurehead and most authoritative voice for Costa Rican Catholicism. Although the archbishop may have the most authority, the bishops in Costa Rica often speak with one unified voice, producing collaborative documents; their relatively small number facilitates this sense of unity. CECOR is also a part of regional bodies, including the Central American Episcopal Secretariat (SEDAC) and the Latin American Episcopal Conference (CELAM). In SEDAC, Costa Rica has played a leadership role. Bishop José Ulloa served as the president of SEDAC from 2002 up until the time of this study, and Bishop San Casimiro began serving as general secretary in 2005. Each of these conferences also has issued statements with critical evaluations of FTAs, documents analyzed in this chapter.

CECOR has consistently declared itself neutral in the trade debate, though it has provided a set of ethical guidelines to engage CAFTA-DR and other economic policies. In spite of its stated neutrality, the Church has challenged CAFTA-DR's claims to promote authentic human development and has criticized aspects of the free trade paradigm (as well as free trade agreements). Both before and during the CAFTA-DR debates, they promoted social welfare programs, calling for an

---

[3] Canada, the United States, and Mexico share NAFTA, as discussed in previous chapters.

[4] The diocese of San José, in addition to representing over 50 percent of the population, also has a number of its own ministries. What happens in this diocese, more than other dioceses, impacts people throughout the country. For example, the city's vicariate office (VEPS) is charged with coordinating social issues in the diocese of San José, although people throughout the country use its materials and resources.

increase in social services from the state. They questioned a process in which economic experts had sole authority over economic policies. Archbishop Hugo Barrantes of San José wrote, "Since the beginning of the 1980s, the social contract that allowed us as a society to construct a different nation has started to run out" (2004a, section III). He critiqued the fact that many state institutions have been damaged and dismantled by the dynamics of global capitalism. Comments like these have drawn fire from both sides of the political aisle. Some pro–CAFTA-DR advocates found the Church too critical and political, and accused it of working against CAFTA-DR. By contrast, anti-CAFTA Catholics bemoaned the failure of the bishops to stand aggressively against a faulty agreement, wanting them to be more prophetic.

Religious and national values have penetrated the free trade discourse in Costa Rica. Especially prominent have been concerns of human dignity, solidarity, the common good, dialogue, and peace. Such values coexist with a conservative theological understanding about the proper role of political voice, an understanding dependent in part on CECOR's hierarchical organizational structure and location in a peaceful Catholic Central American state. This analysis relies on official CECOR (and SEDAC and CELAM) documents, published anti-trade documents, and articles in *Eco Católico* from 2003–2007.

THE POLITICAL RESPONSE OF THE COSTA RICAN BISHOPS

A Time Line of Catholic Discourse on Economic Globalization

At an international level, the Catholic Church has historically and consistently voiced concerns about different aspects of economic liberalism. Stemming from various viewpoints, Burns (1990, 1992) provides an excellent analysis on how past Papal authorities have approached the Church's relationship with economic liberalism, so I will only briefly discuss that history here. Before the turn of the nineteenth century, the Catholic Church had been quite involved in temporal affairs. With the Enlightenment, resistance from European states prompted the Church's retreat from this role (Burns 1992), and with it came a redefining of social issues as distinct from other issues of faith. Catholic social teaching (CST) as a unique development came about in 1891 with the publication of *Rerum Novarum* by Pope Leo XIII.[5] CST encouraged religious engagement with economic and political issues, reaffirming the Church's relevance in social life, while not claiming temporal authority in such areas. Paradoxically, while the creation of CST emphasized the Church's concern for the common good (Palacios 2007), it also signaled a hierarchy of theological concerns where social issues were now distinct from (and less important than) other "spiritual" matters of faith (Burns 1992).

[5] Leo XIII was one of the first popes who could possibly have had an authentic connection with the proletariat, given that the church was no longer part of the ruling elite (Burns 1990).

The first Costa Rican foray into CST followed soon after, with a letter on the just salary penned by Archbishop Theil (1880–1901) (Picado 2007; Williams 1989). Written on the eve of the 1894 presidential elections, the letter expressed concern that day workers were not being paid the true value of their work. Archbishop Theil called for fairer salaries. His doing so established the Costa Rican Catholic Church's moral obligation in economic matters. Although the two Costa Rican archbishops following him, Archbishop Stork (1904–1920) and Archishop Castro (1921–1939), ignored significant social questions, Archishop Sanabria (1940–1952) was politically active and outspoken on economic and social life (Williams 1989). In fact, current bishops still reference his critiques on the economy. He worked with Catholic trade unions, supported state-sponsored social reforms, and even suffered criticisms from some for being too sympathetic to the Marxist party. After Archbishop Sanabria's twelve-year term, however, the Church in Costa Rica was again largely silent on many issues of social concern until the latter part of the 1970s.

This is not to suggest that it was only the change in the archbishops that is the causal explanation for the changed emphasis of the Catholic Church in Costa Rica over time. Bishops are accountable to the Vatican and are charged to interpret Catholic teaching to their particular context. As Hagopian (2009a) argued, to understand the decisions made by bishops, we have to consider both their individual beliefs and the bishops' assessment of political opportunities and risks. That is, the political ties the Church has to the state, the type of society in which the Church operates, and the reactions of the laity to the Church all matter.

The Catholic Church's Vatican II council (1962–1965) brought renewed attention to CST and the responsibility of the Church to speak to social issues, even as they accepted a less powerful role in the political sector (Burns 1992). A decade after Vatican II this new emphasis took hold in Costa Rica. During the latter years of Rodriguez's tenure as archbishop (1960–1979), some of the concerns articulated by Costa Rican bishops today first received critical attention. Bishop Arrieta (who would become the next archbishop) and Bishop Trejos (who later provided strong religious arguments against CAFTA-DR), signed a letter during the 1974 elections that rejected both liberal capitalism and Marxist socialism, critiquing the power of the market in society more generally (CECOR 1974). In 1975, several bishops and priests spoke on the issue of agrarian reform and criticized some of the then-current attempts at privatization (Trejos Picado, Coto Orozco, et al. 1975). Around the time that Bishop Arrieta became the archbishop in 1979, the council itself exhibited greater willingness to engage with political issues (Williams 1989). This discourse both made connections between religious values and political policy for citizens of the Church and also engaged political leaders and the state.

Coinciding with the rise of global capitalism under the Washington Consensus, the Church was addressing many of the issues raised by CAFTA-DR before the treaty came into existence: the role of global capitalism, the national importance of agricultural, state provision of social services, and the need for political participation within the country. Hagopian (2009a) found in her analysis of the region that the Catholic Church throughout Latin America has been vocal on similar issues.

In its lengthy and politically engaged 1994 letter, "Mother Earth," CECOR critiqued the export-oriented focus of the nation that had resulted in a shift toward the production of export crops and increased power and favor for transnational corporations (TNCs) and large businesses. In evaluating the changes that economic globalization had wrought, the bishops called for the government to maintain strong social welfare programs. In 2000, they were integrally involved in efforts to resist the privatization of the electric company. In both of these cases, however, the focus was on the Costa Rican state with less attention to international actors.

The perspective and concerns of the bishops reflect Costa Rica's place in the international political economy. Although Costa Rica has had preferential access to U.S. markets under the Caribbean Basin Initiative, CAFTA-DR sought to deepen those agreements. In doing so, CAFTA-DR required lower tariffs and restrictions on protectionist policies, which impacted the publicly run institutions in Costa Rica. Under CAFTA-DR, transnational corporations and other international business actors gained access to new arenas, such as water, electricity, and the telecommunications industry, that were previously denied.

The bishops' first statement on free trade agreements came in late 2002, even though CAFTA was not the first trade agreement to be debated in Costa Rican society. (The country signed an agreement with Mexico in 1995, Canada in 2002, and Chile in 2002.) A letter by SEDAC condemned the possible harm that would befall peasant farmers under CAFTA: if "forced to choose between money and the person, we choose the person, even though that could mean a possible setback in economic progress" (SEDAC 2002). Following this statement, the bishops in Costa Rica encouraged dialogue within the country over CAFTA. In 2003, the Vicariate in San José brought together a number of people from different sectors to discuss the treaty. That year, three individual pastoral letters were penned voicing concerns about U.S. subsidies and the crisis that already plagued agricultural communities in the country (Caritas 2003; San Casimiro Fernández 2003; Ulloa Rojas and Vargas Varela 2003). The *Eco Católico* also published many articles criticizing CAFTA during that year.

The Catholic Church produced the most literature on CAFTA-DR after Costa Rica's president had signed the treaty, as the nation had to decide whether to ratify the agreement. The Church applauded all those who held forums and contributed to dialogue in society, while also demanding that special attention be paid to those sectors negatively impacted by the treaty. The bishops issued their first corporate and most detailed letter in 2004 (CECOR 2004), and three more letters in 2005 (CECOR 2005a, 2005c, 2005d), in addition to two Church plenary assembly messages and one governmental address (CECOR 2005e,

2006b, 2006c).[6] Although offering values to shape economic policy, CECOR was insistent in declaring itself neutral in debates over CAFTA-DR. In 2007 they issued a letter to priests reminding them of their responsibility to remain neutral in their political proclamations from the pulpit (CECOR 2007a). In their letter issued directly before the referendum on the CAFTA-DR, they encouraged people to vote according to their own conscience, asking "all sectors, agencies and individuals . . . to show respect for the will of the majority" (2007b) and to move forward with an appropriate agenda.

A number of factors coalesced to allow for such political discussion on a specific international economic policy. The year 2002 marked a new era as Barrantes became archbishop, and he has demonstrated more willingness to criticize the state. Second, as Father Jorge Arturo Chaves (a consultant for the bishops) suggested in our interview, the political context of the region is an important part of the story of CECOR's previous silence on similar issues (Chaves Ortiz 2007). The past concerns about the spread of communism and liberation theology – neither of which were adopted by the institutional Church in Costa Rica – contributed to a hesitancy to critique free market policies and agendas.[7] Such concerns are no longer pressing, allowing the Church more freedom to criticize economic policies. Finally, the FTA with the United States was much more significant economically than treaties with smaller countries, stirring a more urgent response.

Three central concerns mark the bishops' discourse over CAFTA-DR, concerns that found expression in earlier statements by the Church in Costa Rica. First, the bishops noted that markets need ethical constraints and guidance. Second, they affirmed the sovereignty of Costa Rica, as well as the responsibility of the state to play a role in managing the economy. Third, they voiced procedural concerns, arguing that dialogue and democratic consensus were essential in policy decisions.

Free Markets Need Ethical Constraints

The bishops supported the role of free markets in contributing to growth, but they noted the failure of free markets alone to achieve real development. Bishop Ulloa clearly asserted, "I am not against free trade. I am for free trade" (Ulloa Rojas 2007) before continuing to comment on the specifics of CAFTA-DR. The bishops commended negotiators for "looking to secure a key aspect in our economy: the exportation of our agricultural products" (CECOR 2004, 21).

---

[6] These are in addition to a 2004 letter issued by the Latin American Episcopal Conference (CELAM) about trade agreements in the region more generally, a 2004 joint letter between the United States bishops and SEDAC, and a 2005 letter by SEDAC.

[7] As noted previously, Christian Smith (1991) has argued that liberation theology was grounded in part on Marxist and dependency theories, even as some challenged these linkages later in the movement.

In the event that CAFTA-DR was not passed, the bishops argued that Costa Rica would have to find other export markets. In a joint statement with bishops throughout Central America, they remarked that FTAs "have the potential to increase productivity, creativity, and economic growth, which can be an important part of integral human growth" (SEDAC 2005). Bishop Barrantes (Barrantes Ureña 2005a) highlighted the need for exports from Costa Rica to have access U.S. markets in a homily celebrating the Day of the Worker.

Although supporting the export-oriented model and the participation of the nation in the global economy, the bishops rejected the dominance of markets in current society, and critiqued the lack of ethical frameworks embedded within the market. Much like CELAM, since the mid-1970s, CECOR has consistently cautioned against the egocentrism of capitalism. For example, its 1974 letter rejected the notion that capitalism or socialism is God-honoring, and its 1994 letter criticized the economic order of Costa Rican society and its impact on agricultural workers.

In the more recent CAFTA-DR discussions, the bishops have argued that the neoliberal agenda pursued by Costa Rica in the recent past has not been fully productive, even as there has been economic growth for the country. In his essay on the Church and development, Archbishop Barrantes echoed the call of "Mother Earth" (CECOR 1994), criticizing the style of economic policy implemented since the 1980s:

> Poverty has not stopped and the inequality in income has grown. This shows that the advantages of the [economic] model are not sufficient to allow social mobility and increased quality of life for persons, but rather allow wealth to accumulate in many cases to serve speculative ends or simply leave the country. Today we confront a choice: Continue the way of the last decades and produce concentrated wealth and escalating poverty, or turn from this development strategy and rebuild a social contract that can be implemented.   (Barrantes Ureña 2004a, section III)

Ultimately, the bishops insisted that economic policies must be guided by an agenda of human development, a value absent within a free market system. A joint letter from the Central American bishops stated, "But let us not forget that while the market has its own logic and efficiency, it does not have its own ethics to assure integral human development" (SEDAC 2005). The bishops insisted that if left unregulated, the market would cause social inequality and leave the poor worse off.

Redistribution was part of the legacy of the Costa Rican democratic state; this helped the poor and other marginalized groups gain a greater share of the economic wealth of the country. Bishop Ulloa preached that free trade and globalization needed to result in a greater sharing of the wealth (2007b). Bishop Barrantes stated, "What worries us [the bishops] the most is whether free trade, such as the CAFTA-DR agreement, is able to bring about a redistribution of wealth and not just produce more wealth, but spread that out far and wide" (*Seminario Universidad* 2006). In an earlier homily, he had preached that

CAFTA-DR should be approved only when the government could guarantee it would benefit the poor (Barrantes Ureña 2004b).

CECOR paid particular attention to the impact of globalization on agriculture, with an emphasis on the consequences for poor workers and small farmers. As mentioned, the bishops had spoken earlier on land rights (1974) and had focused on the impacts of global market dynamics on farmers (1994). Caritas, an international organization that addresses social policies related to development, advocated for Costa Rican agricultural products to receive special attention in trade negotiations (Caritas 2003). Along with other Central American and U.S. bishops, CECOR voiced the following concern:

It seems likely that poor farming communities in Central America will suffer greatly when subsidized agricultural products from the United States expand their reach into these markets. Any reform of such supports should address the needs of small and medium-sized farms and farm workers in the United States and in Central America, for whom farming is the principal means of support
(United States Conference of Catholic Bishops [USCCB] and SEDAC 2004).

The bishops suggested that farmers would be worse off economically when forced to compete with the large subsidized U.S. agricultural industry; a way of life would be changed as farmers moved to other careers as a result.

The bishops also protested the destruction of the environment for economic profit. In a weekly bishops' column from *Eco Católico*, Bishop Ulloa decried "the exploitation of environmental and human resources, resources that the Pope has called 'collective goods.' Resources that we are not able to buy and sell – these should be defended at all costs, because they are the heritage of humanity" (Ulloa Rojas 2000). The bishops insisted on increased environmental protections and regulations under CAFTA-DR.

In a similar vein, the bishops called for more protection of human rights. They had concerns about provisions in CAFTA-DR that governed and allowed for the marketization of human organs. Several Catholic leaders raised this subject in personal interviews, expressing their disgust that organs were mentioned in the CAFTA-DR policy as something that could be bought and sold. Regarding both the environment and the commodification of human life, the main concern was the lack of regulations that bound which activities were allowed within the marketplace. Economic sociologists also have examined concerns about commodification of nonmarket goods and the tensions surrounding these topics: organ donation (Healy 2006), reproductive material (Almeling 2007), and life insurance (Zelizer 1979), all of which have encroached the market in an area previously considered outside the reach of the market. The bishops, however, did not so much want more regulations on how organs or the environment could be morally dealt with in economic transactions; rather, they wanted those matters restricted from trading relationships. Alongside concerns about how to encourage ethical growth, those issues led the bishops to critique CAFTA-DR as a potentially irresponsible extension of the free market without attention to the consequences of growth or the necessary restraints that ethical considerations required.

A State Economy Deserves State Regulation

The Costa Rican bishops charged that CAFTA-DR undermined the power of the Costa Rican state to involve itself in national development tasks. The unequal power relationships between the United States and large TNCs with Costa Rica benefited the former at the expense of the common Costa Rican. They insisted that Costa Rica have more sovereignty in the international political economy, a requirement for the state to promote a complementary development agenda to the treaty. During the initial stages of negotiation, they called for changes in CAFTA that would promote a stronger state. Such a move would allow the government to place necessary limits on the market and shape proper development.

CECOR suggested that CAFTA-DR was of particular concern in comparison to other FTAs precisely because of this unequal relationship. It was an abuse of power. Bishop Ulloa made the following case in a personal interview: "And a third principle is that a free trade treaty should always be founded in justice, that it should be just. That a country, to be powerful, to be grand, to be rich, would take advantage of a developing country, a poor country, to exploit it – No. Justice has to be a fundamental principle" (Ulloa Rojas 2007). The bishops argued nations have to be in equal power relationships when making agreements, although few specifics are ever given about what this concretely looks like (CECOR 2004).

A central concern of the power imbalance was the consequence for the Costa Rican welfare state. CAFTA-DR mandated a number of changes. Publicly run state programs were threatened by provisions that required states to open such industries to private foreign companies. These changes to Costa Rican public institutions and the laws were not guided by national consensus. For the bishops, this translated to a loss of freedom for the country to govern itself.[8]

During discussions about CAFTA-DR, the bishops called for a new social contract that would endorse an increased role for institutions and the government in mitigating some of the current economic problems. They consistently argued that a stronger social welfare state would promote the common good – unlike the free market alone. In an early letter on CAFTA, Bishop San Casimiro warned of CAFTA's potential civic consequences:

---

[8] These fears were in part realized, as the government did have to change some of its laws before the treaty could be enacted. For example, laws governing both the national insurance company and the telecommunications industry – both state monopolies – had to be changed to allow for both national and international competition. This political process delayed CAFTA-DR's implementation in the country until 2009.

We call to the attention of our people the fact that the free trade agreement with the United States is not a simple bilateral agreement like that we would have with another country. It appears in theory to present many opportunities for our country, and also to present many questions. The consequences [of CAFTA] can be negative for vulnerable sectors (like agriculture and transportation) as well as for necessary sectors (like telecommunications) if we do not manage this wisely, and with clear attention to the common good.

(Caritas 2003, 99)

Following the referendum, the bishops continued to speak out, this time tying their suggestions for a more active development agenda more closely to CAFTA-DR: "We have a moral obligation, people and government, not simply to mitigate or compensate those who are affected [negatively by CAFTA-DR], but to make necessary changes to change the general mechanisms of inequality that we find inside this aspect of the economy" (CECOR 2007b). In their discourse, the bishops consistently reiterated that it was the responsibility of the state to promote ethical development, a mandate that required more autonomy than CAFTA-DR provided.

While expressing hope in a more equal power balance, the bishops avoided villainizing the United States, and warned against opposition to the treaty for purely ideological reasons. As Father Francisco Hernández, the head of Caritas in Costa Rica noted, "Whatever issue we have with the United States always brings out passion" (Hernández Rojas 2007). He encouraged sober evaluation of the issues rather than a rejection of the treaty because of feelings about "los gringos." In their calls for greater Costa Rican authority, the bishops critiqued the relationship of Costa Rica with the United States. What made CAFTA-DR a concern, however, was not the presence of the United States, but the dynamics and consequences of the power relationship between the two.

Dialogue and Democratic Consensus Are Essential for Policy Change

Both as a strategy and as part of their discourse, CECOR bishops promoted the idea that the common good, as developed through economic and state policy, must be arrived at through consensus and dialogue. In *A Reflection*, the council enunciated its stance:

The discernment or the ethical reading of an economic medium should be decided in community, in a true dialogue, in a dialogue that examines the economic and social impacts.... It is the way of the church to encourage discernment according to the principles of the Gospel with respect to the socioeconomic and cultural context; this is, to analyze our reality ... in a context of communication, to realize through dialogue our national priorities.

(2004, 25)

Other religious leaders across the Americas shared CECOR's lament over a lack of dialogue. A letter written by the Central American and U.S. Catholic bishops made this point clearly: "There has not been sufficient information and debate in our countries about the various aspects of CAFTA and its impact on our societies.... This lack of dialogue and consensus regarding the treaty is also leading to growing discontent. In Central America, this could lead to violence and other civic unrest" (USCCB and SEDAC 2004).

Indeed, violent political response is a constant possibility in Central America, and bishops have repeatedly warned the populace about the dangers of polarization. As the only country in Central America where civil war has been avoided and democracy is strong, Costa Rica cherishes its history of dialogue. Historically, political equality and democracy have been prioritized over economic equality. Even as the bishops promoted redistribution, a strong state system, and ethical markets, they ultimately championed the collective making such political decisions. This delicate balance assumes and hopes that people will pursue the common good and a pro-poor agenda.

In pursuit of this democratic yet value-influenced society, CECOR lent its support to the referendum as a political tool. They emphasized the importance of individual discernment and responsibility, even as they promoted their particular values framework. Bishop Ulloa explained why the referendum was so important: "I think that this medium is an important one because the people are going to decide and the result will have to be accepted by both parts. Because whoever wins, the loser has to accept it. Why? Because it is the free and democratic will of the people that is going to decide what it is we want for Costa Rica" (Ulloa Rojas 2007).

Supporting such a referendum allowed the Church to assert its religious presence within the policy sector, while still acknowledging the authority of democratic processes within a pluralistic democracy. Inglehart (2009) argued that strong religious voices are compatible within a democracy when they recognize this power of the vote. After the referendum results were announced, the bishops reiterated their support for the democratic decision, calling the vote legitimate and urging opponents to respect the outcome: "the enthusiastic expression of the citizen in this first referendum of the nation's history is the voice of the people toward new ethical goals" (CECOR 2007b).

The support of the referendum reflected not only support for democratic processes, but also support for the democratic government that is in place in Costa Rica. The bishops value their relationship with the government. As Bishop Ulloa stated, even when the Church has spoken out against the state, "The relationship that we have had is a relationship of dialogue, of understanding. Together we search for what is best for Costa Rica" (Ulloa Rojas 2007). Even as CECOR was clearly critical of the CAFTA-DR agreement, they sought to uphold the legitimacy and power of the state.

Surely many bishops were disappointed with CAFTA-DR's acceptance by the public, but they nonetheless projected a consistent understanding of their own authority. They were clearly confident in their theological and ethical positions, and their right to evaluate free trade agreements. Yet they did not attempt to wield technical authority. The Church legitimized the role of technical experts, yet insisted that the latter should not be the only voice. Democracy should reign alongside technical opinion. In their letter to priests across Costa Rica, issued five months before the referendum, the bishops expressed their respect for the democratic process. They reminded priests not to instruct congregations how to vote. The vote cast out of an individual conscience, the bishops argued, would "strengthen our democratic system" (CECOR 2007a). Parishioners needed to freely make their own political decisions. In pastoral letters and other public statements, the bishops repeatedly called for people to vote and take seriously their responsibility to vote – not only in this referendum, but also in other elections. So while they raised political and ethical concerns about CAFTA-DR and called for a strong state, they also focused on enabling the less powerful to speak within the political arena. Their ends were strongly influenced by their religious values, as discussed in the next section.

RELIGIOUS JUSTIFICATIONS AND THE DEVELOPMENT OF DISCOURSE

First and foremost, the Catholic bishops of Costa Rica founded their political analysis of CAFTA-DR in religious authority – specifically the principles of CST. As *A Reflection* states, they analyzed society "from the lens of the Gospel and the social doctrine of the Church" (CECOR 2004, 22). Although Papal social teaching holds special authority, the current bishops also accord authority to past documents from progressive periods in their own national history. Based on a national and international view of CST, the bishops have primarily emphasized the values of human-centered development, solidarity in a search for the common good, and peaceful interactions and dialogue among citizens. Such are central values in CST.[9]

The Human as the Center of Development

A 2004 joint statement between Central American and U.S. bishops stated, "the human person must be at the center of all economic activity. FTAs, such as CAFTA, should be a way of achieving authentic human development that upholds basic values such as human dignity, solidarity, and subsidiarity" (USCCB and SEDAC 2004). These thoughts were echoed in the subsequent SEDAC document on CAFTA-DR (SEDAC 2005), as well as a letter from the Costa Rican bishops in the same year (CECOR 2005d). The value of human-centered development dominated their discourse. CECOR emphasized this theme while CAFTA was initially being drafted, as people were debating

---

[9] As Coleman (2005) argued, even as there is sometimes disagreement on the terms and the centrality of some themes, there are eight principles of CST: human dignity, the social nature of the human, the common good, subsidiarity, solidarity, preferential option for the poor, justice, and integral humanism.

whether it should be passed, and after the Costa Rican referendum. They often made reference to the encyclicals of Paul VI (especially *Populorum Progressio*), and his teachings on human dignity, the person, and true development.[10] Archbishop Barrantes attested to the coherence of this message across time.

In May 2004 and through 2005 we spoke on this theme, and we have always insisted that the human person should be at the center of all economic activity. Our discourse has always been very coherent.... The key for us is the dignity of the human being, and we disagree with leaving it [CAFTA-DR] in the hands of technical experts and economists who see everything at the macroeconomic level.   (*Seminario Universidad* 2006)

The bishops identified their focus on the human as one often at odds with the logic of current market structures. They repeatedly contrasted liberal economic logic to moral ethics. In a SEDAC statement, the bishops from Central America declared that choosing to focus on human welfare was an intentional act: "We do not oppose, on any level, all types of treaties or commercial agreements.... We proclaim with vehemence that between money and the person, we opt for the person, even though this may mean a possible decrease in economic progress" (SEDAC 2002).

To "opt for the person" includes an emphasis on human dignity, the first principle of CST noted by Coleman (2005). Laczniak (1999) also focused on human dignity as the central value of CST for decisions by businesses and individual actors. Human dignity is about understanding the nature, rights, and responsibilities of people and the groups in which they are embedded (Coleman 2005).

In the 2004 statement from CELAM, the bishops linked human development and human dignity, stating, "We propose that the human person is in the center of the integration process.... The fundamental principle is the recognition of human dignity as a central value" (CELAM 2004, 68). Human dignity is upheld when all people, and especially the poor, benefit economically from policies undertaken by the government. According to Bishop Ulloa, "The first principle that we defend, really, is that the person is the end of all human action and also commerce ... [T]he gap between the rich and the poor ... should close so that all have a life of dignity" (Ulloa Rojas 2007). The bishops' commitment to human dignity guided their participation in politics, given the moral implications they saw of economic policies.

Solidarity and the Common Good

The Costa Rican bishops, along with other international Catholic bodies, often evoked notions of "solidarity" and the common good in their pastoral letters.

[10] Palacios (2007) pointed out that this document, *Populorum Progressio*, was written largely in response to the development gap between wealthy and poor countries, and was the first encyclical to significantly address issues of development.

Given the different ways solidarity has been conceived in Catholic thought, the bishops most frequently reference Pope John Paul II – rather than CELAM or other more liberationist sources. Palacios (2007), in discussing how solidarity tends to be defined in CST, highlights two important elements. First, society is the whole of many parts; that is, people are in relationships with one another and dependency exists. Second, this solidarity is often critical of individualism or equality, instead accepting order and hierarchy (Palacios 2007, 44).

In their 2004 letter, *A Reflection*, the bishops argued that the overemphasis of economic policies on the individual was problematic. Solidarity requires an attention to distributive justice, the common good, and subsidiarity. Palacios also noted that solidarity does not demand economic or political equality; that is, although fair wages or treatment of people is mandated, because of differential talents or effort, many supporting solidarity may still accept significant inequality. Rather, this solidarity is concerned that all are treated fairly and with dignity. In a sermon given just months before the referendum vote on CAFTA-DR, Bishop Barrantes highlighted the centrality of human dignity for solidarity: "The critical ethic to judge a free trade agreement is to see if human dignity is one of its principles. This only happens when a free trade agreement is founded on the principles of justice and solidarity" (Barrantes Ureña 2007).

Solidarity was characterized by special attention to the needs of those often ignored. In his 2003 pastoral letter, Bishop San Casimiro declared, "We consider that in these discussions [on CAFTA] social justice should prevail.... The Church is committed in its mission of solidarity, to show itself faithful to Christ, while truly being 'the Church of the poor'" (San Casimiro Fernández 2003, 358). Bishop Ulloa asserted that the values of justice and solidarity require attention to all groups in society, especially those who rights often go unprotected: "We see the need to renew our commitment for the promotion of justice, and to denounce all that is against the life and the dignity of the person. We must protect the rights of every man and woman, of every adult and child . . . of every worker, of every woman, ethnic or social group" (Ulloa Rojas and Vargas Varela 2003).

The bishops repeatedly asserted the need for justice for those who have been marginalized: the small farmer and small businesspeople, the elderly, the unemployed, the disabled, indigenous populations, and children. A society has a responsibility to care about the fate of every single person within it, and only when it does will it achieve a common good. As the bishops wrote, "Of justice, we understand rights and responsibilities together, as an obligation to make things better for the most disadvantaged, as sharing the wealth, with a consciousness of the social oath that weighs on us for the good of all" (CECOR 2004, 26).

As explained earlier, the bishops encouraged parishioners to vote their opinions. But solidarity clashes with self-interest, and the bishops challenged people to avoid making a decision on CAFTA-DR based on their own interests. In one of the first statements written in 2003 on CAFTA, Bishop San Casimiro issued such a challenge for the country to focus on the consequences of CAFTA for the entire country, and "not simply for the benefit of a few economic elites" (Caritas 2003, 99).

This emphasis on solidarity translated into a political process whereby the nation might collectively identify and pursue a common good. This common good should include everybody, both at a procedural level and in the final evaluation of consequences: "In effect, there are many economic situations that hurt our communities. At a macro- and microeconomic level, there is an increase in the social gap, poverty, unemployment, insecurity, problems of early education, water, and environmental damage. Many people are excluded from the opportunity to access the common good.... We are responsible for constructing a common good that includes all of our brothers and sisters" (CECOR 2004, 21–22).

To promote the common good, the bishops also relied on national pride. In their 2006 message before the general assembly of the government, they declared their national fidelity: "Costa Rica is first. In this spirit, given the situation that we confront in the future with CAFTA-DR, we make a fraternal call to leave every type of confrontation and compromise. With a serene spirit, we should always have the common good of Costa Rica in mind, looking for ways of understanding, dialogue, and discernment" (CECOR 2006b).

Further supporting such an idea, Chaves argued that the Vatican charged the bishops with the task of proclaiming and clarifying the gospel and CST, which requires guiding society in finding the common good:

The correct ethical and religious position before problems such as this [like decisions about CAFTA] is a collective one. The discernment of the ethical religious teaching should be made in communities, in collaboration with responsible bishops, in dialogue with other Christian brothers and people of good will, looking for "options and commitments that will promote social, political, and economic transformation that are considered necessary in that case."

(Chaves Ortiz 2003b, citing a letter from Pope Paul VI, *Octagesima Adveniens* [1971])

Many of CECOR's statements similarly assumed that if everyone processed policies together, there could be a shared understanding of the common good. The bishops established core religious principles to guide people as the people themselves decided how to enforce these principles. In a sermon on CAFTA-DR, Bishop Ulloa highlighted the specific role of the Church in bringing about the common good. "The mission of church is not primarily political; it is religious and evangelistic. It offers the strength to unite groups ... to make decisions that affect the collective group" (Ulloa Rojas 2007).

CECOR stood in contrast to many Catholic activists involved in Kairos in Canada, who were more skeptical that a common good would naturally arise from democratic processes. Although the emphasis on the common good is central throughout CST – Barbieri (2001) referred to it as CST's "linchpin" and noted its connection with the other important CST values – CECOR's conception of the common good reflects some national biases. Their 2005 statement on CAFTA differs slightly from a 2004 joint statement issued with the United States and other Central American councils, but this difference is distinctive. The Costa Rican bishops used the exact wording found in the joint letter to endorse human development, yet they diverged when listing the core values that support such development. In place of "human dignity, solidarity, and subsidiarity" (USCCB and SEDAC 2004), the bishops in Costa Rica listed "dialogue, the common good, equality, solidarity, and subsidiarity" (CECOR 2005d, 401). CECOR emphasizes dialogue, the common good, and equality as what makes for true human development.

Peace

Peace is another value championed by the bishops that finds support throughout the Catholic community, but is uniquely shaped and defined by context. In the bishops' discourse, peace is interconnected with their belief in the goodwill of the Costa Rican people, and this value has been a prominent character of much Catholic action within Costa Rica over the years.[11] Peace was an ever-present element in their discourse on CAFTA-DR, and one that increased in importance over time.

At a basic level, calls for peace were calls for nonviolent resolution. In a 2005 letter calling for dialogue in place of polarization, the bishops appealed to Costa Ricans' affinity for peace, reminding the country that, in this specific moment, citizens had the chance to reaffirm their commitment to nonviolence. "Because we know that violence and intolerance are forces that weaken and destroy national unity, we call on all Costa Ricans to solidify their commitment to peace, the fruit of justice and good understanding" (CECOR 2005b, 421).

For the bishops, peace was not just about nonviolence, but also about a lack of conflict and confrontation. Unlike Catholic liberationist thought, the bishops' discourse had little acknowledgment of class divisions, oppression, and struggles within society.[12] Bishop Ulloa emphasized the bishops' rejection of heated conflict, and the value of avoiding relationships involving high tension, in stating, "Ultimately, yes, there are certain themes in which we have had little agreement between the state and the Church. But we have talked, and I think that we have walked well. We have not had confrontations" (Ulloa Rojas 2007).

---

[11] Sawchuk (2004) noted that the tendency to avoid conflict is often more prominent in conservative wings of the church than in liberal ones. This tendency is also especially strong in the Costa Rica context, as it remains one of the only countries in the region to have not undergone significant civil war. Statements by the bishops reveal a sense of pride in that history of democracy and peace.

[12] As detailed later in the chapter, a dominant Catholic response in Costa Rica was to declare that CAFTA-DR must be rejected, acknowledging the reality of strong conflict among segments of society. Such a stance had a similar view of conflict as that held by Kairos actors profiled in the previous chapter.

Although peace often translates to avoiding conflict, the bishops do acknowledge that such peace requires justice and is not just about people being able to
live together. Peace was not separate from calls for human-centered development, solidarity, and the common good. According to the bishops, the true peace
they sought is founded upon justice. They reminded people that "true peace is
the fruit of justice, moral virtue, and legal guarantees that respect rights and
privileges and distribute costs and benefits equally" (CECOR 2005b, 421). Their
calls for peace focused on the fate of the marginalized, even as this concept of
peace could be achieved without much struggle or conflict.

Unlike some of the other values they espoused, the theme of peace became
more prominent in CECOR's discourse as division grew after the 2006 presidential election. The "walking well" with the state referenced earlier has not
been without effort in such a polarized context, where conflict and division have
appeared at high levels. The bishops called for Costa Ricans to pursue peace
first – before any particular CAFTA-DR decision. In a homily delivered at the
Metropolitan Cathedral in downtown San José on the day of the election, the
priest encouraged people to embrace the democratically reached decision.
CECOR released a memo just days after the election that asked voters to peace-
fully accept the results.

Even their own interactions reflected the emphasis on peace as division rose in
the country. Although the earlier individual 2003 pastoral letters by bishops
showed more diversity of thought, once CECOR established a full CAFTA
analysis (in 2004), only joint letters were issued by the bishops on the topic.
Father Hernández explained that even if the bishops came to an issue with
slightly different views, once they had decided on a position, they spoke as one
voice for the sake of peace. He stated, "Normally there is a unity of the bishops,
although you are able to have some bishops who are not initially in agreement,
but if the majority decides something, then all of them accept it" (Hernández
Rojas 2007). Likewise, in personal interviews current bishops readily articulated
the council's position when asked about CAFTA-DR and free trade more generally (Barrantes Ureña 2007; Ulloa Rojas 2007). Peace as a value is balanced
with human dignity and solidarity to shape the bishops' vision of the common
good for Costa Rica.

THE ROLE OF HIERARCHY AND HISTORY IN CECOR'S RESPONSE

The structure of CECOR's hierarchy is different from those of the religious
organizations described in Chapters 2 and 3. The bishops hold significantly more
religious authority than the leaders in the previous cases. Statements of the Church,
as a result, are not intended to represent public consensus, but rather to serve as an
authoritative word for the people. Bishops are charged with discerning and applying CST and the gospel to the national context. In this charge, the bishops have

relied largely on the stance of the official Catholic Church and the Vatican, with local Catholic organizations largely accepting the bishops' position. Among those less connected to the official authority structure within the Church, however, there has been opposition to CAFTA- DR; such opposition often has relied on many of the same Catholic social values that the bishops asserted. Although these differences are due in part to varied understandings of conflict, power, and peace, they also have resulted from the different social locations occupied by these actors.

The eight bishops with authority in the hierarchical structure of the Catholic Church in Costa Rica appealed to official Catholic documents and teaching to legitimate their ethical values and religious commitments. They referenced a number of Costa Rican Catholic documents from the past to demonstrate their consistency in applying CST over the years. For example, in his article on the Church and development, Archbishop Barrantes wrote, "The Catholic Church, under the hand of Monseñor Víctor Manuel Sanabria, understood also the seriousness of the moment and was ready to help in the task of solidarity and justice." He continued to discuss the social policies of the past and present. "This is not to glorify the past, but to extract the lessons that history and experience has left us" (Barrantes Ureña 2004a).

As a national conference, the bishops were responsible for speaking directly to their Costa Rican context. As Palacios (2007) noted, since Vatican II, there has been increased attention to, and freedom for bishops to implement, CST within their own national context, as well as acknowledgment that national churches operate in different contexts. CECOR has not only dealt with FTAs more than many other bishops' conferences, but also has dealt with FTAs from a particular context. The emphasis of the bishops on peace and the common good was in part influenced by a national history of nonviolence over the years.

In relating CST to their national context, the bishops referenced both their own history and the central documents of the global Church. This reliance on Catholic history and authority was especially evident in their formal letters. When President Arias visited the Vatican in 2006, concerned with CECOR's involvement with CAFTA-DR, the correspondence that followed between the Costa Rican bishops and Cardinal Sodano, secretary of the Vatican, revealed CECOR's allegiance to Rome. The bishops stated in their letter to Cardinal Sodano, "We assure you that in no moment have the bishops opposed economic development policies that include legitimate human development; in receiving the teaching of Pope Benedict XVI, we are illuminating the objectives of justice to which all political action should be directed" (CECOR 2006a).

To a lesser degree, the council at times referred to CELAM documents to support their claims, although this process was wrought with care. To be sure, Costa Rica is a member of CELAM, a permanent council that has had five general meetings to date. The Costa Rican bishops, as intimated earlier, did not support the liberationist direction of the group, and have used CELAM documents associated with liberation theology carefully. Williams (1989) detailed the conflicts of

interpretation in Costa Rica of CELAM documents.[13] The SEDAC 2004 statement referenced the 1968 CELAM Conference at Medellín's call for peace, a topic
where the stance of the Costa Rican Church has been quite conservative. When
making claims about the problems of over-empowered TNCs or liberal economies, CECOR cited CELAM's 1979 Puebla conference, most likely because few
documents have discussed TNCs (CECOR 2004). Mostly, however, they relied on
Papal documents of the Church, while also supporting their positions with the
historical tendencies of the Latin American and Costa Rican churches.

Even as they relied on Catholic authority to legitimate their position, the
bishops took seriously the power they had as an important social actor in Costa
Rican political life. Unlike the cases described in Chapters 2 and 3, the bishops
had close ties to the power of the state.[14] For example, in discussions about the
fate of the government-managed electric industry (Instituto Costarricense de
Electricidad, or ICE) in 1999, the bishops helped broker an agreement after
mass demonstrations broke out in response to governmental plans to privatize.
Ultimately, the state agreed to not liberalize the industry.

CECOR strategically used the power they held in Costa Rica to apply CST
values, and used a strategy of neutrality to legitimate their political discourse to
the state. The bishops provided recommendations before the International
Commission of the Legislative Assembly on CAFTA-DR (CECOR 2006c).
Their ability to call for dialogue between both sides of the trade debate was best
illustrated in their forums instituted in 2007 after the referendum was announced.
Each Monday, the Catholic radio channel, Radio Fides, hosted two guests
representing the pro– and anti–CAFTA-DR positions. Such guests included
government officials, university faculty, agricultural experts, and business actors.
To emphasize the impartial nature of such forums, a large screen in the debate
room revealed the exact time that each person had spoken. The bishops also
called for others to promote this type of discussion: "We respectfully invite the
national community, and particularly the public and private universities[15] and
other Christian denominations, to be united in constructing spaces of dialogue"
(CECOR 2005b, 421). They called for priests to give voice to both sides as well, to
serve as ethical guides without promoting their own opinions (2007a).

Such a response must be interpreted in their particular context. Costa Rica
officially remains a Catholic state and is one of the only states within Central
America where the bishops enjoy the status of being officially recognized by the

---

[13] He cites the example of when Caritas in the 1980s published a pamphlet using CELAM documents, and then was accused, primarily by the John XXIII Social School, of being Marxist. The
relationship of these organizations with one another is described in the next section.
[14] In August 2006, for instance, they were granted the honor of speaking in the General Legislative
Assembly regarding their recommendations on CAFTA-DR.
[15] Universities were among those most involved in CAFTA-DR debates. The leader of the anti-
CAFTA-DR movement, Eugenio Trejos, was the rector at the Technological Institute of Costa
Rica. Two prominent universities, the University of Costa Rica and the National University, also
had many outspoken critics of CAFTA and hosted protest events.

state. When comparing the religious identity of citizens in Costa Rica to those of neighboring countries, in Costa Rica Catholicism remains a dominant force. The Catholic Church enjoys strong support from citizens and has strong linkages with the government. CECOR also exists within a society that has a strong civil society and well-functioning democracy. When religious heterogeneity is low and civil society is high, the Catholic Church is freer to pursue its full agenda (as compared to cases where there is more diversity and/or a weak civil society) (Hagopian 2009b). In other words, the strong civil society in Costa Rica would predict that more critical attitudes might be voiced surrounding current policies related to economic globalization.

In addition to promoting dialogue among different factions in Costa Rica, the bishops have prioritized open communication with the government. Their criticisms of CAFTA-DR were framed in terms of what sort of development agenda the country should pursue. In their message to the Church's General Assembly, they invited people to join them in their task: "We are first interested in an institutional transformation of our country ... with the goals of eliminating poverty and inequality, of sustainable development and a life of dignity for all, without forgoing increasing our production or the competitive capacity of Costa Rica at an international level" (CECOR 2006b).

The bishops used the opportunity of high public interest in CAFTA-DR to speak out about development and economic policies more broadly. So, while papal authority was crucial in highlighting the values that CECOR used to legitimate their presence in the CAFTA-DR conversation, the Costa Rican context was important in understanding the ways that they chose to communicate the message and interact with the state. The bishops promoted values central in CST, while also promoting values of dialogue and nonpartisanship that increased their legitimacy among the citizens of Costa Rica.

Central Network Actors in the Production of Discourse

While CECOR speaks on behalf of the Costa Rican Catholic Church, the hierarchy and network of Catholic actors within the state is more complex. Other formal bodies also produce discourse within the Church, and most of these offices have a bishop associated with them.[16]

The vicariate office in San José (VEPS) produced official documents under the oversight of Archbishop Barrantes. Their informational book on CAFTA-DR not only detailed the position of CECOR, but also included a number of homilies on the topic delivered by various bishops. VEPS also maintains an electronic database of these statements.

---

[16] For example, Bishop San Casimiro, as the bishop in charge of Caritas, recently issued a letter that dealt with the high levels of migration between Nicaragua and Costa Rica. The official church organizations within the country, such as Caritas, the John XXIII Social School, and the *Eco Católico*, all have a bishop appointed to oversee them.

Caritas has produced most of the discourse on immigration in the country. Williams (1989) documented the role and history of Caritas in the country, noting that before 1981 the organization was largely focused on social services but after 1981 it became more of a voice for the poor and marginalized in the country, and that it has been one of the more receptive segments of the Costa Rican Church to ideas from CELAM. The former head of Caritas (2002–2006), Father Guildo Villalta, currently heads the VEPS office in San José, and represented the Church officially as part of a national commission appointed by the government in 2002 to study CAFTA. The current head of Caritas in Costa Rica, Father Francisco Hernández, also has made recommendations before CECOR about CAFTA-DR. Although his position toward CAFTA-DR was more neutral and in line with the official position CECOR has articulated, he is notable for leading not only Caritas (since 2006), but also the John XXIII Social School (since 2007).

Even though it is under the same leadership as Caritas, the John XXIII Social School is a very different sort of Catholic organization, and traditionally has been more conservative than Caritas and other parts of the Church. With a staff of more than a hundred, it was initially founded to "teach, defend, and diffuse" CST. It has championed the *solidarismo* movement, which seeks to foster good relationships between workers and employers. "A form of labour organization that renounces collective agreements and the right to strike, *solidarismo* emphasizes the common interests and collaboration of workers and owners," according to Sawchuk (2004, 142), a scholar of labor rights and the Catholic Church in Costa Rica. Such a movement, although professing to work with workers and employers, is actually a vehicle of the employers and sells its services to businesses (Goldin 2007). When Caritas became more concerned with the structural issues affecting the poor in the early 1980s, it was the John XXIII Social School that critiqued their Marxist tendencies (Williams 1989). Given the central role the John XXIII Social School plays within the Church, it is worth noting that the larger *solidarismo* movement in Costa Rica was a prominent leader in the pro-CAFTA-DR movement. The former leader of the John XXIII Social School, Father Claudio Solano, was perhaps more important to the CAFTA-DR story than the institution itself. As head of the Catholic *solidarismo* response after 1971, he became a leader in the pro-CAFTA-DR movement.[17] Several interviewees suggested he was asked to step down at the John XXIII Social School because of his growing power and close relationship with the business community.

The Catholic newspaper *Eco Católico* is under the supervision of the bishops, but has taken a more critical stance toward CAFTA-DR than the bishops themselves. Father Armando Alfaro served as editor for almost forty years, taking office in 1967 and serving until the end of 2006. From its founding, the paper has dealt with political and social issues. This weekly publication has an estimated circulation of about 15,000. It is the print source of the Catholic Church to which most

---

[17] The night of the election, media photographed Solano celebrating predictions of the referendum's passage alongside President Arias.

Catholics in the country had access, sold every Sunday outside the cathedrals. However, the contents of the pastoral letters are still more accessible to citizens, given that they are not only reproduced in national newspapers, often with accompanying background or context, but also read aloud in masses throughout the country. The newspaper serves as both a medium to transmit the official messages from the bishops and a venue for other Catholic voices to express their opinions on social, economic, political, and religious issues.

Father Jorge Arturo Chaves, an economist at the National University and an anti–CAFTA-DR advocate, serves as a consultant for CECOR and the Latin American Catholic bishops. Although he has not headed a Catholic organization in the country, he has played a role in shaping the Church's policy on CAFTA-DR. As an economist, he also has represented the Church on more technical matters. In one interview he was referred to as a "mouthpiece of the Catholic Church" (Cordero Arias 2007). Archbishop Barrantes seemed to affirm this stance (in regard to technical aspects of CAFTA-DR) when he stated that Chaves "is an asset because he is an economist in addition to being a priest. I think that he is the only economist priest that we have, and he has a very clear understanding of all the mechanisms of the economy and everything that comes with globalization" (Barrantes Ureña 2007). Most of the official actors within the Catholic Church in Costa Rica have been faithful (to various degrees) to the position on CAFTA-DR taken by the bishops.

Unofficial Discourse and the Response to CECOR

So far, I have focused on the official position of CECOR regarding FTAs, and CAFTA-DR specifically. Yet, the Catholic position on CAFTA-DR in Costa Rica is far more complex. Some religious actors have been more sympathetic toward CAFTA-DR than CECOR and their supporters, and some religious actors have been vocal in their skepticism toward the CECOR policy. I turn now to the sizable minority of actors who have been vocal in their protest of the CECOR position.

Although the Costa Rican bishops avoided making a definitive statement on CAFTA-DR, other Catholic voices took more definitive stances, a freedom accorded to them in part because of their existence outside the formal structure. Hagopian (2009b), in studying some of the tensions faced by Catholic actors (especially in Latin America), noted that while there is often agreement on general principles, the question of how to divide political attentions to different moral and social concerns is less clear. She also observed that although the Church's ability to mobilize the laity and the perspectives of the laity are important, the political risk the Church faces impacts its decisions. The official Church in Costa Rica has been calculating of political risks and its context, but this seems to be less the case with those who have voiced dissent.

Some of these leaders have had significant authority within the Catholic community, having held past leadership positions in the Church. Although some Catholics within the country championed the cause of CAFTA-DR, of more interest is the sizable faction of those in the Church who opposed it. Unlike those who affirmed CAFTA-DR primarily from their position as citizens, many Catholic anti-CAFTA-DR supporters called for CECOR to promote their agenda as the ethical path. These voices generally shared the same religious values of the bishops but drew different political implications, especially once CAFTA-DR was established and Costa Rica had to accept or reject the treaty.

In February of 2007, groups of priests in two communities in Costa Rica – Alejuela and Tilaron – formally expressed their opposition to CAFTA-DR in print (Álvarez Ruiz et al. 2007; Sota S. et al. 2007). Months later, on the eve of the October 2007 referendum, a cadre of priests throughout the country authored a letter protesting CAFTA-DR (Picado Gatgens et al. 2007). Bishop Emeritus Trejos Picado and former newspaper editor Armando Alfaro were among the signers of this document. Trejos Picado also authored a number of individual letters against CAFTA-DR that called for the Catholic Church to speak against the treaty. Although he had not been an official member of CECOR since 2002, he was still a leader in the Catholic community. As explained earlier, *Eco Católico* gave voice to this segment of the Catholic population.

Those opposing the stance of the bishops still deferred to them in many ways. At the very least, there was a continual respect for the bishops in power. Bishop Emeritus Trejos Picado, for example, has a picture of Archbishop Barrantes set up in his office right next to one of the pope. He stated, "I respect, but do not share, the position of my brother bishops, because I love them. But that does not keep me from speaking about the Costa Rica that I love deeply" (Trejos Picado 2007b). He and other CAFTA-DR opponents often referenced the current bishops in articulating their own position, highlighting the points at which they agreed. Authority and legitimacy were still important for this unofficial group. In talking about their concerns in regard to democracy, for example, they noted, "Remember also what the archbishop of San José, Bishop Hugo Barrantes wrote: 'The lack of transparency is the main threat and obstacle to a national agreement'" (Picado Gatgens et al. 2007). Most notably, they presented their opposition to CAFTA-DR "in obedience" to the bishops, referencing their "duty" as priests: "We have considered it a duty of conscience to publish this 'Ethical Valuation of CAFTA-DR' to be submitted on the referendum. We do this in obedience to the provisions of our Bishops, who have invited us to pronounce and guide believers, with the sole restriction of not doing this during liturgical celebrations" (Picado Gatgens et al. 2007).

This nonofficial voice, while noting their obedience to the bishops in some regards, ultimately rejected the analysis of the bishops. In the same letter, the group argued that the development agenda promoted by the bishops would be impossible if CAFTA-DR passed:

In the case that Yes wins in the referendum, it will be impossible for a humane, sustainable, and integral agenda of development to occur, as desired by the bishops, our pastors; [it will be impossible] to formulate and draft an agenda for our own particular economy, to coordinate the economic and social policies to stop the increasing social gap and consequential impoverishment of the Costa Rican people.... It is regrettable that if CAFTA-DR is ratified, this legitimate aspiration of solidarity would be completely unobtainable. (Picado Gatgens et al. 2007)

This group, has a similar desire to the bishops to legitimate their position based on CST, and shared a concern for authentic human development and human dignity. Yet, the anti-CAFTA-DR movement argued that they upheld CST *better* than the bishops. To this end, Bishop Emeritus Trejos Picado referenced the same Costa Rican religious history as his colleagues in CECOR to support his anti-CAFTA-DR position: "The Catholic priests who signed below have satisfied our conscience in communicating this ethical judgment on the Free Trade Agreement inspired by the Gospel and the social doctrine of the Church and after consulting the best experts in the country" (Picado Gatgens et al. 2007). The letter argued that CAFTA-DR denied true human dignity:

It [CAFTA-DR] is a sin. It goes against God, it goes against the person, against the family, against common interests, against the interest of the people. I would be a traitor if I placed myself on the yes side.... If I am a minister of Christ, and Christ died to bring us all to God, I must be faithful and not only express my opinion.... We must not agree with those who promote the culture of death. (Picado Gatgens et al. 2007)

As ministers of Christ (an authority even higher than the bishops), the priests were compelled, then, to speak out regarding the devaluing of human life they perceived within CAFTA-DR. The letter from the bishops in Tilaron further declared that the correct, religious, and ethical position was for people to be part of a collective force protesting the agreement (Álvarez Ruiz et al. 2007).

While anti–CAFTA-DR advocates, like the bishops, espoused the values of human dignity, this group did not place the same emphasis on the democratic process or finding a common solution. Although they also supported solidarity, they tended to note that conflict existed. More in line with liberationist thought, they acknowledged that some people benefit at the expense of others, which complicates the possibility of consensus around a common good. They charged that transparency was not upheld within CAFTA-DR, that the United States received concessions that Costa Rica was denied, and that items were included in the treaty that did not belong. The inclusion of such items mandated an ethical rejection of the treaty. Emeritus Bishop Trejos Picado named, in particular, the concerns about the environment: "CAFTA-DR will also rob us of the water that maintains us.... We are not going to be robbed of those things that God has given us, and He has given us His gift of nature" (Trejos Picado 2007b). These anti-CAFTA Catholics saw the treaty as misappropriating environmental resources that God had given to the Costa Rican people.

Perhaps just as important as the two sides' different views of consensus were their understandings of how the Church should connect their moral and ethical values with political engagement. The protestors and bishops diverged largely in how they sought to analyze policy. While the Catholic Church officially declared that they were not technical experts and could not evaluate the treaty, many opposed to CAFTA-DR in the Church argued that there was no question that the treaty went against Catholic values. While the bishops saw their role as enforcing religious doctrine, opposition leaders emphasized a moral responsibility to protect values through policy engagement. In many ways, these protestors had more in common with the Presbyterians from Chapter 3, who called for religious experts to be involved in evaluating economic life, than they did with the bishops. The anti–CAFTA-DR advocates charged that workers would suffer, and many groups would be hurt by the devastation resulting from CAFTA-DR; they did not just assert that this *might* happen. In adopting deregulatory policies, the current model of Costa Rican life would be lost. Transnational organizations would be given power over indigenous matters, even making decisions about the seeds used by farmers. Protestors raised concerns over how the bishops could propose an agenda to promote solidarity when the FTA at its core destroyed solidarity.

Thus, while agreeing with the official position on the value of human dignity, those outside the hierarchical structure mobilized to make claims about the effect of the treaty, an action those with authority refused to take. This strategy was influenced both by their position outside the official Costa Rican Catholic Church structure, and by different understandings of peace and consensus. Both of these factors shaped their views of appropriate and ethical political engagement.

CONCLUSION

The neutral but politically engaged position of the Catholic bishops in Costa Rica regarding CAFTA-DR was a strategic decision by the Church. In not promoting a clear path for the political future of CAFTA-DR, the Catholic bishops were able to concentrate on key theological and social values. This strategy allowed them to highlight values shared by many Costa Ricans and to maintain a level of authority within society. Perhaps their criticisms were taken even more seriously by the public and the government than they would have been if considered mere ideologues in the debate. It would be naïve to argue that the Church was solely responsible for the referendum and its accompanying dialogue, but Church officials were central actors in legitimating this process, even declaring the referendum results valid after the election and praising the process.[18] The bishops' political strategy allowed them to promote their ideal of a common good and retain their role as leaders in establishing that common good.

---

[18] The bishops, however, would not advocate a stance of letting the people decide on all issues. On abortion, for example, the bishops have not called for people to vote on new laws, but have insisted that current antiabortion laws must stand. This probably has something to do with the distinctions within CST, where issues of "faith and morals" take precedence over "social" ones.

This is not to suggest that the model of political involvement employed by the bishops was the best model possible, but rather that the position flowed from the values espoused. That is, this lack of political advocacy for specific policies was shaped in part by values that impacted the ways in which the bishops thought about the political process. As Hart wrote, "the way we do politics manifests our identity and moral convictions" (2001, 3–4); for CECOR, their values emphasized the democratic process above a specific political goal. In the next chapter I compare the different political strategies of the religious communities in promoting political change, arguing that values about the process are central to understanding variation in political advocacy. Procedural values explain more of the variations than general values about economic life, given many of the principles shared by the three cases in this book.

Using their authority, the bishops argued first and foremost for an ethical framework to trade debates. They highlighted the values of human dignity, solidarity, justice, and peace. They accessed their moral authority from these religious values and from religious texts influenced by CST, as it has been understood in the international and the Costa Rican settings. Their central political goal was to make and keep such Catholic values and ethics relevant to trade policy decisions. The bishops did not attempt to evaluate the CAFTA-DR policy, but rather to provide the tools for others in society to do so.

The bishops' political objective of remaining both neutral and critical may seem contradictory. They simultaneously criticized the specifics of CAFTA-DR while still refusing to oppose it. They protested unrestrained markets and condemned the commodification of life and land, suggesting that such would occur under CAFTA-DR. They repeatedly called on Costa Rica to assert its sovereignty and not bow to U.S. pressure, demanding that democratic processes and dialogue occur as part of the CAFTA-DR decision-making process. But even in the complexity of its position, CECOR was clear in promoting its main message: Whether or not CAFTA-DR was implemented, Costa Rican society needed a new social contract and a reorientation of human development. By airing its criticisms through impartial forums and strategic dialogue, the Church avoided polarizing the nation any further and retained its position of authority in the midst of conflict.

5

The Political and Economic Discourse
of Religious Communities

All the religious organizations discussed in this book engaged in public discourse about free trade with the intent of social change, albeit in different ways. In this chapter, I first focus on why these groups became involved in political debates and what sustained their involvement. Noting some common theological principles, I also discuss the importance of transnational identity (in spite of national differences) in prompting each group's engagement. Second, I examine how understandings of authority and organizational structures significantly shaped both the processes of discourse production and the discourse itself. Finally, I investigate the different models for engagement that these religious communities employed. Although the groups shared some values and perspectives, they applied them to public life in diverse ways.

Table 5.1 provides an overview of their political stances. GATT-Fly/ECEJ/ Kairos, the Presbyterian Church (USA), and the Costa Rican bishops (CECOR) shared some common concerns within their political discourse on free trade agreements (FTAs), even as they all articulated different proposed solutions. CECOR's official position on the fate of FTAs was neutral, although they expressed their concerns for economists and citizens to consider. The PCUSA took the further step, in 2003 and 2004, to ultimately reject the Central America–United States Free Trade Agreement (CAFTA) and other FTAs. The Canadian coalitions, from their inception, not only rejected specific agreements but also crusaded against Canada's participation in the export-oriented international capitalist model.

Kairos and its predecessors largely took an *alternative* approach to the market – that is, they rejected FTAs and criticized free trade, calling for a new economic paradigm. They advocated for more inward-oriented economies and promoted their own economic model of self-sufficiency. These religious actors rejected the role of the central players in the current economic order, attacking the growing power of transnational corporations (TNCs) and the hegemony of the United States and international financial institutions (IFIs). The coalitions

TABLE 5.1 *Responses of Religious Organizations*

Religious Organization	Political Positions	Economic Application
GATT-Fly/ECEJ/ Kairos (Canada)	*Alternative Approach* The international economic order needs to be restructured. Canada should adopt a system of self-reliance.	Markets must benefit the poor. Local governments and people need power to make decisions. States should manage markets.
PCUSA (United States)	*Reformative Approach* The international economic order needs to be reformed. Empirical research shows that FTAs are flawed and need adjustment.	Regulations are needed to avoid human-rights violations. Economic well-being is a basic human right. International global governance is necessary.
CECOR (Costa Rica)	*Complementary Approach* Trade agreements should be evaluated based on ethical concerns. The lack of democratic decision making is a problem with creation of FTAs.	FTAs need an accompanying development agenda. Land and culture are not for sale. Costa Rica needs a strong welfare state.

charged that those with power were conspiring against developing states, and they consistently called for developing states to have more sovereignty and ability to control their own economies. Central to these criticisms was the understanding that markets and all economic policies should benefit the poor and that local governments and people within local communities should be making policy decisions. So the Canadian coalitions consistently sided with local communities in their disputes with TNCs.

The PCUSA, by contrast, called for a reform of the current international economic system. Although they pointed out problems within capitalism as a system, they did not reject the model but sought to reform specific policies in order to promote more ethical markets. To this end, they called for more standards and regulations in the market to limit labor and human-rights violations by businesses and other market actors. They also argued for a more expansive conception of rights that included the economic welfare of individuals; to protect these economic rights, they favored policies of redistribution. Finally, they endorsed a stronger role for the United Nations (UN) and other international organizations to ensure regulation of the market.

CECOR did not reject the international capitalist system or specific FTAs but raised concerns about some potential impacts of capitalism. This practice was consistent with the views of the international Catholic hierarchy. The bishops advocated for Costa Rica to develop a complementary development agenda, alongside any FTA, that would focus on human welfare in the country. While remaining neutral in the national debates over CAFTA-DR, they voiced potential problems with the agreement and encouraged a more democratic decision-making process. In addition to concerns for the marginalized, the bishops also protested the inclusion of land and other sacred aspects of culture within the pages of an FTA. Ultimately, they provided a set of ethical values to guide policy but encouraged public dialogue over CAFTA-DR as they demanded that people should have a greater political voice in evaluating the treaty.

Even as they shared many of the same criticisms about FTAs, often noting similar problems (as outlined in Table 5.1), the groups varied in their perspectives on capitalism, the international political economy, the requirements of state economic policy, and the role of local communities and international governing bodies. They ultimately disagreed in their assessments of FTAs – that is, CECOR mostly critiqued them, the PCUSA demanded significant changes, and Kairos ultimately rejected them, both in principle and in practice.

VALUES AND MOTIVATION FOR ACTION

Although they come out of different theological traditions, these communities espouse similar core values. The most central of these is community (which is particularly notable, given the increasing attention in the social science literature to the role of religious individualism). The emphasis on community is closely connected with justice and right relationships among people. Table 5.2 highlights the different religious values of the organizations explored throughout this book. Note how closely related these values are to the concept of community.

TABLE 5.2 *Theological Values of Religious Organizations*

Religious Organization	Religious Tradition	Central Theological Values
Kairos, etc.	Liberation theology Social gospel	Solidarity with the poor Empowerment and equality Sacredness of creation
PCUSA	Reformed theology	God's sovereignty Covenant and community Hope
CECOR	Catholic social teaching	Human as the center of development Solidarity and the common good Peace and dialogue

Community as an Ethical Starting Point

Research on religious life in America has noted the increasing focus on individualism within the lives of all participants (Bellah et al. 1985); this has especially been the case concerning work on the political activism of evangelicals. Individualism has been found to influence people's political and social beliefs, and religious individualism has been tied to a lack of attention to structural concerns in society (Emerson and Smith 2000; Hart 1992). Yet all of the organizations studied in this text did focus on structural issues, and they did so in part by contesting the individualism they identified as governing market decisions. Such evidence challenges the deeply embedded assumption that the growing religious individualism in Western religious communities today characterizes most religious communities.

To be fair, in some instances individualism can *inspire* communalism. Hart (2001) argues that the Durkheimian idea of individual human dignity has been the basis for collective goals and responsibility to society; here, the search for the common good requires a human-rights framework that relies on a "cultural analysis, emphasizing the collective, historical, and suprarational character of the culture of human rights" (202). All of the groups discussed in this book linked individual rights and human dignity with a commitment to community.

Lichterman (1995, 1996) has similarly proposed that in a commitment to the common good, individuals and personalism may often play an important role. He provides the example of members of a local Green party, arguing that many activists became engaged in community action as a result of a "personalized sense of political responsibility" (1996, 3). So although the Green movement worked for community goals, it was personalism that motivated the action of members. All of the cases detailed in these pages required that people be involved in designing and deciding upon a public good.[1] To that end, all of the groups argued politically for more rigorous democratic procedures, insisting that individuals need to collectively make decisions about general aspects of economic policy.

For the three case studies, the community was much more than the aggregate of individuals, even as this commitment to the community was framed and motivated by the value placed upon individuals. This stands out considering that appeals to the common good within U.S. public discourse are often more about the sum of individual interests than the community as an entity (Lamont and Thévenot 2000, 12–13). Relationships among people were central; people were responsible for their neighbor, and special attention was to be given to

---

[1] By contrast, Lichterman (1995, 1996) also discussed the case of HAT (Hillviewers Against Toxics), a group focused on eliminating sources of toxic hazards from their mostly low-income neighborhood. He argued that communal belonging was critical to motivating the action of members. Such a group also emphasized the community, although egalitarianism in decision making was not a priority. That is, it was a commitment to a community, and not a personal sense of activism, that motivated the politics.

those who were vulnerable. As Gordon Douglass (a Presbyterian pastor and economist involved in PCUSA trade-policy research) wrote, "Community, rather than individualism, is the proper starting point of a biblical ethic" (2001, 1).

Even so, the organizations had different understandings of what defined the common good of a community. CECOR maintained that the common good was determined and sustained through dialogue in society. The PCUSA based its understanding of community on the theology of covenant, which prioritizes the relationships that people have with God and one another. For Kairos, their central value of solidarity meant that prioritizing the community equaled prioritizing the poor and marginalized.

All of the groups agreed, however, that a corporate response was needed in order to promote community. They universally critiqued the lack of attention to the poor and marginalized in current economic structures, and each also supported increased governance of the market and laws to establish guidelines to protect the community.

Not only was this message of community clear and influential for each of the organizations, but also much of the protest their messages evoked from their religious adherents was associated with a tension between community and individualism. This seems to verify what Douglass wrote: "Calls for freedom of commerce as the standard for all economic relationships bring into focus more clearly than most economic issues the strain between individual and community values" (2001, 2). Those adherents who supported free markets often critiqued the notion that the community should be a focus of the market, even as they would agree with community as a value. Their objections revealed an understanding of markets as efficient and value-neutral structures for the distribution of goods. Many of these actors who challenged the responses of the three religious organizations focused more on what it meant to be moral *within* markets than on the morality of the markets themselves.[2] Yet, for those leading CECOR, the PCUSA, and Kairos, the failure of markets to properly value and respect community characterized them as immoral structures in need of change.

National Values

Even as the case studies highlight some of the nuanced theological arguments promoting and shaping the involvement of these organizations in the public realm, when examined together, national values emerge as another source of differing attitudes among these three organizations. That is, the groups relied on different nationally influenced values in their political discourse. CECOR lifted up peace as a paramount value, the Canadian coalitions appealed to human

---

[2] Examples include Father Claudio Solano in Costa Rica and *The Presbyterian Layman* in the United States.

rights, and the Presbyterians in the United States placed a high value on ration-alization and research, and right governance solutions.

The Costa Rican Catholic bishops actively promoted peace and dialogue. They emphasized these values not only more than Kairos and the PCUSA, but also more than their co-religionists in Latin America and North America. To be certain, peace and dialogue have been espoused by the Catholic Church everywhere, and have been referenced repeatedly in Papal documents. Within Costa Rica, how-ever, these values were central values of the trade debate. As argued in Chapter 4, peace was highly valued in the Costa Rican state; they have no standing army and they have avoided the conflicts and civil wars experienced by other nations in the region. A priority on preserving the peace led to the bishops' neutral declaration, as their contribution to a "peaceful dialogue" within society prevented them from taking an oppositional stance toward CAFTA-DR.

The *solidarismo* movement in Costa Rica is one example of how values of peace have influenced the work of the Church. Originally a secular movement, when Father Solano took charge of the John XXIII Social School in 1971, *solidarismo* became a staple of CST in Costa Rica. This movement emphasized peace (between employees and employers) over polarization. The premise was that a common goal could exist among parties, and conflict was avoidable. Catholic social teaching (CST) in Costa Rica has been marked historically by an emphasis on peace over conflict.

For Kairos, discussion of human rights has served an important role in political dialogue, albeit less central than peace did for CECOR. It was unique to the Canadian experience to find ecumenical coalitions (attracting those from various denominations) centered on rights issues with such depth and breadth. The former chair of the Kairos board, Rev. Paul Hansen, highlighted the unique role that Canada played in leading the ecumenical movement worldwide, as such coalitions sprang up in the wake of Vatican II. These coalitions sprang up to deal with a specific abuse or violation of human rights.

Although an emphasis on human rights was based in part on theological claims of the sacredness of God's creation and calls to empower individuals, it also was clearly recognized as a national value. Kairos employed appeals to human rights to relate their work to the broader Canadian public. References to rights were strategic; calls for action and speeches before the parliament often used such rhetoric.

For both Canada and Costa Rica, their national values were also connected with an explicit recognition of national identity, and a stated pride in their own nation. Just as Anderson (1983) noted that shared understandings and symbols make the nation a meaningful concept, for those in Costa Rica, being Costa Rican was defined in part by valuing peace. Likewise, for Kairos, part of their national identity was about valuing human rights, especially in contrast to perceived perspectives in the United States.

In the United States, national values were often unidentified and unrecog-nized. That is, although their rhetoric was just as influenced by national values as the other two cases, the PCUSA was less explicit in recognizing nationalistic tendencies. For example, the documents of the PCUSA did not clearly articulate national values, though implicit values of research and rationalism are consistent throughout the discourse. A rational focus, and a desire to appear objective, was more valued in the U.S. context than within the broader international Reformed community and the other two cases in this book. There was an acceptance of traditional sources of wisdom and a focus on the logical and empirical over personal narrative or feeling. Research was the central strategy the church employed in pursuing social change; research was the process by which policy was created.

Although the PCUSA has its intellectual and religious founding in European history, it also was influenced by its historical development within the United States. The Great Awakening shaped the Reformed tradition in America – Smith has argued that the event caused splits within the community, as some opposed revival because of its "socially disruptive effects" (1999, 213). The tension over individual and corporate responses to social ills that emerged in the eighteenth century is still present. Within the PCUSA, an emphasis on research has meant engaging a diverse set of political views, sometimes polarized, on issues of social policy.

Finally, understandings of the common good also are correlated with nationalistic ideas of community and individualism. Much like scholars of racial, ethnic, and gender identity have noted, membership in a minority group tends to increase one's recognition of group identity as important to understanding self-identity (see Howard 2000 for an overview of formation and maintenance of such identities). This seems to be no less the case for national identity, as the U.S. Presbyterians stand out in their relatively limited references to their national location, or in their identification as citizens of a particular state. Somers (1994) noted the ways people define themselves by locating themselves in social narratives. Public narratives play an important role in identity; such public narratives about nationality and national belonging are strongest and most explicit in Costa Rica and weakest and less referenced in the United States.

A Transnational Identity and a Global Perspective

Transnational networks were extremely important for these religious communities' efforts toward the common good. Their networks included civil society actors, local international communities, and religious actors. National antitrade alliances were central partners for the coalitions in Canada, the PCUSA had strong relationships with other Reformed churches worldwide, and CECOR was part of the global Catholic Church. As I argued in each of the case study chapters, these networks brought religious resources to the groups and impacted their perspectives. Consequently, these national organizations had a transnational character that differentiated them from others in civil society in both their outlooks and their approaches to analysis.

The values that guided the religious organizations were themselves products of transnationalism, given the international religious traditions that influenced their doctrines. Casanova (1994, 125) has noted that liberation theology, for example, is really a product of networks, as many of the priests in Latin America developing the theology were themselves European and products of European culture. This is important, because as these three groups have dealt with the disorder of globalization (Swidler 1986; Wuthnow 1989), the theological tools they have relied on have often been international. By the disorder of globalization, I am referring to the fact that contemporary globalization efforts have raised a number of questions, and increasingly efforts to increase economic globalization and liberalization are contested. For example, in his review of the literature on globalization, Guillen (2001) noted that questions are raised about how much of globalization is really new, whether it is prompting countries to similar developmental paths, and how (and if) it harms the authority of states. These are all big questions; people have to both evaluate what changes have been wrought by globalization today as the power of economic and political actors changes, and also assess the impacts of those changes.

Since the end of the nineteenth century, there has been a recognized international body of CST that Catholics in many countries have utilized, and Casanova (1994) has argued that since Vatican II, it makes sense to think of Catholicism as a somewhat unified international community with similar goals. (This is not to deny that there are significant areas of debate and contention within the Catholic Church.) The Presbyterian Church is also part of an international global community. As noted in Chapter 3, although the theology of the PCUSA is not identical to the theology of Reformed churches on other continents, there are a number of overlapping principles shared by members of the Reformed community. As Philpott (2009) stated, such religious values are often in existence a priori to the state or other nationalistic values.

Although each case in this book was part of a global religious community, none of them suggested that they spoke *for* their global community. As Lichterman (1996) found (in his study of Green Party activists), serving a global community is different from seeing oneself as its voice. The Costa Rican bishops did speak to some extent on behalf of their national community as Costa Rica engaged in trade dialogue with international partners. By contrast, both the PCUSA and Kairos spoke more *to* their nations as they tried to bring global voices into the dialogue occurring in their religious communities. Part of this difference is attributed to the fact that the PCUSA and Kairos were located in powerful G8 countries often setting the trade agenda, as well as the privileged historical position the Catholic Church in Costa Rica has held in connection with the state and society.

Strong institutional linkages and experiential networks facilitated the transnational identities of these religious actors. Institutional linkages were especially important in the case of the Costa Rican bishops. CECOR has, in addition to participating in regional conferences, issued statements on trade with other bishops in Central America (SEDAC 2005), with Central American and U.S. bishops (USCCB and SEDAC 2004), and with bishops in Latin America. Although part of less formal structures, the PCUSA endorsed the ACCRA Confession of the World Alliance of Reformed Churches (WARC), *Covenanting for Justice in the Economy and the Earth* (2004), and has been part of various international discussions. The Canadian coalitions have been active in the World Council of Churches, with ECEJ authoring a piece entitled "Justice: The Heart of the Matter" for the Council on issues of finance and development (2001).

As was argued in Chapters 2 and 3, personal relationships were often more important than the existence of formal linkages in facilitating dialogue about global issues and bringing people into global networks. Personal experiences were critical in activating such networks and in allowing for the flow of information across networks to have an impact. When people and communities had personal linkages with institutional or noninstitutional partners, these linkages often served to broaden perspectives as information flowed from person to person. For the PCUSA and coalitions in Canada, such relationships were critical to their economic discourse. All of the early leaders within GATT-Fly/ ECEJ/Kairos had had significant experiences overseas. These experiences not only made development issues a priority for GATT-Fly as it began, but also introduced activists to the tradition of liberation theology. And for many within Kairos, their connections to liberation theology were extremely personal, embodied by their relationships with the actual theologians.

Transnational networks helped provide information to these religious communities that ultimately impacted their strategies of political action. Chapter 2 revealed how Kairos changed their political agenda (to advocate for alternative policies in place of higher sugar prices) because of their experiences with sugar workers in the developing world. Likewise, within the PCUSA, it was those who heard the stories of partners in Bolivia who ultimately put forth the 2003 resolution against the Free Trade Area of the Americas (FTAA) before the General Assembly. As Andrew Kang Bartlett recounted in Chapter 3, the two presbyteries that submitted the 2003 resolution against the FTAA to the General Assembly were both connected with their Joining Hands partner in Bolivia and had sought additional education on trade and its economic impacts.

Ultimately, the strategies employed by these groups, although influenced by transnational relationships, were often aimed at their national communities. For example, they all directed much of their discourse toward the citizens – and governments – of their states. As Philpott (2009) argued, as religious actors involve themselves in the politics of a particular state, they do so in reference to their larger international community. The work of Casanova is instructive for understanding this play between the global and the local or national. He discussed the tension "between a global orientation to human civil society and public involvement in the public sphere of a particular civil society" (1994, 226). The cases in this text demonstrate how this global orientation exhibited by a religious community often goes alongside the action happening in local communities. The global is sometimes more abstract; as noted in Chapter 3, some of the early Presbyterian focus on the global community demonstrated the overbroad strokes with which such a community was painted. The PCUSA, like the other cases, became more informed about the global community over time. This occurred through networks with international actors and partners, as information was shared to educate the churches on global realities. This information and the increased international experiences motivated the religious communities to become more engaged in, informed about, and morally concerned about the international political economy and those in their global networks. This was done, however, within their own national context, as the audience of these religious communities is most often the faithful within their own state borders.

THE INFLUENCE OF ORGANIZATIONAL CONTEXT ON DISCOURSE PRODUCTION

Context plays an important role in shaping discourse. Differences among the internal structures and perspectives of these three groups were an importance aspect of differences among their words and actions. First, these three cases differed in their internal approaches to discourse: that is, *who* discourse should represent and *how* it should be developed. The processes of developing discourse were both theologically and institutionally influenced. Second, beyond different understandings of religious authority, these cases had different external levels of authority, due to different relationships with their host states.

Perspectives on Their Own Voices

Table 5.3 highlights different aspects of discourse production in the three religious organizations. While CECOR aimed to represent the official and moral word of a timeless church, the PCUSA intended to represent their ever-changing religious community. Kairos did not claim to represent any large body, and they made the fewest claims about the authority behind their discourse. As a result, they were able to make more challenges to the status quo and more easily participate in broader social movements for change. At the other end of the spectrum, CECOR, being charged with interpreting Catholic social policy for Costa Rica, was more conservative in their pronouncements. In making statements, then, representatives of organizations were shaped both by who they represented, and the processes by which discourse was created and evaluated.

Although both CECOR and the PCUSA intended their discourse to represent official stances, that process was a hierarchical one for CECOR and a democratic one for the PCUSA. Both a democratic and hierarchical approach can restrict the freedom of discourse, albeit for different reasons. This is especially true for religious groups wanting to speak politically, as shared theological

TABLE 5.3 *The Production of Political Discourse*

Religious Organization	Who Discourse Represents	Development of Discourse
Kairos, etc.	Unofficial arm of Protestants, Catholics	Staff and partner-created research and policies
	Speak for themselves (social movement)	Member-based feedback
		Staff-led action/protest
	No or little oversight	
PCUSA	Official Protestant denomination	Policy via democratic body
	Speak for church body in a particular time	Consensus-developed research
		Staff-designed programs
	No international oversight	
CECOR	Official Catholic body	Bishop issued statements
	Speak for Costa Rican Church	Consultants as experts
	Oversight by Vatican	Priest-led programs (with bishop oversight)

concepts rarely translate into politically homogenous ideologies. As Hofrenning has noted, in cases where disagreement within a policy may be high, religious lobbyists are less likely to make such issues salient (1995).

Expert Voices Challenging the Status Quo. Kairos (or its earlier forms) did not suggest that they spoke for all Christians in Canada. Unlike the PCUSA and CECOR, members of Kairos chose to join because of some shared political and social concerns. Their research, protected by the weasel clause explained in Chapter 2, did not face institutional oversight from Protestant denominations or the Catholic Church.[3]

Staff created the policies of Kairos. An identity piece on GATT-Fly from 1984 stated that the staff "try to work as a collective," although it did admit this work might be unequal, as "responsibility for tasks is generally shared by about two or more staff people, one with principal responsibility and the other(s) acting in a support role." The coalition then cited this logic as a "major reason we haven't named specific authors for our publications" (GATT-Fly 1984, 2). Policies of equal remuneration among staff regardless of their training and responsibilities did equalize relationships at some level, even when tasks were not the same.

That said, not all staff were equal. Some members had a high level of influence within the organization, and it was a few staff members who largely developed the research on economic globalization: John Dillon, John Mihevc, and Rusa Jeremic. This is not to say that democratic processes were absent, or that such individuals would retain authority if they changed their political ideologies. In

---

[3] Since 2001, however, when the various coalitions merged into Kairos, Protestant and Catholic member denominations do have to approve official policies.

the early stages of GATT-Fly, board members were often involved in helping staff to create and think about policies, and even today, committees exist to provide feedback to the staff. In reality, however, specific staff members have often been the key source of ideas and main authors of the committees' written presentations.

Kairos rarely focused on maintaining the boundaries of their own organiza-tion (like CECOR did) and often spoke through their participation in other alliances. As presented in Chapter 2, many of the staff held leadership roles in secular organizations at the same time they served with GATT-Fly, ECEJ, or Kairos. For the staff with joint positions, their identities with the two organiza-tions were not distinct. Likewise, the group often used resources from partners and reproduced these materials as their own. This was enabled by a lack of democratic, representative, or highly authoritative constraints on the production process.

More recent internal changes have increased the oversight by religious insti-tutions over Kairos, and the results reveal how religious authority structures can constrain the position of an organization. After becoming Kairos in 2001, policies had to be approved by a board of member denominations, so official policies became more restricted, even as the research of the coalition continued to reflect many of the same ideas and political positions. Although staff have still presented an alternative economic order at the World Social Forum since 2001, they have had a harder time making a clear statement against free trade than they had as GATT-Fly in the 1980s.

Speaking on Behalf of Members. By contrast, the PCUSA had both different aims of representation as well as different structures in place for producing discourse collectively. Although the Bible is authoritative for this community, it is the job of the community to interpret ancient scripture for today's context. The General Assembly (GA) was created for this purpose – to approve policy and process research. And policies were meant to represent the church's response at a particular point in time. Admittedly, the research that informed policy, and was mandated from policy, was not purely the result of democratic processes. Such research required that different experts within the community be brought into consultation with one another. This process balanced the desire for special-ization in different fields with a desire for diversity of thought that could better represent the whole community. As reports on globalization suggest, this greater diversity can present challenges for consensus.

Given the rather wide range of theological and political beliefs among its members, the PCUSA's emphasis on democracy made it difficult for the church to create policy that addressed the contentious issues of the day. At the same time, global trade has not been as divisive a topic as same-sex marriage, for instance, and democratic procedures about it have not derailed policy initiatives. Still, balancing a priority of democracy with an emphasis on specialization has clearly been a challenge; as noted in Chapter 4, one commissioner raised the issue of whether staff really supported and followed policy or whether they directed or even ignored policy, thus subverting the democratic process. The fact that the specific workings of democracy were questioned revealed that there was some tension in balancing democratic policy and reliance on the work of experts. At the same time, there was a clear consensus among members of the PCUSA that policy *should* be the result of a democratic process and not just decided by religious or technical authorities.

The PCUSA had fewer qualms about working ecumenically than did CECOR, and once the church polity approved social policy to pursue an agenda, the church staff were encouraged to act ecumenically in their efforts. Catherine Gordon of the Washington, DC, office and Andrew Kang Bartlett of the Presbyterian Hunger Program affirmed the centrality of ecumenical work at a lobbying level, esteeming both the work of groups like the American Friends Service Committee and interfaith alliances (of which the PCUSA is a central actor).

Although they worked ecumenically, because policies and research were meant to represent their community, the church still produced their own reports, created through PCUSA channels. When they did use materials from their partners, as was the case with some of their trade materials from the Hunger Office, they altered these to make sure the products they disseminated agreed with the Presbyterian tradition. Bartlett, for example, noted the process he went through to make the worship guide for the global week of trade, produced by the international Ecumenical Advocacy Alliance (EAA), Presbyterian ready. He noted that the product of the EAA was a bit more radical than the perspective of most Presbyterians. He "Presbyterianized" this EAA resource for his community by doing things like inserting statements from the PCUSA, changing some recommended actions, and adding more specific stories from the PCUSA's Bolivian partners (Bartlett 2007).

Leaders Interpreting Official Policies. The bishops of CECOR are leaders meant to represent the Catholic Church in Costa Rica and to speak authoritatively to the community within the country. High understandings of their own religious authority constrained the bishops from making more specific political statements about complex issues, especially ones that could be contested. Even so, they raised many of the same concerns about the treaty that the other religious communities raised. The fact that it was an emeritus bishop who opposed CAFTA-DR the most vocally, ultimately rejecting the treaty, was indicative of the constraints of representation. Guided by many of the same values as his fellow bishops, Monsignor Trejos Picado spoke without the same institutional Catholic constraints regarding his position.

The Costa Rican Catholic Church never suggested that they were democratically governed. The bishops were responsible for clearly laying out the moral values to guide the nation; even as they spoke authoritatively to Catholics, they also addressed their speech and teachings to the broader society. CECOR was meant to represent and to govern a specific religious community. Interviewees clearly expressed that they did not see themselves as part of a broader ecumenical alliance, even as they worked with partners on certain issues and expressed respect for the work of other religious communities and actors in civil society.

Given the emphasis on a unified stance among them, the bishops had to engage in substantial dialogue to develop a unified Costa Rican position. In doing so, they consulted other experts – for example, the economist priest, Father Jorge Arturo Chaves, who was critical in helping inform their position. Minutes from CECOR meetings reported input from others, such as the current head of Caritas, Father Hernández. In this way, members of the Catholic Church with knowledge on particular issues informed the stance of the bishops. But once a position was reached, even the bishops held it above their own ideas. Father Hernández has noted how the bishops spoke with one voice even when there was disagreement in developing a singular position. And within my interviews, bishops often gave me the stance of the conference when I asked for their own position and ideas.

State Authority versus Religious Authority

Chaves (1993) has described the decreasing authority that religious bodies have within their own organizations as "internal secularization," a term borrowed from Dobbelaere's (1981) notion of religious change. Chaves identified religious authority as something based in traditional sources, while authority emanating from an agency structure has a more rational basis. However, I would argue that religious authority may often be defined in part by rational authority, especially among traditions like the PCUSA, where community consensus serves as a source of religious authority.

The three religious groups studied here occupied different places within their respective national power structures. They all enjoyed a level of legitimacy within the state, though their power varied (the Catholic Church had a more powerful role vis-à-vis the government than did the Presbyterians or Kairos). Recognizing and respecting the power of the state, they directed at least some of their strategies at governing bodies, lobbying those in power. They all also focused on grassroots mobilization and community education to various degrees, even as appeals to the national government were always part of the repertoire. The Catholic bishops represented the official religious voice within Costa Rica. The Presbyterians were one of a number of established Protestant mainline religious organizations in a nation where religious groups have an important public voice. Kairos has not historically represented the church at an institutional or formal level and, as a result, has been more limited within a modern state.

Casanova has argued that understanding power in relation to the state is central to understanding the public role of religion: "The public character of any religion is primarily determined by the particular structural location of that religion between state and society" (1994, 9). He uses the examples of the

Spanish, Polish, and Brazilian churches in the era before Vatican II to illustrate how these varied national locations contributed to diverse public identities.[4]

Yet, as Casanova also noted, in the wake of Vatican II, there has been within the Catholic Church an increasingly shared understanding of how to engage the state. This has impacted not only the Church in Costa Rica, but also Kairos. In similar fashion, the Reformed community to which the PCUSA belongs became more similar in the middle of the twentieth century. These changes have lessened the degree of national variation within denominations. That is, although national identity and national location are important for the public role of religion, the internal organizational structure and theological traditions are equally, if not more, important.

Outsiders to Power. Kairos was the most critical of those in power, had the weakest connection with institutionalized religious communities, and was the least likely to lobby the government in efforts for social change. As GATT-Fly, the group had a reputation as a pestering influence on the government. They viewed themselves as being on the cutting edge, leading society in the creation and discussion of economic alternatives. As Dillon attested, they chose to be less formally tied to denominations and churches so that they would have more autonomy to take radical political positions. A lack of institutionalized connections to either religious or governmental authorities meant few restrictions for the organization.

Although they wrote letters to the government and encouraged people to practice their power of political voice, reform was never the main strategy of GATT-Fly (or ECEJ or Kairos). Instead, they strived to replace the current economic order with a new economic order through grassroots activism. Instead of endeavoring to change international policy, they aimed to have communities and states choose different developmental paths entirely. Unlike the other two groups, Kairos, at least in its origin as GATT-Fly, might best be considered a social movement, precisely because of its noninstitutional challenge to power (Goodwin and Jasper 2003).

Inside Reformers. Not only is the membership of the PCUSA located in one of the richest countries, but they also are socioeconomically privileged in relationship to other U.S. citizens. Like other mainline traditions, the denomination retains a privileged demographic position. As Smith and Faris (2005) reported, the PCUSA remains one of the most well-educated and wealthiest denominations in terms of individuals, ranking only behind the smaller Jewish, Unitarian, and Episcopal denominations. Historically they have spoken to the U.S. system of

---

[4] The Spanish Catholic Church violently strived to maintain its status as the national church in an era of liberalism. The Polish Catholic Church existed as a "territorial national church in search of a nation-state" (Casanova 1994, 71). And the Brazilian Catholic Church was painted as a national church working with the government in its development of national goals. These models illustrate three different relationships with the state and three different understandings of what it means to be a public church.

power and have consistently enjoyed overrepresentation in governmental offices. Perhaps this helps explain why they were more likely than Kairos to accept the position of those in power. Lobbying government was a central way they sought reform, and social policies called on members to write letters to Congress in an effort to promote change. Although this may not have been the most effective strategy (we have little proof that members of Congress, for example, changed positions based on the teaching of the PCUSA), it fits with their emphasis on speaking prophetically to power. As Hofrenning noted, prophetic lobbyists often define their success differently: They want "to preach as much as they seek to lobby" (1995, 117); being faithful in the long term is more prized than short-term success. The PCUSA was also the strongest supporter of global institutions such as the UN. Their discourse expressed few qualms about those currently in power being part of establishing a common good, or at least involved in enforcing such a good.

State Affirmation. The Costa Rican bishops enjoyed a high level of respect within society and have historically been brought into governmental accords as a trusted civil society actor. In helping broker accords between the Costa Rican state and the electric company back in 2000, they claimed an identity as "citizen bishops," directing society to a peaceful discovery of Costa Rica's common good. Regarding FTAs, they expressed hope in an ability to shape an economic agenda that the society would eventually adopt. They did not want to alienate the government, even though (as noted in Chapter 4) many of their stances invited the criticism of the government. The relationship of the Catholic Church with the state, especially in Latin America, often influences how critical the Church is and which social and economic issues it champions (Hagopian 2009b). CECOR largely affirmed the state and validated the political processes at work within the country. They publicly applauded the referendum process and, amid some disagreement in Costa Rica about how to proceed, supported the legitimacy of referendum results. Even in raising concerns about the direction that the state should take on the Central America–Dominican Republic–United States Free Trade Agreement (CAFTA-DR) policy, the bishops showed a high level of trust in the state to pursue the common good.

Is it important to understand not only the power that these religious actors had within their own states, but also the power that such states had in the international community. It was not coincidental that the organization in the United States was the one least willing to critique the capitalist system. (The contrast of PCUSA policy with the political stance of WARC made this support of capitalism more apparent.) To be sure, some religious groups in the United States would protest capitalism more strongly than did the PCUSA. However, part of the reason the PCUSA was less critical of capitalism than other reformed groups have been is the influence of national location. They were a privileged group in a privileged state. By contrast, the Costa Rican church considered capitalism to be a broken international system, which led to their insistence that Costa Rica not give up too much power to the United States.

RELIGIOUS APPROACHES TO THE ECONOMIC REALM: FRAME, LENS, AND PRACTICE

Although values and structures influenced the content of discourse, just as important as content were the strategies of engagement. The different frames that religious communities have for understanding their public roles speak to the power of religion in economic life. These groups employed three distinct models for how religion and economics should interact: religion as a framework to shape policy (CECOR), religion as a lens to evaluate policy (PCUSA), and religion as practices to dictate policy (Kairos). CECOR aimed to provide moral guidance that did not deny the unique authority of economic experts, viewing religion as a general guide for policy. By contrast, Kairos saw their religious authority as able to displace economic authorities in dictating proper economic practices. The Presbyterian Church took a view in between these two cases in treating religion like a lens, advocating for religious leaders to work with economists to design policy. Each strategy was essentially influenced by a different evaluation of the power of economic experts and the legitimacy of secular voices. Those evaluations, in turn, determined how each group conceived of its religious authority operating in the economic arena.

All of the groups exhibited what Casanova (1994) termed a "deprivatization" of religion; that is, they all engaged with the modern state, but in a way that did not threaten the modern, secular notion of sphere differentiation. Yet, they differed in how they understood what it meant to be deprivatized; different boundaries existed between the sacred and the profane. And although each case brought religion to bear on the economy in different ways, they all challenged the notion that the boundary between religion and economics is nonporous.

As discussed in Chapter 1, it is often taken for granted in modern society that the market is the domain of technical experts and economists. This assumption faces some contestation, but the model of economic liberalism implemented in the late twentieth century has affirmed the power of technocrats. Even so, there is national variation in what credentials are valued. The United States and Canada value as experts those with economic expertise and traditional training. The same is true in Latin America, but more skepticism exists there over the wisdom of liberal economic policies, even as more deference is shown to technocrats and those with sphere-specific authority (Centeno 1994; Roberts 2008).

Respecting Realm Boundaries

The framework model of engaging with the economy, which was most clearly evidenced in Costa Rica, is the approach that is most respectful of the traditional separation of economic and religious authority. In this model, the authority of religious experts is in the religious realm, and economic experts should be in charge of the economic realm. Religious leaders are encouraged to articulate values to guide economic experts, even as such experts bring their unique knowledge to the policy decisions.

In the example of the Costa Rican Catholic bishops, Papal documents and other statements by bishops' conferences had authority, and the opinions of those with legitimacy in the Catholic hierarchical structure were most highly regarded. Wuthnow (1994b) has highlighted the important role that centralization, training, and rationalism play in religious hierarchies, and the CECOR case demonstrated the importance of such values, especially the importance of one strong centralized religious voice.

Catholic religious values are intended to dictate a broad framework for thinking about all spheres of life that follows from the assumption that God is in charge of all realms. As religious leaders, the bishops, working out of the Catholic tradition, supplied the values of development that people and policy makers should consider. In this view, secular authorities, though valid, need to follow rules from the sacred realm. In the CECOR case, religious leaders supported technical authority and specialization, but they also demanded that technical decisions uphold religious values. Still, definitional to this model is that decision making over policy occurs in the secular realm; the Church is a guiding light shining into that realm. Throughout recent history the Catholic Church has reprimanded groups that have become too political, just as it censured liberation theologians in Latin America. Nevertheless, when religion is used as a frame, both experts in the religious and economic realms are recognized as authoritative, and religion has authority in the realm of moral values.

Viewing the Economy through the Lens of Religion

In the second model, religious and economic experts are also both valued, but the boundaries between the two are not as strong. Religion's role is to serve as a lens through which to view economic matters, and religious leaders are given more freedom and authority to speak about economic issues. This stems from an understanding that religion *is* economic, that social issues are an important part of theology, and that sphere differentiation is not tightly bound. This model is founded on the idea that religious authority is developed in community as people engage in public life. Unlike the authority that Chaves (1993) noted being placed in traditional sources, rational processes contribute to moral authority in this model. One task of religious leaders is to process social life with experts from other fields.

The PCUSA served as an example of this second model. The Presbyterian Church, like CECOR, provided values for economic experts to heed. These values, however, were not produced by leaders in religious authority but rather were developed within community. For the PCUSA, it was the job of the church at large to evaluate and take a stance on political and social issues. As they clearly stated in *Resolution on Just Globalization*:

When the church addresses economic realities, it does not claim the technical competence of specialized institutions, though it gains insight from members in those organizations. The church as a body can and should, however, engage in an ethical analysis of economic laws, customs, and proposals; denounce morally unacceptable economic outcomes; name the sin that is causing pain; and insist that more fair and humane policies be sought and implemented.   (Advisory Committee on Social Witness Policy [ACSWP], 2006, 10)

In this model, religion has to engage with its social context, and religious actors are required to grapple with complex social issues.

Thus, the Reformed tradition identified the social ethic as the work of Christ, as equally important as His Person. For the PCUSA, the social was not secondary, as it is for CST. They operated out of the belief that the church could and should make definitive statements about policy. In producing the research that should guide policy, they brought theologians, CEOs, and economists together. The authority of different spheres was recognized, but alongside a belief that the best results emerge when those experts engage with one another and speak jointly in the development of policy.

Religion as Economic Practice

The third model is not primarily about values that must be enacted or debated by economists or other experts. Instead, the practices demanded by true religion *are* authoritative for the economic realm, and such practices can be used to create policy. Liberation theology served as a prime example of this model, where religious leaders developed a theology that was political at its core. Although it would be too reductionistic to argue that religion is defined by practice alone in this model, I agree with Smith's (1991) characterization of liberation theology – that it was more about the action of liberation than about doctrine, and the theology of the movement consisted mostly of reflection on the action.

Kairos embodied this model. The practices of Christ were central over the person of Christ for the organization, which explains the coalition's lack of concern about the religious beliefs of their staff. In a 1985 document on biblical justice, GATT-Fly stated, "We believe that it is through our active participation in the struggles of oppressed groups for justice that we encounter Christ, come to know God and offer the kind of fast that is truly pleasing to God." Unlike the other two groups, both of whom highlighted the person of Christ as divine, Kairos and its predecessor organizations rarely discussed the relational aspect of the divine at the institutional level.[5] As reported in Chapter 3, they were mostly

---

[5] This does not mean that a person of God is not an important concept for those within the organization, just that it is not an important characteristic of the organization. One example would be the chair of the board, Father Paul Hansen, who frequently referred to Christ as "the Beloved," and to relationship with the Beloved.

concerned in staff selection about whether someone shared their vision of solidarity and could represent the beliefs of member churches.

Kairos called for markets to be composed of these religious practices, and there was little engagement with traditional economists. Similar to the scenarios that Evans (2009) studied,[6] members of Kairos did not reject the field of economics, but rather the current paradigms that dominate the field. That is, Kairos protested the expertise and authority accorded to neoclassical economists and proponents of free markets. Kairos, in many ways, challenged the very theories and assumptions behind economic "expertise." It called for economic markets to be guided by concerns over solidarity and meeting basic needs, rejecting the current guiding concern of seeking economic growth.

Notable about all three of these models was that religious actors must be knowledgeable about economic claims. Even as some of the economists I encountered in my research claimed that religious leaders were simply wrong or uninformed about economics, the leaders of the religious organizations I studied had at least a cursory understanding of the arguments being made, and demonstrated very intentional efforts to engage with economic logic. The Costa Rican Catholic bishops, who engaged the least with technical experts, still pointed out the impacts that certain policies could have and made use of empirical and economic data in making their case. They were briefed on trade by a consultant and priest who taught economics at the National University.[7]

A Typology of Religious-Economic Engagement

How applicable are these models for other religious groups within the economy? Although the typology is not exhaustive, it does provide a helpful tool for evaluating different ways that religious communities engage within the political economy and, in doing so, extend previous work in this area.

In Chapter 1, I discussed Neibuhr's typology of Christ and culture, as he found that religious communities have different understandings of the relationship of the divine to culture. This study shows some of the variance in how communities think about their own relationships to culture, and suggests that that culture or society should be more nuanced in such a typology. Economic

---

[6] Evans discussed how some conservative Christians that protest current ideas about evolution or climate change rely on alternative scientific evidence to protest commonly accepted "facts."

[7] In the international Catholic arena, a 1999 document (addressed to the World Trade Organization [WTO]) from the Pontifical Council revealed copious knowledge of trade policy. It discussed issues such as the differential treatment of imports from developing countries, the current standards on genetically modified organisms, food aid under the Food Aid Convention, and the relationships between international property rights and transfers of technology; all of this occurs with extensive reference to specific sections of trade agreements, WTO proposals, and UN declarations.

markets, the family, and political structures, although all part of culture, are not the same. The area of social life being discussed is important.

In this book, I am suggesting that to understand how religious communities think about their relationship to economic life, one must understand how such institutions think about the realm of economic life, and not just their own relationship to the culture. Second, among those actors who would have religious communities interacting with and redeeming culture, they do that in different ways, depending on how they the define boundaries of each.

Scholars such as Hart, Lichterman, and Wood have noted a difference between religious communities that are conservative and those that are more progressive in their public engagement and economic action. Each scholar has added important information to what we know about those actors. Hart's work found that there are not clear linkages between theologies and economic platforms. Both Hart (2001) and Lichterman (2005) noted that progressive communities often struggle to connect theology with economic life, and that frequently discourse avoids religious rhetoric. Wood (2002) noted many of the challenges of more orthodox religious communities in engaging in material justice efforts. All of this work has been important in drawing attention both to the way that religious communities are involved in economic change and to the hindrances that often exist.

The typology presented in this chapter suggests that another nuance to examine among the more progressive religious communities would be their views of the authority of the economic realm, and of their relationship with that realm. This typology highlights the ways that a religious community's understanding of its own authority has implications for how it speaks to other types of authority. As Burawoy (2014) noted, the encroachment of the market into all areas of public life is one of the central challenges for justice actors (and, he argued, applied sociologists) in the twenty-first century. As a result, understanding the different ways groups speak to that encroachment, and the ways that religious actors bring moral authority to that debate, becomes even more important now than in the past.

CONCLUSION

Although many economic sociologists have concentrated on the influence of traditional financial actors, other scholars of this subfield (most notably Viviana Zelizer 1979, 1994, 2005) have examined the ways that nontraditional cultural actors influence the economy. And I would argue that understandings of culture outside the economic realm have economic implications for how particular markets are structured. Differentiation in modern society, however, has meant that religion and other sectors of civil society are considered distinct – and unimportant – for the functioning of the state or the market. At best, some would argue, they fill in for the failures of these official institutions.

Religion is even further separated from the market because it is considered the domain of the sacred, which, Douglas (1966) would argue in Durkheimian fashion, is by definition that which is not profane and common (as the market would be). Many who have studied discourse, for example, have tended to follow such a distinction: Jasper (1992), in his discussion about moralistic arguments, mentioned how moral arguments might trump instrumental ones that lack emotional punch. This statement is based on an assumption that the instrumental can be divorced from the moral because they exist in separate realms. But religious groups play a vital role in contributing to discussions about justice in society (Wuthnow 1994b, 17). And sometimes that justice is economic justice. Kairos, the PCUSA, and CECOR believed they had an obligation and responsibility to be involved in the public arena, and as international actors, they brought a global perspective to their national situations. These cases, although diverse in their responses to FTAs, all rejected the notion that religious groups should be silent on economic matters. Secularization has led to modern states in which religious organizations rarely control the state and the market, but this does not mean they have accepted political silence.

For the religious cases in these pages, religious values shaped moral understandings about the market as well as conceptions about authority and the role of religious communities in public life. Vital to crossing the boundaries of sacred and profane was a theological emphasis on community, one that these three actors saw as contradictory to the ideological basis of current market structures. This perspective prompted each of these groups to challenge market paradigms and the role of economic experts as the architects of economic policy. They argued that markets are not amoral and divorced from moral guidelines, and they each presented a moral alternative to the current state of affairs, with strong transnational identities influencing their opinions.

In trying to understand variation in discourse among these communities, this chapter has highlighted the different institutional contexts and public theologies of the groups. CECOR, with its hierarchical structure, had more constraints on what they were able to say. And the organization with the flattest decision-making structure, the PCUSA, also was constrained, by democracy, as a politically diverse group of people had to agree on policy recommendations.

Although such internal organizational characteristics are important, ties to one's external social and political context are also influential. The relationship each group had with the state further shaped its ability or willingness to speak. Those with authoritative power were more cautious in their discourse than were more marginal actors. The organization with the weakest power vis-à-vis the state, Kairos, was the most radical in their position; that is, they had the least to lose by opposing current policies. By contrast, CECOR, who was a partner in state negotiations, spoke cautiously and voiced more muted critiques of free trade.

The most prominent sources of variation among these cases were the different ways in which they engaged the experts on the economy. Although all rejected the idea that religious experts and economic experts were separated by an impermeable boundary, each employed a distinct model of religious actors speaking to economic policy makers: They either tried to guide their analysis, evaluated their policies and worked alongside them, or challenged the very theories that grounded their decisions. I have argued that these three models interpret religion as a frame, a lens, and a set of practices, respectively. These same three models could be applied to any other moral agencies and nontraditional economic actors who seek to challenge the sovereignty of economic life from other social spheres. The typology of religion as frame, lens, and practice contributes further to our understanding of how the values of nontraditional economic actors connect to market structures.

As the analysis in this chapter reveals, the three organizations profiled in this book varied on almost every measure. Beyond differing in aspects of theology, structure, and location, their political discourses varied in nature, stance, and scope. They took different political stances (and employed different strategies) in regard to the issue of free trade; they spoke to different audiences; they have had varied historical trajectories regarding their involvement in the political economy. Yet, the similarities between them merit as much attention and analysis as do their differences. Their religious warrants which overlapped significantly, were used to challenge current market structures and provide possibilities for how the market system could (and should) be different. They all argued that religious groups, although nontraditional market actors, are an important part of the economy. These cases are a testimony to the ways in which religion remains a public force.

6

Encouraging Religious Communities to Promote the Common Good

Each of the religious communities I studied for this book engaged in meaningful political discourse over free trade agreements (FTAs). Each also faced significant challenges in mobilizing their communities. In this final chapter, I consider some of the challenges for religious communities involved in transnational advocacy efforts, especially relating to economic life.

Wuthnow (1994b) has argued that an important role of religious groups is to advocate for justice in the public arena. A prominent way religious communities engage in such a task is to question the existing social structures and institutions, as well as the philosophies that undergird them. This book has outlined the specific concerns raised by three unique religious communities in regard to international capitalist markets and the individualism inherent in today's economic systems.

Religious organizations writ large, however, have not been fully effective in their quests to raise broad social concern over the structure and ideology of economic markets. Often they have not, as this book has shown, even succeeded in rallying their own members to the causes promoted by leadership. This is because many people (religious and nonreligious) still believe that it is not appropriate for religious actors to speak to the "social" issues of the day. Of those who would acquiesce that religious leaders *can* and *should* speak to and engage with politics, some view the current economic system as positive in its values, or as value-neutral. To advocate, then, with any efficacy, religious groups must first overcome this initial barrier.

I argue that religious groups *do* have something important and necessary to say about the market. Markets are social and cultural constructions based on values, and current market structures often prioritize individualism and efficiency over community and solidarity. Kairos, PCUSA, and CECOR are all, in different ways, advocating for an emphasis on the common good to shape (or even replace) current market notions and practices.

How can religious groups effectively enter this dialogue in order to impact social change? First, they must recognize the centrality of *community* and relationships to religious moral-political dialogue. Second, they need to confront the skepticism about their ability to speak on social issues by clarifying the notion of religious (and secular) *authority*. Third, although religious groups have been successful at producing rich resources on political issues, ultimately they must encourage *personal experiences* that make such resources meaningful to members and other citizens, and demystify market-related concepts. Finally, I suggest that groups should engage in more *ecumenical* activity to strengthen their voice within political-economic discourse.

COMMUNITY AND RELATIONSHIPS IN THE MARKET

Christian communities that do not discuss relationships with one's "brothers and sisters" in Christ are scarce. Rather, numerous Christian traditions reference Old Testament scriptures and gospel teachings to show God's concern for the alien, the poor, and the oppressed. Religious traditions, thus, have a rich fabric to draw upon in constructing community as a theological value. Whether they made use of claims of covenant (PCUSA), solidarity (Kairos), or the common good (CECOR), all of the cases studied declared that caring about one's neighbors obligated women and men to challenge the individualism esteemed by current market structures.

Religious institutions, however, need to do more to communicate and enforce this central teaching about community; and, in doing so, they should not be afraid to use religious language. Members may disagree over the implications of their faith or specific hermeneutics, but for the most part they accept central theological themes that unite communities. In order to mobilize this theological force into real social change, religious principles must be translated into policy, and policy constantly reassociated with its theological foundation. Leaders must flesh out what it is that a commitment to community entails. Who is part of the community, what does it mean to be "in community," and what responsibilities does being in community entail?

Defining Community

Is community an inclusive or exclusive concept? According to DiMaggio (1997), the concept of community, and collective identity, is often created through the use of an "us" and "them" dichotomy. Such appeals, theorists have argued, are often about constructing imagined communities and connecting people to them (Lichterman 1996; Goodwin, Jasper, and Polletta 2001; Anderson 1983). Often, communities may be defined as much by who is included as who is excluded.

Part of the reason for these exclusive definitions and conceptions of community is that the broader, inclusive notion of community – one that is all-encompassing – often fails to take hold. Massengill (2013) found that the concept is often a nebulous one; that is, there is little reflection on what *community* means to people appealing to the term. Lichterman (1996), in his study of progressive political action, found it was easier for people to be involved in global goals when they identified themselves with a concrete global community. Social movement theorists tell us that people do not join movements because of the ideology of the cause alone; networks and personal interests are central in these decisions (Diani and McAdam 2003; Munson 2008; Snow et al. 1980).

Indeed, we see each organization in this book highlighting the plight of people within its own borders. Consider, especially, the PCUSA when it first entered the dialogue, CECOR in the debate over CAFTA-DR, and GATT-Fly in its call for self-sufficiency. Yet, on balance, the powerful transnational networks and traditions to which these groups belonged were more foundational for their conceptions of community than national values. When religious organizations challenge economic paradigms, they must bring in the perspective of a broad (inclusive) community, especially given the exclusive nature of the term in much public discourse.[1]

Inclusion, as evidenced by the cases in this book, also means an emphasis on those who are forgotten within a community. Although these religious organizations accentuated different marginalized people, all played a vital role in reminding their members of those who are often overlooked by more popular definitions of community. Eliasoph observes that people serving their communities often seek to avoid talking in the name of "strifeless harmony and mutual aid, acceptance, and comfort." They are often "doing something without needing to talk about it" (1998, 244–245). As a result, talk of public interest is often missing. Religious communities must articulate clear definitions of who is included in community.

Prioritizing Community

Perhaps just as important as defining community, religious organizations can contribute to a public dialogue about what it means to prioritize community, especially in a free-market system. These three organizations talked about seeking the common good and practicing right relationships among people. What does that mean in terms of behavior in the market?

Within the current political and economic situation, economic freedom is often characterized by its individualistic nature. That is, economic freedom has been equated with the autonomy of individuals to make their own decisions freely within the marketplace. In the United States, political debates at election time often invoke themes of such freedom – described largely as people's ability to do whatever they want with "their" money.

---

[1] As Kirkpatrick (2007) has noted, within the PCUSA, experiences are starting to link people more closely with others in the global community, and this trend appears to apply beyond the boundaries of the PCUSA.

Development economist and Nobel prize winner Amartya Sen has written about economic freedom from a different perspective. He defined freedom as something that "helps to advance the general capability of a person" (1999, 10). In this understanding, promoting economic freedom is connected with increasing the economic opportunities available to people to participate in the market and within their communities. Poverty and high levels of inequality threaten this notion of economic freedom. The religious organizations examined in these pages discuss a similar notion of economic freedom. Like other actors engaged in progressive politics, they have understood notions of human rights to serve as a basis for the common good and the community (Hart 2001).

For the cases in this study, practicing community is connected with this broad understanding of promoting the economic freedom of others. As mentioned in Chapter 4, the PCUSA, in *Hope for a Global Future*, concisely identified what it means to care about others in the community – to care about the human dignity of others. They noted that the ability to provide for basic needs, to participate in economic and political life, and to be afforded legal protections are all part of a robust understanding of such dignity (ACSWP 1996). Kairos also focused on the importance of protecting the rights and dignity of others. As they noted in their evaluations of current economic policies, we must ask how policies "enhance or inhibit the ability of ordinary people, and of governments, to provide for the common good, understood in terms of adequate food, shelter, clothing, employment, education and health care" (Ecumenical Coalition for Economic Justice [ECEJ] 1991, 1). In similar fashion, CECOR connected the promotion of the common good with upholding individual dignity: a task, they noted, that requires basic educational, employment, and health opportunities for all.

SPHERES OF AUTHORITY: THE IMPORTANCE
OF PROPHETIC VOICE

For some communities, the social and the moral serve as two separate (and distinct) spheres informed by faith and religious beliefs. In each of these cases, the social was central to religious teaching and practice, even as the importance of social issues vis-à-vis religion. Kairos, CECOR, and the PCUSA are unified in their belief that religious organizations should speak to economic life, that markets are moral constructions, and that such social issues are of theological importance.

Yet, as several scholars of politics have found, religious communities engaged in progressive politics have been reticent to bring in faith issues (Hart 2001; Lichterman 1995, 1996). These scholars have observed that progressive politics is often lacking strong moral arguments. This trend may also be impacting the discourse of politically conservative religious communities who are increasingly making appeals to nonreligious arguments for their religiously influenced beliefs. For example, those leading the religious opposition to gay marriage and abortion sometimes use a "natural law" approach to dismiss the idea that theirs is just a religious argument. Dr. Robert George has led this movement in many respects, especially within the Catholic community (Kirkpatrick 2009). Likewise, Klemp (2012) has shown that Focus on the Family increasingly has backed up their political claims with secular arguments. Reliance on natural law has been one way that some conservative religious actors have tried to bring together a movement, and avoid discussions about theology.

A reliance on religious authority, however, is critical for any religious community dealing with questions of market injustice. Such a community should rely *more* on religious and ethical language and authority, not less. This is especially true as the community engages with its religious constituencies. If markets are social constructions predicated on moral values, then a discussion of the market must address the type of moral fabric upon which we want to construct society. Yet current discussions of economic equity and justice are often lacking in their inclusion of ethical and moral discourse (Hart 2001). Although I am not suggesting that religious leaders control such discussions, many religiously influenced values – like community, justice, and solidarity – seem to have the best chance of entering into public discussions when religious actors are championing them.

In studying mainline Protestant communities in the United States, Steensland (2002) noted that perhaps one of their key challenges is to help parishioners make connections between their religious and policy beliefs (233–234). It is less important that these groups articulate a clear position than that they help people think about these connections. Eliasoph (2005) also has found that people have difficulty connecting their personal lives with the political and that talk of the public interest is much less accessible than individualistic rhetoric (259–260). This may explain why Wuthnow found that, even among the religious, economic life is rarely influenced by religious ideas; when religion is discussed, it often is used to legitimate existing structures or help people make sense of life rather than to guide their action (1994a).

One of the results (although not a tenant) of Catholic social teaching (CST) is that individuals often dichotomize moral issues from the social. Areas of personal morality (for example, procreation) are considered spiritual, while those that impact social relationships or society (for example, proper wages) are considered nonspiritual. Even as the leadership of all three religious organizations have rejected this divide, those whom they represent have not done so to the same degree. Social issues are often viewed as divisive, and societal authorities (such as economists) are often accorded deference in social areas.

A central challenge seems to be convincing religious members that market issues are religious issues. This assertion can be a source of contention within religious communities, as seen in this study. In the case of Kairos, some of their statements ultimately brought them into conflict with the Canadian Council of Catholic Bishops. Likewise, the Presbyterian Lay Committee frequently critiqued the work of the PCUSA in political life, and Father Claudio Solano in Costa Rica protested the notion that Christians need to be critical of an FTA.

Religious organizations have to make the case that their authority extends to the market realm. That is, they should assert that biblical mandates of community and just economic relationships are relevant for decisions in the political economy. This is one of the strengths in the Catholic Church's position in Costa Rica. The official Church position was to promote different theological values, and to claim that such values matter in decisions about policies. They faced claims that their message had been watered down because they did not make religious claims regarding which policies best enforced religious values. But they clearly made an authoritative claim that Christians must think ethically about market life and market policies.

The study of discourse in this book reveals the fact that churches play a key role in trying to recast markets as a sacred place. To raise moral questions, to make the market part of one's religious consciousness, *is* a central task of a church. The cases in this book are examples of groups who are using their prophetic voices to open up a conversation about how markets should be constructed. If successful, such discourse could contribute to the type of robust debate and discussion that Hart (2001) has deemed vital to democracy.

DEMYSTIFYING THE MARKET THROUGH PERSONAL EXPERIENCES

At a minimum, markets deserve religious attention because of the relationships embedded within them. That is, markets shape our interactions with one another and affect our treatment of others. This poses the question of what it means to be relationally responsible in the market. How does one love one's neighbor, practice community, and promote the freedom described earlier?

Connecting the market with relationships is a vital task of religious communities. An erosion of personal relationships in the market has led to complacency about the power differentials and inequality embedded in economic relationships (Reynolds 2013). The commodity fetishism that Marx decried increases when people are disconnected from the products they sell (which is a feature of modern markets) (Lyon 2006). We buy, sell, and trade with little thought about with *whom* we are conducting our transactions. The farmer in El Salvador, the factory worker in China, and the child working the mines in Tanzania are rarely integrally connected with the coffee, shirts, or the jewelry we buy.

One difficulty in addressing the general concept of the market is the lack of agency that individuals, particularly consumers, perceive that they have. People often see themselves as part of a larger system in which they have no control, and which they have no ability to change. As those working on the ground with different justice ministries in the PCUSA discussed, one way to counteract this perception is to provide concrete opportunities for people to become involved. Religious organizations often have the resources to connect people with opportunities such as the Presbyterian Coffee Project or Sweat-Free Ts, and thus once again connect products with the production process and producers. Often, it is easier to mobilize people into participation in such activities than directly into advocacy work.

A second way to demystify the market is to encourage personal relationships with those occupying positions in the global marketplace different from one's own. This is in many ways one of the aims of the programs just mentioned. When we consider those who are active in trade-related issues, the common unifying factor usually is not a particular field of study, but rather experiences with global neighbors. The case of Kairos perhaps showed this more strongly than any other. All of those involved in leading the organization had had significant life experiences while abroad that motivated their current action on globalization. Other work on social activism confirms the importance of these networks: Experiences with Central Americans during the 1980s, for example, played a central role in mobilizing U.S. citizens in the Central America peace movement (Smith 1996).

Recall the narratives of many of the individuals in these pages who came to economic activism based on personal relationships, especially those religious activists in Canada and the United States (countries that occupy a privileged position in the international economy). Among Kairos leaders, the stories abound, especially among the most committed members. Joe Gunn worked with Jesuits in Central America, John Mihevc with church leaders in Sub-Saharan Africa, Paul Hansen with the Maryknolls in Venezuela. GATT-Fly itself was founded by those present at the Santiago, Chile, United Nations Conference on Trade and Development (UNCTAD) meetings of 1972. Their work and research over the years were sustained by relationships with those outside Canada. Mexican delegations in 1988 examined the impact of free trade zones; delegations in 2005 followed up on the implications of Canadian mining companies (Howlett 1994; Kairos 2005c).

Evidence from the case study on the PCUSA also suggests that these networks and experiences with those in different economic situations really matter. Similar to Kairos, the head of the just trade program (at the time of this research), Andrew Kang Bartlett, spent time overseas and with diverse communities in the United States. He worked in Japan on issues of civil rights in the 1980s, and had experience with the indigenous in Latin America. Yet, beyond the activists themselves, specific *political action* on trade within the PCUSA could be traced to such connections, as noted in Chapter 4. Those promoting the first social policy to critique the Central America–United States Free Trade Agreement (CAFTA) were congregants connected with the Joining Hands program in Bolivia. Some of the churches most active in immigration issues are those on the border that come into contact with immigrants on a regular basis.

The implications of connecting people to market decisions cannot be underestimated. The alternative trade paradigm has been as successful as it has because of such connections; research has found that exchange of knowledge, through relationships, has been critical to the commitment and success of ventures like fair trade (Hudson and Hudson 2003; Lyon 2006). Personalization recasts political and economic decisions as not just an exercise in efficiency and profit but also a choice of how to treat one's neighbor. Such personalization also has the potential to challenge our acceptance of larger macro-level structures. In previous research, I found that the faith commitments of a Christian coffee business and network led to increased personalization of impersonal trade transactions – and ultimately, to criticism of dominant commodity trade structures (Reynolds 2013). Although religion does not automatically prompt more personal views of the market, religious traditions often encourage a love of neighbor and value on community. Combined with personal experiences, people may start to question the assumption of markets as merely technical structures.

AN ECUMENICAL MOVEMENT TOWARD CHANGE

The call for religious organizations to develop a robust vision of community, embrace a prophetic political voice, and personalize a depersonalized market requires resources and energy. Unfortunately, as students of religion are aware, the liberal Protestant and Catholic actors profiled in this book are dealing with challenges similar to those of many like-minded congregations. Many religious communities are struggling to maintain their role in society and to keep members. Those tasks can occupy so much energy that it is difficult to have any energy left for efforts to expand the reach of their work. Throughout the interviews, a common theme that emerged was the difficulty groups encountered in recruiting activists and motivating religious adherents to embrace their social causes.

Many of the activists I interviewed began their political engagement in regard to concerns about the international political economy more than thirty years ago. Several spoke of the excitement and energy when they joined. One could argue that for each of these communities, sizable energetic groups of potential religious recruits no longer exist. The Protestant mainline is experiencing decline, and in most places throughout Central America, the Catholic Church is rapidly losing its favored status among states and citizens.

Groups must engage religious nonactivists with their message. Many individuals who share the doctrines of the religious actors profiled in this book do not share their conviction that reforming markets is a matter of faith. In others words, many emerging religious leaders are not passionate about the cause of economic justice. Rather, it is the religious activists of decades past who continue to be the leading voices. Kairos is a prime example. The PCUSA, as is true with many mainline Protestant denominations, is not only losing members, but also losing churches. Although PCUSA members rarely object to the policies on trade or the economy (as noted in Chapter 5), many are ignoring them. Members frequently characterize the leadership as having political ideological bents and perspectives that prevent them from being taken seriously. In Costa Rica, a growing evangelical church corresponds with people exiting the Catholic Church. CECOR, like other Catholic bodies in Latin America, has become focused on engaging Catholics in a more active faith.

Part of the struggle of these communities is connected to a tendency, in general, among Protestant communities involved in these social movements to become less religious over time (Martin 1985). Unlike the other two cases, Kairos was part of a broader community, and the original interchurch coalitions became quickly affiliated with a larger, nonreligious movement. Alliances with nonreligious communities are not problematic; however, only having alliances with nonreligious communities appears to be. Why have there not been more religious groups united in common efforts? What might such a community look like? As the previous chapter pointed out, these groups share several similar commitments in their actions, such as a commitment to community and right economic relationships, and aim to approach economic issues from a transnational perspective. These values are not unique to the religious communities on these pages, but are shared by those in many different religious traditions.[2]

Miroslav Volf (2011b) calls for religious actors to become more engaged in promoting the common good. Even as his discussion has focused on Christian communities, he has noted that Christian and Islamic communities share many of the same ethical commitments, and calls for more ecumenical action.[3] Many scholars of economic development have found that religious communities offer important values that emphasize community. Padwick and Lubaale (2011) have highlighted the importance of the concept of *ubuntu* (men-and-women-in-community) as a spiritual resource of African Independent Churches. Many religious communities focus on the marginalized actors, and think about "the extent to which the last person is included" (Tyndale 2011, 215).

Although not focused on engagement in economic issues, Volf has suggested that religious communities must engage in the public square. He has rebuked what he sees as the idleness of religious communities that think faith is mainly about the enrichment of their individual souls. Although he has refuted the idea that there is a common core among religious communities, he has noted that they often have overlapping values. He has further suggested that religious communities have an important argument to offer the public arena:

Maybe the most difficult challenge for Christians is to actually *believe* that God is fundamental to human flourishing.... We must believe it as a rock-bottom conviction that shapes the way we think, preach, write, and live.... *That*, I think is today's most fundamental challenge for theologians, priests and ministers, and Christian laypeople: to *really mean* that the presence and activity of the God of love, who can make us love our neighbors as ourselves, is our hope and the hope of the world – that this God is the secret of our flourishing as persons, cultures, and interdependent inhabitants of a single globe.

(2011b, 74)

---

[2] Moving outside of the Christian tradition, for example, Islamic prohibitions against interest have often been driven by concerns of equity in the distribution of resources (Ozsoy 2011).

[3] In *Allah: A Christian Response* (2011a), Volf has argued that Christians and Muslims share many religious ideals (including a commitment to the one God), and has offered suggestions for how these groups can work together toward the common good.

This call echoes that of Warren (2001), who has noted that the theological traditions of justice and liberation have a potential to transform politics. His study of African American Protestantism highlighted the important role of religious communities for democratic revitalization.

The evangelical community may be an important partner in efforts toward this conception of human flourishing that calls us to examine our economic structures. To be fair, in my initial analysis of religious organizations (as reported in Table A.1) I did find that many evangelical congregations throughout the Americas are silent when it comes to discussions about the economy. Yet, there is evidence to suggest that evangelicals are often important actors in critical efforts toward reforming the economy. Although the evangelical community is often associated with the political right in popular parlance, this association is not always valid and is becoming increasingly problematic (for example, see Davis and Robinson 1999 or Freston 2004, who show the lack of connection between conservative theological beliefs and politics in Europe and the global South). Research has found an increasing involvement in progressive market-related issues among Pentecostals and evangelicals in the global South (Miller and Yamamori 2007). Even within the United States, Wuthnow (2007) has noted that younger evangelicals seem to exhibit more critical stances toward a liberalized economy. Lichterman (2005) has argued (in concurrence with Hunter) that evangelicals' rhetoric on social issues often acknowledges the existence of structural sin, and even though individualistic language is sometimes employed by such groups, it is not a monolithic block (237). This is especially be true of the relief and development community, where ideas of transformational development have relied on structural understandings regarding poverty, and critical attention to economic policies (Reynolds and Offutt 2013).

The leaders in the organizations in this book seemed to recognize this possibility at some level. In interviews with leaders, evangelicals emerged as a potential ally. Kairos, as it deals with a declining and aging membership, is finding that new religious activists are not joining. But they have had interest from evangelicals. The head of the Christian Coalition of Relief and Development Organizations (CCRDO), a Canadian evangelical relief and development group, was very active in his regional Kairos community; and during one of my visits to an annual meeting, I met Baptists who were considering joining the organization officially for the first time. Within the PCUSA, although economic progressives were often painted as theological liberals, I found several serving on various task forces who were affiliated with a broader evangelical population, and who very much endorsed the engagement of the church with economic markets. Finally, in speaking with members of CECOR, several interviewees mentioned some of their work with Protestant churches. Although a clear divide still exists between Catholics and Protestants in Costa Rica, they have come together in the past on social issues.

This does not mean that all (or most) evangelicals are strong potential allies in a movement for a more just economic order, much like mainline Protestants and

Catholics are not always aligned with causes highlighted in this book. Significant numbers of the population of the religious communities studied in this book rejected the intrusion of religious values into economic policy discussions. But, as John Fife of the PCUSA pointed out, ecumenical opportunities, at least among Christian communities, appear to be a way forward:

> And free trade is once again right at the top of the agenda, only it's all the questions about it, not the ideology of it. Back in the '90s, the ideology of free trade was there and everybody was in favor of it and everybody was pushing it.... Now it's reversed.... We have all the theology and sociology and economics of that in our social witness policy. So we can begin to deal with those questions, the Presbyterians. And certainly the National Conference of Catholic Bishops can [deal with these same questions], and they've got solid social witness policy on this. And the Evangelicals are beginning to talk.   (2008)

SAVING A FALLEN MARKET

The question of how to reform economic markets, and recast market structures as objects of religious reflection, is likely to remain a permanent challenge in the modern world. After thirty years of movement toward a freeing of the economy from the state management of the mid-twentieth century, we confront a moment of crisis. The twenty-first century has brought with it questions about how we should regulate the economy, and what it means to have an economy that benefits all citizens around the world. The Occupy Wall Street movement that began in 2011, alongside the economic crisis, has in some ways moved a discussion of the economy more blatantly into the public realm. Actors who can provide an ethical framework are vital. As discussion occurs about how to construct new economic policies, religious actors have something important to contribute to the conversation. Through being willing to speak prophetically about the theological importance of community and concern for neighbor, religious organizations may contribute to the public discourse about the economy. Their articulation of ethical critiques of current markets – based on religious understandings of the common good and true human flourishing – are a necessary and important part of a broader society being able to develop a robust moral-political vision of economic markets for a continually globalizing world.

Primary Sources

Kairos (Chapter 2)

Bula, Omega. 2007. Interview (not recorded). March, Toronto, Ontario.

Canadian Church Leaders. 1973. "Development Demands Justice." Pp. 231–240 in *Canadian Churches and Social Justice*, 1984, edited by John R. Williams. Toronto: Anglican Book Centre.

Clarke, Tony. 2008. Interview. May 27, Ottawa, Ontario.

Common Frontiers. 2002. FTAA: It's Hazardous to Your Health. http://www.common frontiers.ca/oldsite/call-out_eng_colour%20_final.pdf.

Cormie, Lee. 2004. "CEJI & Ecumenical Coalitions: Hope for a New Beginning in History." Pp. 300–322 in *Intersecting Voices: Critical Theologies in a Land of Diversity*, edited by Simon & Schweitzer. Ottawa, ON: Novalis.

Dillon, John. 1973. Limitations of the Trade Issue. Unpublished Report. Toronto: Kairos Archives.

———1976. New International Economic Order. Unpublished Report. Toronto: Kairos Archives.

———1987. "Alternatives to Free Trade." Pp. 9–11 in *Free Trade or Self-Reliance: Report of the Ecumenical Conference on Free Trade, Self-Reliance, and Economic Justice, February 26–March 1, 1987, Orleans, Ontario*. Conference Publication. Toronto: GATT-Fly.

———1996. "Challenging Free Trade in Canada (the Real Story)." *Economic Justice Report* 7(2): 1–8.

———1997. *Turning the Tide: Confronting the Money Traders*. Toronto: ECEJ; Ottawa: Canadian Centre for Policy Alternatives.

———2007. Interview. May 31, Toronto, Ontario.

Ecumenical Coalition for Economic Justice (ECEJ). 1990a. "GATT-Fly Changes Its Name." *Economic Justice Report* 1(1): 4.

———1990b. *Recolonization or Liberalization: The Bonds of Structural Adjustment and Struggles for Emancipation*. Toronto: ECEJ.

———1991. "Ethical Reflections on North American Economic Integration." *Economic Justice Report* 2(3): 1–16.

———1992. Background Paper on Economic Integration of the Americas. Overview of the Americas Initiative. Toronto: Kairos Archives.

————1993a. Background Paper on Economic Integration of the Americas. *Notes on Canadian Legislation*. Toronto: Kairos Archives.

————1993b. Intellectual Property Rights in NAFTA. Toronto: Kairos Archives.

————1994. Economic Integration of the Americas: Education/Action Kit. Toronto: Kairos Archives.

————1995. Remandating documents. Toronto: Kairos Archives.

————1996. *Promises to Keep, Miles to Go: An Examination of Canada's Record in the International Year for the Eradication of Poverty*. Toronto: ECEJ.

————1999a. "Redistribution of Wealth and Jubilee Vision for Global Village." *Economic Justice Report* 10(3): 1–16.

————1999b. Remandating documents. Toronto: Kairos Archives.

————2000a. "Development and Democracy: The WTO Fails to Deliver." *Economic Justice Report* 11(1): 1–16.

————2000b. "Idolatry and Exclusion: Theological Perspectives on Globalization." *Economic Justice Report* 11(2): 1–16.

————2001a. "Justice: The Heart of the Matter. Report prepared for the World Council of Churches." Reproduced in *Economic Justice Report* 11(4): 1–20.

————2001b. "Kairos: Canadian Ecumenical Justice Initiatives." *Economic Justice Report* 12(2): Insert.

————2001c. "Putting People Before Profits: A Ten Point Justice Agenda for the Americas." *Economic Justice Report* 12(1): 1–16.

ECEJ and ICCHRLA (Stephen Allen and Joe Gunn). 1999. A letter to International Trade Minister Pierre Pettigrew on the occasion of the FTAA Summit of Trade Ministers of the Americas in Toronto. November 1. Toronto: Kairos Archives.

Episcopal Commission for Social Affairs, CCCB. 1983. "Ethical Reflections on the Economic Crisis." Pp. 88–98 in *Canadian Churches and Social Justice*, 1984, edited by John R. Willians. Toronto: Anglican Book Centre.

————1987. *Ethical Choices and Political Challenges: Free Trade at What Cost?* Ottawa, Ontario: Episcopal Commission.

————1997. Letter to the Minister of Finance. April 17. Ottawa, Ontario: Episcopal Commission.

————2002. "Trading Away the Future: Concerns Arising from the Investor-State Mechanism of the North American Free Trade Agreement and Its Extension Throughout the Americas." A Background Paper prepared for the Conference on Humanizing the Global Economy (Joint Conference with CCCB, USCCB, and CELAM), Washington, D.C., January 28–30.

GATT-Fly. 1973a. *GATT-Fly: An Interchurch Initiative for an Alternative Trade Policy*. Toronto: UCC/University of Victoria Archives.

————1973b. *GATT-Fly Notes*. Toronto: UCC/University of Victoria Archives.

————1977. *Paying the Piper: How Working People Are Saddled with the Debt from Huge Resource Projects while the Banks and Corporate "Pipers" Call the Tune*. Toronto: GATT-Fly.

————1978a. *Canada's Food Trade: By Bread Alone?* Toronto: GATT-Fly.

————1978b. *Sugar and Sugarworkers: A Popular Report of the International Sugarworkers Conference*. Toronto: GATT-Fly.

————1979. *Canada's Food: The Road to Self-Reliance*. Toronto: GATT-Fly.

————1980a. "Export Oriented 'Development' – Who's It For?" *GATT-FLY Report* 1(5): 1, 4.

————1980b. *GATT-Fly Report* 1(2): 1–4.

————1981a. *The Power to Choose: Canada's Energy Options.* Toronto: Between the Lines.

————1981b. "Unions Propose Self-Reliant Plan for Textile Clothing Sector." *GATT-Fly Report* 2(2): 3.

————1983a. *Ah-Hah: A New Approach to Popular Education.* Toronto: Between the Lines.

————1983b. "How to End the Depression: Self-Reliance and Economic Independence." *GATT-Fly Report* 4(5): 1–4, 6.

————1984. "GATT-Fly: What We Do and Who We Are." *GATT-Fly Report* 4: 1–4.

————1985a. "A Biblical View of Poverty and Justice." *GATT-Fly Report* 6(1): 3.

————1985b. "Free Trade or Self-Reliance." *GATT-Fly Report* 6(2): 1–2, 4.

————1985c. "Free Trade vs. Self-Reliance – The Fight Ahead." *GATT-FLY Report* 6(3): 3–4.

————1986a. "Churches Urged to Oppose Free Trade with the U.S." *GATT-Fly Report* 7(1): 1–6.

————1986b. "Farmers and Free Trade." *GATT-Fly Report* 7(3): 1–6.

————1986c. "U.S GATT Strategy Threatens Canada and Third World." *GATT-Fly Report* 7(2): 3–4.

————1987a. "Bleed Them to Death: The Promise of Free Trade in Rural Canada." *GATT-Fly Report* 8(3): 1–4.

————1987b. "Building Self-Reliance in Canada." *GATT-Fly Report* 8(1): 1–8.

————1987c. *Free Trade or Self-Reliance: Report of the Ecumenical Conference on Free Trade, Self-Reliance, and Economic Justice, February 26-March 1, 1987, Orleans, Ontario.* Conference Publication. Toronto: GATT-Fly.

————1988a. "Action Needed to Stop the Deal." *GATT-Fly Report* 9(3): 1–4.

————1988b. "Canada's Churches and the Free Trade Agreement." *GATT-Fly Report* 9(1): 1–6.

————1989. "Free Trade Budget Will Increase Unemployment." *GATT-Fly Report* 10(2): 1–4.

————1990. Remandating documents. Toronto: Kairos Archives.

Graham, Julie. 2008. Phone interview (not recorded). March 6, Toronto, Ontario.

Gunn, Joe. 2008. Interview, May 28, Ottawa, Ontario.

Hansen, Paul. 2008. Interview. March 27, Toronto, Ontario.

ICCHLA (Interchurch Coalition on Human Rights in Latin America) (Central America Delegation). 1996. Letter to the Central American presidents and Canadian Prime Minister on the occasion of free trade talks in Ottawa. May 15. Toronto: Kairos Archives.

Jeremic, Rusa. 2005. Remarks before the Subcommittee on Trade, Trade Disputes, and Investment (SINT) regarding Chapter 11. February 12. www.kairoscanada.org.

————2006a. *Canada–Central America Free Trade Negotiations: It's Time to Get it Right.* Submission to the Standing Committee on International Trade, on Behalf of the Kairos and Americas Policy Group. June 21. Www.kairoscanada.org/. . ./CAFTA_APG_Submission_June06.pdf.

————2006b. "Free Trade at the Crossroads: Time for a New Approach." Kairos Policy Briefing Paper 6: 1–2. http://www.kairoscanada.org/sustainability/global-finance/kairos-briefing-paper-6-free-trade-at-the-crossroads-time-for-a-new-approach/.

————2007. Phone interview (not recorded). April 28, Toronto, Ontario.

Kairos. 2003a. Becoming KAIROS Liturgy. www.kairoscanada.org.

———2003b. Bible Study: Reflecting on Scripture. www.kairoscanada.org/fileadmin/fe/
files/PDF/WhoWeAre/KairosBibleStudy.pdf.

———2003c. "Free Trade Deals: What You Don't See May Be What You Get." *Global
Economic Justice Report* 2(1): 1–12.

———2003d. North American Churches Consultation on Globalization. Discussion Paper.
www.councilofchurches.ca/documents/social_justice/faith-economy/ChurchPolicy
Background.pdf.

———2004a. Action Alert against FTAA. www.kairoscanada.org.

———2004b. "Food, Farmers, and Global Trade: The Real Story. *Global Economic
Justice Report* 3(4): 1–16.

———2004c. Kairos Brief for the International Policy Review. August. www.kairosca
nada.org/fileadmin/fe/files/PDF/Publications/policyReview.pdf.

———2005a. Brief to the House of Commons Standing Committee on Foreign Affairs on
Canada's International Policy Statement. November 2. www.kairoscanada.org/fil
eadmin/fe/files/PDF/Letters/2005/Statement_Brief_SCFAIT_IPS_2Nov05.pdf.

———2005b. Bulletin insert on the WTO. http://www.kairoscanada.org/fileadmin/fe/
files/PDF/WorshipReflctn/WTObulletinInserto511.pdf.

———2005c. A Cry for Justice: The Human Face of NAFTA's Failure in Mexico:
Canadian Church Leaders' Delegation to Mexico. March 11–19, 2005. www.kairo
scanada.org/fileadmin/fe/files/PDF/HRTrade/Trade-commerce/Delegation_FINAL
FullReport_Aprilo5.pdf.

———2005d. Kairos Invites You to Join Global Action for Just Trade. www.kairoscanada.
org/fileadmin/fe/files/PDF/Publications/GlobalWeekofAction_Flyer_Jano5.pdf.

———2005e. Letter to Prime Minister Martin. November 2. www.kairoscanada.org/
fileadmin/fe/files/PDF/Letters/2005/ltrMartinSummitofAmericaso51102.pdf.

———2005f. *Trade E-Bulletin* 2(1).

———2006a. Bad Deal Is Bad News: WTO Inches Forward in Hong Kong. *Global
Economic Justice Report* 4(4): 1–16.

———2006b. It Is Still Ours to Plant the Seeds: A Kairos Worship Service for Hope in
Action. www.kairoscanada.org.

———2006c. "Little Information – Lots of Concern." *Trade E-Bulletin* 3(2,3): 1–3.

———2006d. Look Before Leaping: Canada–Central America Free Trade Agreement
Fundamentally Flawed. www.kairoscanada.org/fileadmin/fe/files/PDF/Letters/2006/
LetterJoint_civilsociety_CAFTA_21June06.pdf.

———2006e. *Trade E-Bulletin* 3(1).

———2006f. Worship Guide for Kairos Sunday. www.kairoscanada.org/fileadmin/fe/
files/PDF/WorshipReflctn/KAIROSSunday06_OrderService.pdf.

———2008. Statement on the Report of the Secretary-General on Business and Human
Rights (Dr. John Ruggie), entitled "Protect, Respect, and Remedy: A Framework for
Business and Human Rights." June. www.kairoscanada.org.

Lind, Christopher. 1987. "Ethical Reflections on Trade and Self-Reliance." Pp. 40–41 in
*Free Trade or Self-Reliance: Report of the Ecumenical Conference on Free Trade,
Self-Reliance, and Economic Justice, February 26–March 1, 1987, Orleans, Ontario*.
Conference Publication. Toronto: GATT-Fly.

Luttrell, Bill. 1987. "Self-Reliance in Canada." Pp. 29–31 in *Free Trade or Self-Reliance:
Report of the Ecumenical Conference on Free Trade, Self-Reliance, and Economic
Justice, February 26–March 1, 1987, Orleans, Ontario*. Conference Publication.
Toronto: GATT-Fly.

Mihevc, John. 1995. *So the Market Tells Them So: The World Bank and Economic Fundamentalism in Africa.* London: Zed Books.

———2007. Interview. March 27, Toronto, Ontario.

Reeve, Ted. 1992. "A Challenge to Economic Power: The Work of the Canadian Ecumenical Coalition for Economic Justice." A paper prepared for Life & Peace Institution session on Economics, Power, and Human Rights. Toronto: Kairos Archives.

Smith, Jane. 2002. Letter to Prime Minister Chrétien on the occasion of the G8 Summit. www.kairoscanada.org.

Ten Days for Development. 1993. Development on Trial. Toronto: Kairos Archives.

United Church of Canada, Division of Mission in Canada. 1988. *Responding to Free Trade from a Christian Perspective.* Toronto: United Church of Canada.

United Church of Canada. 2006. *Living Faithfully in the Midst of Empire.* Toronto: United Church of Canada.

Vandervennen, Paul. 1996. Letter to Central Americans Presidents and Canadian Prime Minister: On the Occasion of Free Trade Talks in Ottawa. May 15. ICCHRLA.

PCUSA (Chapter 3)

Adams, Mark. 2008. Interview. January 17, Douglas, Arizona.

Advisory Committee on Social Witness Policy (ACSWP), PCUSA. 1994. *Sustainable Development, Reformed Faith, and U.S. International Economic Policy.* Advisory Committee on Social Witness Policy, Louisville.

———1996. *Hope for a Global Future: Towards Just and Sustainable Development and Study Guide.* Office of the General Assembly (PCUSA), Louisville.

———2006. *Resolution on Just Globalization: Justice, Ownership, and Accountability.* Office of the General Assembly (PCUSA), Louisville.

Advisory Council on Church and Society (ACCS), PCUSA. 1976. "Economic Justice Within Environmental Limits: The Need for a New Economic Ethic." *Church and Society: The Journal of Just Thoughts.* September/October 67(1): 5–56.

———1985. *Toward a Just, Caring, and Dynamic Political Economy.* ACCS, New York.

Bartlett, Andrew Kang. 2007. September, Louisville, Kentucky.

Borst, Marilyn. 2007. Interview. May 18, Atlanta, Georgia.

Broyles, Vernon. 2007. Interview. September 19, Louisville, Kentucky.

Committee on Social Witness Policy of PCUSA (CSWP). 1990. *Restoring Creation for Ecology and Justice.* Office of the General Assembly (PCUSA), Louisville.

———1991. Prospectus for a Task Force: Sustainable Development, Reformed Faith, and U.S. International Policy. Unpublished document.

———1994. *Why and How the Church Makes a Social Policy Witness.* Office of the General Assembly (PCUSA), Louisville.

Costa, Ruy O. 2003. *Globalization and Culture.* Advisory Committee on Social Witness Policy, PCUSA, Louisville.

Douglass, Gordon. 2001. *The Globalization of Economic Life: Challenge to the Church.* Advisory Committee on Social Witness Policy of the PCUSA, Louisville.

General Assembly, PCUS. 1948. "On Trade." *Minutes of the General Assembly.* Office of the General Assembly (PCUS), Atlanta.

———1953. "On Trade." *Minutes of the General Assembly.* Office of the General Assembly (PCUS), Atlanta.

——1954. "On Trade." *Minutes of the General Assembly*. Office of the General Assembly (PCUS), Atlanta.

——1955. "On Trade." *Minutes of the General Assembly*. Office of the General Assembly (PCUS), Atlanta.

——1977. "On Investment in Africa" and "On Lowering Trade Barriers." *Minutes of the General Assembly*. Office of the General Assembly (PCUS), Atlanta.

——1980. "The Presbyterian Church in the United States and America's Role in International Economic Justice." *Minutes of the General Assembly*. Office of the General Assembly (PCUS), Atlanta.

General Assembly, PCUSA. 1983. "Transnational Corporations." *Minutes of the General Assembly*. Office of the General Assembly, New York City.

——1984. "Christian Faith and Economic Justice," "Committee on a Just Political Economy," "Addressing International Concerns Beyond the U.S.," and "Just Political Economy Town Meetings." *Minutes of the General Assembly*. Office of the General Assembly, New York City.

——1985. "On Investment in Africa" and "Towards a Just, Caring, and Dynamic Political Economy." *Minutes of the General Assembly*. Office of the General Assembly, New York City.

——1987. "Affirmation on Global Hunger" and "Infant Formula Manufacturer's Compliance with WHO Guidelines." *Minutes of the General Assembly*. Office of the General Assembly, New York City.

——1989. "Third World Debt and the Churches' Responsibility." *Minutes of the General Assembly*. Office of the General Assembly, Louisville.

——1990. "Guatemalan Bishops' Pastoral, 'The Clamor for Land,'" "Purchase of Salvadoran Coffee," and "World Food Day." *Minutes of the General Assembly*. Office of the General Assembly, Louisville.

——1992. "Free Trade Agreement" and "Maquiladoras along the U.S.-Mexico Border." *Minutes of the General Assembly*. Office of the General Assembly, Louisville.

——1993. "Why and How the Church Makes a Social Policy Witness" and "Implementation of NAFTA." Minutes of the General Assembly, Office of the General Assembly, Louisville.

——1994. "Just and Compassionate U.S. Immigration Policy." *Minutes of the General Assembly*. Office of the General Assembly, Louisville.

——1995. "Humanitarian Aid to Africa." *Minutes of the General Assembly*. Office of the General Assembly, Louisville.

——1996. "Hope for a Global Future: Toward Just and Sustainable Human Development." *Minutes of the General Assembly*. Office of the General Assembly, Louisville.

——1997. "Global Economy: Brazil and South Korea." *Minutes of the General Assembly*. Office of the General Assembly, Louisville.

——1998. "Jubilee 2000." *Minutes of the General Assembly*. Office of the General Assembly, Louisville.

——1999. "Encounter with New Neighbors," "Farm Crisis," and "International Working Conditions." *Minutes of the General Assembly*. Office of the General Assembly, Louisville.

——2000. "Mission in Partnership." *Minutes of the General Assembly*. Office of the General Assembly, Louisville.

——2001. "Fair-Traded Organic Coffee and Sugar." *Minutes of the General Assembly*. Office of the General Assembly, Louisville.

————2002. "Affirmation of the Declaration of Debrecen (World Alliance of Reformed Churches)." *Minutes of the General Assembly*. Office of the General Assembly, Louisville.

————2003. "On Opposing the FTAA." *Minutes of the General Assembly*. Office of the General Assembly, Louisville.

————2004. "Opposition to CAFTA" and "On Celebrating the 'Social Creed' and Considering a 21st Century Social Creed." *Minutes of the General Assembly*. Office of the General Assembly, Louisville.

————2006. "Just Globalization." *Minutes of the General Assembly*. Office of the General Assembly, Louisville.

General Assembly, UPCUSA. 1976. "On Trade." *Minutes of the General Assembly*. Office of the General Assembly (UPCUSA), New York City.

General Assembly, UPCUSA and PCUS. 1979. "Challenge of Development." *Minutes of the General Assemblies*. Office of the General Assembly (UPCUSA and PCUS). New York City and Atlanta.

General Assembly Mission Council, PCUSA. 1984. "The Presbyterian Church and Transnational Corporations." *Church and Society: The Journal of Just Thoughts*. March/April 7–36.

Fife, John. 2008. Interview. January 17, Tucson, Arizona.

Former commissioner for GA. 2007. Interview. May 19, Atlanta, Georgia.

Gordon, Catherine. 2007. Interview. June 13, Washington, D.C.

The International Labor Rights Fund. 2001. *The Employment Effects of Free Trade and Globalization*. Advisory Committee on Social Witness Policy, PCUSA, Louisville.

Kernaghan, Ron. 2007. Interview. August 14, Pasadena, California.

Kirkpatrick, Clifton. 2007. Interview. October 9, Princeton, New Jersey.

Livezey, Lois. 2007. Interview. May 1, New York City, New York.

Office of Ecumenical Affairs. 2001. *Voices from Korea, USA, and Brazil: The Reformed Faith and Global Economy*. PCUSA, Louisville.

Presbyterian Hunger Program. 2005. *Worship Guide on Trade and Globalization*. PCUSA, Louisville.

————2007. Just Trade Website. www.pcusa.org/trade.

Presbyterian Lay Committee. 2007. *The Layman Online: Objectives and Mission*. www.layman.org/abousus/objectives_and_mission_statement.aspx.

Stivers, Robert I. 2003. *Globalization and the Environment*. Advisory Committee on Social Witness Policy, PCUSA, Louisville.

Taylor, Stuart. 2008. Interview. January 16, Tucson, Arizona.

Ufford-Chase, Rick. 2007. Interview. March 29, Princeton, New Jersey.

World Alliance of Reformed Churches (WARC), 2004. *The ACCRA Confession: Covenanting for Justice in the Economy and the Earth*. Available online at www.warc.ch.

Costa Rican Catholic Church (Chapter 4)

Álvarez Ruiz, Ervin et al. (18 priests in Tilarán). 2007. Porque Queremos Una Costa Rica Solidaria. February 16. [*Why We Want a Costa Rica with Solidarity*].

Arrieta Villalobos, Mons. Román. 1993. Nueva Evangelización y Promoción Humana: Excmo.y Revdm. Mons. Román Arrieta Villalobos. [*The New Evangelization and Human Promotion*]. Pp. 228–260 in *La Palabra Social de Los Obispos Costarricenses (1893–2006)*, edited by Miguel Picado Gatjens. San José: CECOR.

Barrantes Ureña, Mons. Hugo. 2004a. El Trabajo, Un Medio Para Construir Una Sociedad Justa y Solidaria. [*Employment, a Means to Construct a Just Society*]. p. 51 in *Iglesia y TLC: Documentos Episcopales*, edited by Edwin Aguiluz Milla. San José: VEPS.

————2004b. Iglesia, Etica y Desarrollo. [*The Church, Ethics, and Development*]. Presentation from *Dialogo Nacional Para Una Ética del Desarollo*, March 2004. www.iadb.org/etica.

————2005a. Mensaje de Mons. Hugo Barrantes Ureña, al Mundo del Trabajo. May 1. [*Message on the Day of the Worker*]. Pp. 57–59 in *Iglesia y TLC: Documentos Episcopales*, edited by Edwin Aguiluz Milla. San José: VEPS.

————2005b. No a La Exploitación Salvaje. [*No to Savage Exploitation*]. *Eco-Católico*, January 20.

————2005c. No Busquen entre los Muertos al que Vive [*Do Not Look for the Dead among the Living*]. March 27. Pp. 55–56 in *Iglesia y TLC: Documentos Episcopales*, edited by Edwin Aguiluz Milla. San José: VEPS.

————2006. La Doctrina Social de la Iglesia, una Luz para el Trabajo Pastoral. [*CST of the Church, a Light for Pastoral Work*]. Pp. 435–439 in *La Palabra Social de Los Obispos Costarricenses (1893–2006)*, edited by Miguel Picado Gatjens. San José: CECOR.

————2007a. Homilía Visita Arquidiócesis de San José a la Basílica de Los Ángeles. July 28. [*Homily in San José Basilica*]. Copy from CECOR personnel.

————2007b. Interview. August 1, San José, Costa Rica.

Caritas, Costa Rica. 2003. Mons. Ángel San Casimiro and Father Guido Villalta Loaiza. Comunicado de la Pastoral Social – Caritas Con Motivo del Tratado de Libre Comercio. May 15. [*Communication of Caritas with Regards to CAFTA*]. Pp. 99–102 in *Iglesia y TLC: Documentos Episcopales*, edited by Edwin Aguiluz Milla. San José: VEPS.

Chaves Ortiz, Arturo Jorge. 2000. ¿En Cual Lancha Seguir? [*In Which Way to Follow?*] *Eco-Católico*, June 11.

————2001. ¿Le Importa Quién esté al Mando? [*Who Is in Command?*] *Eco-Católico*, March 4.

————2003a. Editorial: ¿Por qué un Tratado Commercial Interesa a la Iglesia? [*Why Does a FTA Interest the Church?*] *Eco-Católico*, December 7.

————2003b. ¿Iglesia y TLC: A Favor o en Contra? [*The Church and CAFTA: For or Against?*] *Eco-Católico*, December 7.

————2007. Interview. August 3, San José, Costa Rica.

CECOR (Episcopal Conference of Costa Rica). 1974. Declaración de la Conferencia Episcopal Sobre las Elecciones del 3 de Febrero de 1974. [*Declaration of CECOR on February 1974 Elections*]. Pp. 120–122 in *La Palabra Social de Los Obispos Costarricenses (1893–2006)*, edited by Miguel Picado Gatjens. San José: CECOR.

————1979. Evángelización y Realidad Social de Costa Rica. [*Evangelism and Socia Reality in Costa Rica*]. Pp. 138–159 in *La Palabra Social de Los Obispos Costarricenses (1893–2006)*, edited by Miguel Picado Gatjens. San José: CECOR.

————1981. Iglesia y Momento Actual: Carta Pastoral del Episcopado Costarricense sobre la Situación Actual del País y la Campana Electoral. [*The Church and Today: Pastoral Letter from CECOR on the Current Situation in the Country*]. Pp. 165–175 in *La Palabra Social de Los Obispos Costarricenses (1893–2006)*, edited by Miguel Picado Gatjens. San José: CECOR.

———1994. Carta Pastoral Madre Tierra. Mensaje de los Obispos de Costa Rica sobre la Situación de los Campesinos y los Indígenas. [*Mother Earth: Message of the Bishops of Costa Rica on the Situation of Farmers and the Indigenous*]. Pp. 261–287 in *La Palabra Social de Los Obispos Costarricenses (1893–2006)*, edited by Miguel Picado Gatjens. San José: CECOR.

———1997. Comunicado de los Obispos sobre la Situación Actual de Costa Rica. [*Communication of the Bishops on the Current Situation in Costa Rica*]. Pp. 300–308 in *La Palabra Social de Los Obispos Costarricenses (1893–2006)*, edited by Miguel Picado Gatjens. San José: CECOR.

———2000. Mensaje de la Conferencia Episcopal de Costa Rica ante la Situación que Vive el País. March 23. [*Message of CECOR on the Situation in the Country*]. *Eco Católico*, April 2.

———2004. Una Reflexión sobre el Tratado de Libre Comercio a la Luz de Principios cristianos: Justicia, Equidad, y Solidaridad para Todos. May 30. [*A Reflection on CAFTA in Light of Christian Principles: Justice, Equality, and Solidarity for All*]. Pp. 21–28 in *Iglesia y TLC: Documentos Episcopales*, edited by Edwin Aguiluz Milla. San José: VEPS.

———2005a. Con o sin TLC, Necesitamos una Agenda Nacional de Desarrollo: Mensaje de la Conferencia Episcopal de Costa Rica sobre el TLC. September. [*With or Without CAFTA, We Need a Development Plan: Message of CECOR on CAFTA*]. Pp. 409–410 in *La Palabra Social de Los Obispos Costarricenses (1893–2006)*, edited by Miguel Picado Gatjens. San José: CECOR.

———2005b. Democracia, Politica y Honestidad. Con Ocasión de la Campana Electoral 2005–2006. October 3. [*Democracy, Politics, and Honesty. On the Occasion of the 2005–2006 Electoral Campaign*]. Pp. 411–419 in *La Palabra Social de Los Obispos Costarricenses (1893–2006)*, edited by Miguel Picado Gatjens. San José: CECOR.

———2005c. Dialogo Si, Polarización No. November. [*Dialogue Yes, Polarization No*]. Pp. 420–421 in *La Palabra Social de Los Obispos Costarricenses (1893–2006)*, edited by Miguel Picado Gatjens. San José: CECOR.

———2005d. Los Obispos de Costa Rica y El Tratado de Libre Comercio con los Estados Unidos de América. May 23. [*CECOR and CAFTA*]. Pp. 401–402 in *La Palabra Social de Los Obispos Costarricenses (1893–2006)*, edited by Miguel Picado Gatjens. San José: CECOR.

———2005e. Mensaje de los Obispos de Costa Rica en 89 Asamblea Ordinaria de Costa Rica. February 25. [*Message of the Bishops in the 89th Assembly*]. Pp. 29 in *Iglesia y TLC: Documentos Episcopales*, edited by Edwin Aguiluz Milla. San José: VEPS.

———2006a. Carta de los Senores Obispos de Costa Rica al Cardenal Ángelo Sodano con Relación al TLC. June 21. [*Card of the Senior Bishops to Cardinal Angelo Sodano regarding CAFTA*]. www.iglesiacr.org.

———2006b. Costa Rica, Primero: Mensaje de los Obispos en 92 Asamblea Plenaria. [*Costa Rica First: Message of the Bishops in the 92nd Plenary Assembly*]. Copy from CECOR personnel.

———2006c. Ni a favor ni en contra del TLC: Recomendaciones de la Conferencia Episcopal de Costa Rica a la Comisión de Asuntos Internacionales de la Asamblea Legislativa sobre el Tratado de Libre Comercio enter Centroaméricanos, República Dominicana y Estados Unidos de América. October 9. [*Recommendation of CECOR to the International Commission of the Legislative Assembly on DR-CAFTA*].

Pp. 432–434 in *La Palabra Social de Los Obispos Costarricenses (1893–2006)*, edited by Miguel Picado Gatjens. San José: CECOR.

——2007a. De la Conferencia Episcopal de Costa Rica a los Sacerdotes Diocesanos y Religiosos. May 3. [*From CECOR to Priests*]. Copy from CECOR personnel.

——2007b. Mensaje de la Conferncia Episcopal en las Circunstancias Actuales del País Unidos como Hermanos, Construyamos Costa Rica. October. [*Message of CECOR on the Current Situation: United as Brothers, We Will Construct a Better Costa Rica*]. *Eco-Católico*, October.

CELAM (Latin American Episcopal Conference). 1995. Economicismo causea de injustice. [*Economic Liberalization Causes Injustice*]. May. *Eco-Católico*, May 14.

——(Department of Justice and Solidarity). 2004. Declaración Final del Encuentro del CELAM sobre Tratados de Libre Comercio. August 13. [*Final Declaration of CELAM on FTAs*]. Pp. 67–73 in *Iglesia y TLC: Documentos Episcopales*, edited by Edwin Aguiluz Milla. San José: VEPS.

Cordero Arias, Luis Alberto. 2007. Interview. July 27, San José, Costa Rica.

Eco-Católico. 2000. Obispo Fraterno con los Agricultores [*Bishop Trejos Picado Sends Brotherly Message to Agricultural Workers*]. *Eco-Católico*, May 21.

Loría Garita, Mons. Guillermo. 2006. Homilía en la Jornada Mundial de Oración por la Paz. January. [*Homily on Worldwide Day of Peace*]. Pp. 60–61 in *Iglesia y TLC: Documentos Episcopales*, edited by Edwin Aguiluz Milla. San José: VEPS.

Hernández Rojas, Francisco. 2007. Interview. July 20, San José, Costa Rica.

Madrigal Salas, Alfredo. 2007. Interview. July 13, San José, Costa Rica.

Picado Gatjens, Miguel et al. 2007. Valoración Ética del TLC. October. [*Ethical Evaluation of CAFTA-DR*].

Rodríguez G, Martín. 2003a. Iglesia Perfila Posición ante TLC. [*Church Takes a Position against CAFTA*]. *Eco-Católico*, February 23.

——2003b. Obispos Asumen Posiciones en Temas Claves. (Mons. San Casimiro y Mons. Ulloa). [*Bishops Take Position on Key Principles*]. *Eco-Católico*, March 2.

——2004. Obispo Apoya Eliminación de Subsidios (Mons. San Casimiro). [*Bishop Helps Eliminate Subsidies*]. *Eco-Católico*, March 21.

San Casimiro Fernández Mons. Angel. 2003. Mensaje del Presbiterio de la Diócesis de Ciudad Quesada. April 17. [*Message of Cuidad Quesada*]. Pp. 357–359 in *La Palabra Social de Los Obispos Costarricenses (1893–2006)*, edited by Miguel Picado Gatjens. San José: CECOR.

——2007. Mensaje a Nuestra Senora de los Ángeles. August 2. Cartago.

SEDAC (Central American Episcopal Secretariat). 1995. Obispos Atacan al Neoliberalismo. October. [*Bishops Attack Neoliberalism*].

——2002. Al Pueblo de Dios que Camina en Centro América. [*To the People of God Walking in Central America*].

——2005. Declaración de Los Obispos de América Latina y El Caribe Sobre los Tratados de Libre Comercio. September 9. [*Declaration of Central American Bishops on CAFTA*].

Seminario Universidad. 2006. Interview with Hugo Barrantes Urena. *Seminario Universidad*. Summer.

Sodano, Cardinal. 2006. Secretary for the State of Holiness, Vatican. Letter to Mons. José Francisco Ulloa Rojas, President of CECOR. Pp. 65–66 in *Iglesia y TLC: Documentos Episcopales*, edited by Edwin Aguiluz Milla. San José: VEPS.

Solano Cerdas, Claudio. 2007. Mensaje a los Trabadores. [*Message to the Workers*]. Flyer, October 5.

Sota S., José Francisco et al. (32 priests in Alajuela). 2007. Pronunciamiento contra el TLC de Curas de Alajuela. February. [*Pronouncement against CAFTA from Alajuela*].

Trejos Picado, Mons. Ignacio. 1990. A los Fieles de mi Diócesis. [*To the Faithful in My Diocese*]. Pp. 214–216 in *La Palabra Social de Los Obispos Costarricenses (1893–2006)*, edited by Miguel Picado Gatjens. San José: CECOR.

———1991. Carta Pastoral Iluminados por la Fe. A Propósito del Centenario de la Encíclica *Rerum Novarum*. [*Pastoral Letter Illuminating the Faith*]. Pp. 288–299 in *La Palabra Social de Los Obispos Costarricenses (1893–2006)*, edited by Miguel Picado Gatjens. San José: CECOR.

———2000. Con su Permiso?, Don Julio.[*With your Permission, Don Julio?*] *Eco-Católico*, March 12.

———2007a. A Maria Solidaria. August. [*In Solidarity with Mary*]. Personal Correspondence.

———2007b. Interview. July 28, Cartago, Costa Rica.

———2007c. Mensaje Frente al Tribunal Supremo de Elecciones. July. [*Message in Front of the Election Tribunal*]. Personal Correspondence.

———2007d. Mensaje Sobre el Tratado de Libre Comercio. April. [*Message on CAFTA*]. Personal Correspondence.

———2007e. Nuestra Arma: el Poderoso Boligrafo. July. [*Our Weapon: The Pen*]. Personal Correspondence.

———2007f. ¡Pura Vida! June. [*Pure Life!*]. Personal Correspondence.

Trejos Picado, Mons Ignacio and Alvaro Coto Orozco, et al. 1975. Declaración del Obispos y los sacerdotes de la Diócesis de San Isidro de el General sobre la "reforma agraria." [*Declaration of the Bishops and Priests from the San Isidro Diocese Regarding "Agrarian Reform."*] Pp. 123–124 in *La Palabra Social de Los Obispos Costarricenses (1893–2006)*, edited by Miguel Picado Gatjens. San José: CECOR.

Ulloa Rojas, Mons. José Francisco. 2000. Globalización Golpea Peligrosamente. [*Globalization Hits Hard*]. *Eco-Catolicó*.

———2004a. Homilia en la Solemnidad de Nuestra Senora de los Ángeles. August 2. [*Homily in Honor of the Virgin of Los Ángeles*]. Pp. 54 in *Iglesia y TLC: Documentos Episcopales*, edited by Edwin Aguiluz Milla. San José: VEPS.

———2004b. Mesaje en el Día del Trabajador. [*Message on the Day of the Worker*]. Pp. 52–53 in *Iglesia y TLC: Documentos Episcopales*, edited by Edwin Aguiluz Milla. San José: VEPS.

———2007a. Interview. July, San José, Costa Rica.

———2007b. Sermon on CAFTA.

Ulloa Rojas, Mons. José Francisco and Gerardo Vargas Varela. 2003. El Trabajo un Medio para Construir una Sociedad Justa y Solidaria. [*Employment as a Means of Constructing a Just Society*]. Pp. 51 in *Iglesia y TLC: Documentos Episcopales*, edited by Edwin Aguiluz Milla. San José: VEPS.

USCCB (United States Conference of Catholic Bishops) and SEDAC (Central American Episcopal Secretariat). 1987. Social Development and World Peace. usccb.org/issues-and-action/human-life-and-dignity/global-issues/latin-america-caribbean/central-america/united-states-catholic-conference-uscc-episcopal-secretariat-of-central-america-panama-sedac.cfm.

———2004. Joint Statement Concerning the United States–Central American Free Trade Agreement by SEDAC and USCCB. July 21. http://old.usccb.org/sdwp/international/jointtradestatement.shtml.

References

Alexander, Jeffrey. 2003. *The Meanings of Social Life: A Cultural Sociology*. New York: Oxford University Press.

Almeling, Rene. 2007. "Selling Genes, Selling Gender: Egg Agencies, Sperm Banks and the Medical Market in Genetic Material. *American Sociological Review* 72(3): 319–340.

Ammerman, Nancy. 2005. *Pillars of Faith*. Berkeley: University of California Press.

Anderson, Benedict. 1983. *Imagined Communities: Reflections on the Origin and Spread of Nationalism*. New York: Verso.

Avery, William. 1996. "American Agriculture and Trade Policymaking: Two-level Bargaining in the North American Free Trade Agreement." *Policy Sciences* 29(2): 113–136.

Barbieri Jr, William. 2001. "Beyond the Nations: The Expansion of the Common Good in Catholic Social Thought." *The Review of Politics* 63(4): 723–754.

Bartley, Tim. 2007. "Institutional Emergence in an Era of Globalization: The Rise of Transnational Private Regulation of Labor and Environmental Conditions." *American Journal of Sociology* 113(2): 297–351.

Baum, Gregory. 1991. "The Originality of Catholic Social Teaching." In *Rerum Novarum: One Hundred Years of Catholic Social Teaching*, edited by John Coleman and Gregory Baum. Philadelphia: Trinity Press International.

Bellah, Robert. 1973. *Emile Durkheim on Morality and Society: Selected Writings*. Chicago: University of Chicago Press.

Bellah, Robert, Richard Masden, William Sullivan, Ann Swidler, and Steven Tipton. 1985. *Habits of the Heart: Individualism and Commitment in American Life*. Berkeley: University of California Press.

Benford, Robert and David Snow. 2000. "Framing Processes and Social Movements: An Overview and Assessment." *Annual Review of Sociology* 26: 611–639.

Bennett, Scott. "American and Canadian Assessments of NAFTA." *American Behavioral Scientist* 47(10): 1285–1318.

Berger, Peter. 1967. *The Sacred Canopy: Elements of a Sociological Theory of Religion*. Garden City, NJ: Doubleday.

Best, Jacqueline. 2003. "Moralizing Finance: The New International Financial Architecture as Normative Discourse." *Review of International Political Economy* 10(3): 579–603.

————2005. "The Moral Politics of IMF Reforms: Universal Economics, Particular Ethics." *Perspectives on Global Development and Technology* 4(3–4): 357–378.

Best, Jacqueline and Wesley Widmaier. 2006. "Micro- or Macro- Moralities? International Economic Discourses and Policy Possibilities." *Review of International Political Economy* 13(4): 609–633.

Bhagwati, Jagdish. 2008. *Termites in the Trading System: How Preferential Agreements Undermine Free Trade.* New York: Oxford University Press.

Boice, James. 1985. "The Future of Reformed Theology." In *Reformed Theology in America: A History of Its Modern Development,* edited by David Wells. Grand Rapids, MI: Eerdmans.

Boltanski, Luc and Laurent Thévenot. 2006. *On Justification: Economies of Worth,* translated by Catherine Porter. Princeton, NJ: Princeton University Press. (Orig. pub. 1991.)

Brignoli, Hector and Yolando Martinez. 1983. "Growth and Crisis in the Central American Economies, 1950–1980." *Journal of Latin American Studies* 15(2): 365–396.

Buckman, Greg. 2005. *Global Trade: Past Mistakes, Future Choices.* London: Zed Books.

Burawoy, Michael. 2014. "Sociology as Vocation: Moral Commitment and Scientific Imagination." *Current Sociology* 62(2): 279–284.

Burns, Gene. 1990. "The Politics of Ideology: The Papal Struggle with Liberalism." *American Journal of Sociology* 95(5): 1123–1152.

————1992. *The Frontiers of Catholicism: The Politics of Ideology in a Liberal World.* Berkeley: University of California Press.

Cameron, Maxwell and Brian Tomlin. 2000. *The Making of NAFTA: How the Deal Was Done.* Ithaca, NY: Cornell University Press.

Carney, Martin. 2001. *An Analysis of Gregory Baum's Theology of the "Preferential Option for the Poor" as a Via Negativa Which Addresses Important Critiques of the Preferential Option.* PhD Dissertation, Fordham University.

Carpenter, Joel. 2013. "What's New about the New Evangelical Social Engagement." Pp. 265–279 in *The New Evangelical Social Engagement,* edited by Brian Steensland and Philip Goff. New York: Oxford University Press.

Casanova, José. 1994. *Public Religions in the Modern World.* Chicago: University of Chicago Press.

Cavanagh, John, Sarah Anderson, and Karen Hansen-Kuhn. 2001. "Crossborder Organizing Around Alternatives to Free Trade: Lessons from the NAFTA/FTAA Experience." Pp. 149–162 in *Global Citizen Action,* edited by Michael Edwards and John Gaventa. Boulder, CO: Lynne Reinner Publishers.

Centeno, Miguel. 1994. *Democracy within Reason: Technocratic Revolution in Mexico.* University Park: Pennsylvania State University Press.

Centeno, Miguel and Joseph Cohen. 2010. *Global Capitalism: A Sociological Perspective.* Malden, MA: Polity.

Centeno, Miguel and Patricio Silva, eds. 1998. *The Politics of Expertise in Latin America.* New York: Macmillan Press.

Chaves, Mark. 1993. "Intraorganizational Power and Internal Secularization in Protestant Denominations." *American Journal of Sociology* 99(1): 1–48.

Cima, Lawrence and Thomas Schubeck. 2001. "Self-Interest, Love, and Economic Justice: A Dialogue between Classical Economic Liberalism and Catholic Social Teaching." *Journal of Business Ethics* 30(3): 213–231.

Clarke, Tony. 1995. *Behind the Mitre: The Moral Leadership Crisis in the Canadian Catholic Church*. Toronto: HarperCollins.

Coalter, Milton. 1999. "Confession of 1967." Pp. 65–66 in *Dictionary of the Presbyterian and Reformed Tradition in America*, edited by D. G. Hart and Mark Noll. Downers Grove, IL: Intervarsity Press

Cohen, Jean and Andrew Arato. 1992. *Civil Society and Political Theory*. Cambridge, MA: MIT Press.

Colburn, Forrest and Arturo Cruz. 2007. *Varieties of Liberalism in Central America: Nation-States as Works in Progress*. Austin: University of Texas Press.

Cole-Arnal, Oscar. 1998. *To Set the Captives Free: Liberation Theology in Canada*. Toronto: Between the Lines.

Coleman, John. 2005. "Making the Connections: Globalization and Catholic Social Thought." Pp. 9–27 in *Globalization and Catholic Social Thought: Present Crisis, Future Hope*, edited by John Coleman and William Ryan. Maryknoll, NY: Orbis.

Coleman, John and William Ryan, eds. 2005. *Globalization and Catholic Social Thought: Present Crisis, Future Hope*. Maryknoll, NY: Orbis.

Come, Arnold B. 1983. "The Occasion and Contribution of the Confession of 1967." *Journal of Presbyterian History* 61: 13–32. Reproduced in 2001 in *Journal of Presbyterian History* 79(1): 59–71.

Cone, James. 1970. *A Black Theology of Liberation*. Philadelphia: J.B. Lippincott Company.

Cormie, Lee. 1994. "Seeds of Hope in the New World (Dis)order." Pp. 360–377 in *Coalitions for Justice; the Story of Canada's Interchurch Coalitions*, edited by Christopher Lind and Joe Mihevc. Ottawa: Novalis.

Daudelin, Jean and W. Hewitt. 1995. "Churches and Politics in Latin America: Catholicism Confronts Contemporary Challenge." *Third World Quarterly* 16(2): 221–236.

Davis, Nancy and Robert Robinson. 1999. "Their Brothers' Keepers? Orthodox Religionists, Modernists, and Economic Justice." *American Journal of Sociology* 104(6): 1631–1665.

Diani, Mario and Doug McAdam. 2003. *Social Movements and Networks: Relational Approaches to Collective Action*. New York: Oxford University Press.

Dicken, Peter. 1998. *Global Shift: Transforming the World Economy*. London: Paul Chapman.

DiMaggio, Paul. 1994. "Culture and Economy." Pp. 27–57 in *The Handbook of Economic Sociology*, edited by Neil Smelser and Richard Swedberg. Princeton: Princeton University Press.

———1997. "Culture and Cognition." *Annual Review of Sociology* 23:263–287.

Dobbelaere, Karel. 1981. "Secularization: A Multi-Dimensional Concept." *Current Sociology* 29: 1–216.

Douglas, Mary. 1966. *Purity and Danger: An Analysis of the Concepts of Pollution and Taboo*. New York: Routledge & Kegan Paul.

Dunkley, Graham. 2000. *The Free Trade Adventure: The WTO, the Uruguay Round and Globalism – A Critique*. London: Zed Books.

Ebaugh, Helen and Janet Chafetz. 2002. *Religion Across Borders*. Walnut Creek, CA: Altamira Press.

The Economist. 2005. "Britain: Who're You Calling Naive? The Church of England." 375: 28. April 30.

Eliasoph, Nina. 1998. *Avoiding Politics: How Americans Produce Apathy in Everyday Life*. New York: Cambridge University Press.

Emerson, Michael and Christian Smith. 2000. *Divided by Faith: Evangelical Religion and the Problem of Race in America*. New York: Oxford University Press.

Evans, Curtis, ed. 2001. *The Social Gospel Today*. Louisville: Westminster John Knox Press.

Evans, John. 2009. "An Empirical Test of Religion and Science Conflict Narratives." *Presentation at Society for the Scientific Study of Religion*. Denver, Colorado.

Evans, Peter. 1979. *Dependent Development: The Alliance of Multinational, State, and Local Capital in Brazil*. Princeton: Princeton University Press.

Ferree, Myra Marx. 2003. "Resonance and Radicalism: Feminist Framing in the Abortion Debate in the United States and Germany." *American Journal of Sociology* 109:304–44.

Ferree, Myra Marx, William Anthony Gamson, Jürgen Gerhards, and Dieter Rucht. 2002. *Shaping Abortion Discourse: Democracy and the Public Sphere in Germany and the United States*. New York: Cambridge University Press.

Fligstein, Neil. 2004. "The Political and Economic Sociology of International Economic Agreements." Pp. 183–204 in *The Handbook of Economic Sociology*, 2nd edition, edited by Neil Smelser and Richard Swedberg. Princeton, NJ: Princeton University Press.

Fourcade, Marion. 2007. "Theories of Markets and Theories of Society." *American Behavioral Scientist* 50(8): 1015–1034.

Fourcade, Marion and Kieran Healy. 2007. "Moral Views of Market Society." *Annual Review of Sociology* 33:285–311.

Forrester, Duncan. 1997. *Christian Justice and Public Policy*. New York: Cambridge University Press.

Freston, Paul. 2004. *Evangelicals and Politics in Asia, Africa, and Latin America*. New York: Cambridge University Press.

Friedland, Roger and Robert Alford. 1991. "Bringing Society Back In: Symbols, Practices, and Institutional Contradictions." Pp. 223–262 in *The New Institutionalism in Organizational Analysis*, edited by Walter Powell and Paul DiMaggio. Chicago: University of Chicago Press.

Friere, Paulo. 1970. *Pedagogy of the Oppressed*. New York: Continuum

Gereffi, Gary. 1994. "The Organization of Buyer-Driven Global Commodity Chains: How U.S. Retailers Shape Overseas Production Networks." Pp. 95–122 in *Commodity Chains and Global Capitalism*, edited by Gary Gereffi and Miguel Korzeniewicz. Santa Barbara: Greenwood Press.

———1996. "Global Commodity Chains: New Forms of Coordination and Control among Nations and Firms in International Industries." *Competition and Change* 1(4): 427–439.

Gereffi, Gary and Miguel Korzeniewicz. 1994. *Commodity Chains and Global Capitalism*. Santa Barbara: Greenwood Press.

Goldin, Adrian. 2007. *Estudio Sobre Los Arreglos Directors en Costa Rica*. Consultation study for the International Labor Organization. Print.

Goodwin, Jeff and James Jasper. 2003. *The Social Movements Reader: Cases and Concepts*. Malden, MA: Blackwell Publishing.

Goodwin, Jeff, James Jasper and Francesca Polletta, eds. 2001. *Passionate Politics: Emotions and Social Movements*. Chicago: University of Chicago Press.

Guillen, Mauro. 2001. "Is Globalization Civilizing, Destructive, or Feeble? A Critique of Five Key Debates in the Social Science Literature." *Annual Review of Sociology* 27: 235–260.

Guitierrez, Gustavo. [1973] 2006. *A Theology of Liberation*, 15th Anniversary Edition. Maryknoll, New York: Orbis Books.

Hagopian, Frances. 2009a. "The Catholic Church in a Plural Latin America: Toward a New Research Agenda." Pp. 439–466 in *Religious Pluralism, Democracy, and the Catholic Church in Latin America*, edited by Frances Hagopian. Notre Dame: University of Notre Dame Press.

———2009b. "Social Justice, Moral Values, or Institutional Interests? Church Responses to the Democratic Challenge in Latin America." Pp. 257–331 in *Religious Pluralism, Democracy, and the Catholic Church in Latin America*, edited by Frances Hagopian. Notre Dame: University of Notre Dame Press.

Hart, Stephen. 1992. *What Does the Lord Require? How American Christians View Economic Justice*. New York: Oxford University Press.

———2001. *Cultural Dilemmas of Progressive Politics*. Chicago: University of Chicago Press.

Healy, Kieran. 2004. "Altruism as an Organizational Problem: The Case of Organ Procurement." *American Sociological Review* 69: 387.

———2006. *Last Best Gifts: Altruism and the Market for Human Blood and Organs*. Chicago: University of Chicago Press.

Hertzke, Allen. 1988. *Representing God in Washington: The Role of Religious Lobbies in the American Polity*. Knoxville: University of Tennessee Press, 1988.

Hildebrand, Dale. 1987. *The Inter-Church Coalition GATT-Fly, Theological Praxis and the Option for the Poor: Towards a Canadian Contextual Theology*. Master's Thesis, University of St. Michael's College.

Hirschman, Albert O. 1977. *The Passions and the Interests: Political Arguments for Capitalism Before Its Triumph*. Princeton: Princeton University Press.

———1981. *Essays in Trespassing: Economics to Politics and Beyond*. New York: Cambridge University Press.

Hoffman, Kelly and Miguel Centeno. 2003. "The Lopsided Continent: Inequality in Latin America." *Annual Review of Sociology* 29: 363–390.

Hofrenning, Daniel. 1995. *In Washington, But Not of It: The Prophetic Politics of Religious Lobbyists*. Philadelphia: Temple University Press.

Hopkins, Charles. 1940. *The Rise of the Social Gospel in American Protestantism, 1865–1915*. New Haven, CT: Yale University Press.

Howard, Judith. 2000. "Social Psychology of Identities." *Annual Review of Sociology* 26: 367–393.

Howard-Hassman, Rhoda and Claude Welch. 2006. *Economic Rights in Canada and the United States*. Philadelphia: University of Pennsylvania Press.

Howlett, Dennis. 1994. "The Ecumenical Coalition for Economic Justice." Pp. 99–116 in *Coalitions for Justice; the Story of Canada's Interchurch Coalitions*, edited by Christopher Lind and Joe Mihevc. Ottawa: Noval.

Huber, E. 2002. *Models of Capitalism: Lessons for Latin America*. University Park: Pennsylvania State University Press.

Hudson, Ian and Mark Hudson. 2003. "Removing the Veil? Commodity Fetishism, Fair Trade, and the Environment." *Organization and* Environment 16(4): 413–430.

Hug, James. 2005. "Economic Justice and Globalization." Pp. 55–71 in *Globalization and Catholic Social Thought: Present Crisis, Future Hope*, edited by John Coleman and William Ryan. Maryknoll, NY: Orbis.

Inglehart, Ronald. 2009. "Cultural Change, Religion, Subjective Well-Being, and Democracy in Latin America." Pp. 67–95 in *Religious Pluralism, Democracy, and the Catholic Church in Latin America*, edited by Frances Hagopian. Notre Dame: University of Notre Dame Press.

Jasper, James. 1992. "The Politics of Abstractions: Instrumental and Moralist Rhetorics in Public Debate." *Social Research* 59(2): 315–344.

———1997. *The Art of Moral Protest: Culture, Biography, and Creativity in Social Movements*. Chicago: University of Chicago Press.

Katz, Michael. 1986. *In the Shadow of the Poorhouse: A Social History of Welfare in America*. New York: Basic Books.

Kahl, Sigrun. 2009. "Religious Social Doctrines and Poor Relief: A Different Causal Pathway." Pp. 267–295 in *Religion, Class Coalitions, and Welfare States*, edited by van Kersbergen and Manow. New York: Cambridge University Press.

Kaufman, Robert and Alex Segura-Ubiergo. 2001. "Globalization, Domestic Politics, and Social Spending in Latin America – A Time-Series Cross-Section Analysis, 1973–97." *World Politics* 53(4): 553–587.

Keck, Margaret E. and Kathryn Sikkink. 1998. *Activists Beyond Borders: Advocacy Networks in International Politics*. Ithaca, NY: Cornell University Press.

Klemp, Nathaniel. 2012. *The Morality of Spin: Virtue and Vice in Political Rhetoric and the Christain Right*. Lanham, MD: Rowman and Littlefield.

Kirkpatrick, David. 2009. "The Conservative-Christian Big Thinker." *New York Times Magazine*. December 16.

Kniss, Fred and David Campbell. 1997. "The Effect of Religious Orientation on Relief and Development Organizations." *Journal for the Scientific Study of Religion*. 36(1): 93–103.

Laczniak, Gene. 1999. "Distributive Justice, Catholic Social Teaching, and the Moral Responsibility of Marketers." *Journal of Public Policy & Marketing* 18(1): 125–129.

Lakoff, George. 2006. *Thinking Points: Communicating Our American Values and Vision: A Progressive's Handbook*. New York: Farrar Straus and Giroux.

Lamont, Michele and Laurent Thévenot. 2000. "Introduction: Toward a Renewed Comparative Cultural Sociology." Pp. 1–23 in *Rethinking Comparative Cultural Sociology: Repertoires of Evaluation in France and the United States*. New York: Cambridge University Press.

Larson, Rebecca. 1988. *Ten Days for World Development: A Case Study in Development Education*. PhD Dissertation, University of Calgary.

Lechner, Frank and John Boli. 2005. *World Culture: Origins and Consequences*. Malden, MA: Blackwell Publishing.

Levitt, Peggy. 2001. *The Transnational Villagers*. Berkeley: University of California Press.

Lichterman, Paul. 1995. "Beyond the Seesaw Model: Public Commitment in a Culture of Self-Fulfillment." *Sociological Theory* 13:275–300.

———1996. *The Search for Political Community: American Activists Reinventing Commitment*. New York: Cambridge University Press.

———2005. *Elusive Togetherness: Church Groups Trying to Bridge America's Divisions*. Princeton: Princeton University Press.

Lind, Christopher and Joe Mihevc. 1994. *Coalitions for Justice; the Story of Canada's Interchurch Coalitions*. Ottawa: Novalis.

Lipset, Seymour. 1990. *Continental Divide: Values and Institutions of the United States and Canada*. New York: Routledge.

Lizano, Eduardo. 2005. "El Tratado de Libre Comercio con los Estados Unidos de América, la Iglesia Católica y Otros Iglesias." Academia de Centroamerica, Document 13.

Luker, Kristin. 1984. *Abortion and the Politics of Motherhood*. Berkeley: University of California Press.

Lyon, Sarah. 2006. "Evaluating Fair Trade Consumption: Politics, Defetishization and Producer Participation." *International Journal of Consumer* Studies 30(5): 452–464.

Mainwaring, Scott and Alexander Wilde. *The Progressive Church in Latin America*. South Bend, IN: University of Notre Dame Press.

Manow, Philip and Kees van Kersbergen. 2009. "Religion and the Western Welfare State – The Theoretical Context." Pp. 1–38 in *Religion, Class Coalitions, and Welfare States*, edited by Kees Van Kersbergen and Philip Manow. New York: Cambridge University Press.

Martin, David. 1985. "Religion and Public Values: A Catholic-Protestant Contrast." *Review of Religious Research* 26(4): 313–331.

Martin, John Levi. 2002. "Power, Authority, and the Constraint of Belief Systems." *American Journal of Sociology* 107: 861–904.

Massengill, Rebekah. 2013. *Wal-Mart Wars: Moral Populism in the Twenty-First Century*. New York: New York University Press.

Massengill, Rebekah and Amy Reynolds. 2010. "Moral Discourse in Economic Contexts." Pp. 485–501 in *The Handbook of the Sociology of Morality*, edited by Steven Hitlin and Stephen Vaisey. New York: Springer.

McKeon, Robert. 2003. *The Canadian Catholic Social Justice Paradigm: Birth, Growth, Decline and Crisis*. PhD Dissertation, University of St. Michael's College.

McCloskey, Herbert and John Zaller. 1984. *The American Ethos: Public Attitudes toward Capitalism and Democracy*. Cambridge, MA: Harvard University Press.

Mehta, Jal and Christopher Winship. 2010. "Moral Power." Pp. 425–438 in *The Handbook of the Sociology of Morality*, edited by Steven Hitlin and Stephen Vaisey. New York: Springer.

Michael, Lorraine. 1994. "Relinquishing Control." Pp. 351–359 in *Coalitions for Justice; the Story of Canada's Interchurch Coalitions*, edited by Christopher Lind and Joe Mihevc. Ottawa: Novalis.

Miller, Donald and Tetsunao Yamamori. 2007. *Global Pentecostalism: The New Face of Christian Social Engagement*. Berkeley: University of California Press.

Moffatt, Jeanne. 1994. "Ten Days for World Development" Pp. 151–168 in *Coalitions for Justice; the Story of Canada's Interchurch Coalitions*, edited by Christopher Lind and Joe Mihevc. Ottawa: Novalis.

Mohr, John. 1994. "Soldiers, Mothers, Tramps, and Others: Discourse Roles in the 1907 New York City Charity Directory." *Poetics* 22: 327–257.

Monsma, Stephen. 2006. "The Relevance of Solidarity and Subsidiarity to Reformed Social and Political Thought." Paper presented at the International Society for the Study of Reformed Communities, Princeton, New Jersey.

Mooney, Margarita. 2006. "The Catholic Bishops Conferences of the United States and France: Engaging Immigration as a Public Issue." *American Behavioral Scientist* 49(11): 1455–1470.

Munson, Ziad. 2008. *The Making of Pro-Life Activists: How Social Movement Mobilization Works*. Chicago: University of Chicago Press.

Nazar, David. 1987. *Bishops as Theologians*. Master's Thesis, University of Toronto.

Neibuhr, H. Richard. 1951. *Christ and Culture*. New York: Harper.

Nelson, Robert H. 2001. *Economics as Religion: From Samuelson to Chicago and Beyond*. University Park, PA: Pennsylvania State University Press.

Noll, Mark. 1992. *A History of Christianity in the United States and Canada*. Grand Rapids: Eerdmans.

Nuñez, Emilio. 1985. *Liberation Theology*. Chicago: Moody Press.

Ozsoy, Ismail. 2011. "Islamic Banking: Background, Theory, and Practice." Pp. 159–182 in *Religion and Development: Ways of Transforming the World*, edited by Gerrie ter Haar. New York: Columbia University Press.

Padwick, John and Nicta Lubaale. 2011. "Harnessing Populatio Visions for Social Transformation: The Experience of the OAIC and its Work with African Independent Churches." Pp. 315–330 in *Religion and Development: Ways of Transforming the World*, edited by Gerrie ter Haar. New York: Columbia University Press.

Palacios, Joseph. 2007. *The Catholic Social Imagination: Activism and the Just Society in Mexico and the United States*. Chicago: University of Chicago Press.

Philpott, Daniel. 2009. "Has the Study of Global Politics Found Religion?" *Annual Review of Political Science* 12:183–202.

Picado Gatjens, Miguel. 2007. *La Palabra Social de los Opispos Costarricenses (1893–2006)*. San José, Costa Rica: Conferencia Episcopal de Costa Rica.

Pointer, Richard. 1999. "Presbyterians and Capitalism." Pp. 54–56 in *Dictionary of the Presbyterian and Reformed Tradition in America*, edited by D. G. Hart and Mark Noll. Downers Grove, IL: Intervarsity Press.

Polanyi, Karl. 1944. *The Great Transformation: The Political and Economic Origins of Our Time*. New York: Farrar & Rinehart.

Ponte, Stefano. 2002. "Standards, Trade, and Equity: Lessons from the Specialty Coffee Industry." *CDR Working Paper*. Copenhagen: Centre for Development Research.

Presbyterian Church (U.S.A.), Research Services. 2006a. The Presbyterian Panel: The November 2005 Survey – The Social Creed. Louisville, KY: PCUSA.

———2006b. Presbyterian Panel Data for November 2005 Survey. Louisville, KY: PCUSA.

Putnam, Robert. 1993. "Diplomacy and Domestic Politics: The Logic of Two-Level Games." Pp. 431–468 in *Double-Edged Diplomacy: International Bargaining and Domestic Politics*, edited by Peter Evans, Harold Johnson, and Robert Putnam. Berkeley: University of California Press.

Ragin, Charles. 1987. *The Comparative Method: Moving Beyond Qualitative and Quantitative Strategies*. Berkeley: University of California Press.

Reynolds, Amy. 2010. Saving the Market: The Role of Values, Authority, and Networks in International Trade Discourse, PhD Dissertation, Princeton University.

———2013. "Networks, Ethics, and Economic Values," *Latin American Research Review* 48(1): 112–132.

Roberts, Kenneth. 2008. "The Mobilization of Opposition to Economic Liberalization." *Annual Review of Political Science* 11: 327–349.

Rodrik, Dani. 1997. *Has Globalization Gone Too Far?* Washington, D.C.: Institute for International Economics.

Rosenberg, Mark and Luis Solis. 2007. *The United States and Central America: Geopolitical Realities and Regional Fragility*. New York: Routledge.

Ruttan, Brian. 1987. *The Interchurch Project GATT-Fly: A Reconstruction*. PhD Dissertation, Trinity College (Toronto).

Sawchuk, Dana. 2004. *The Costa Rican Catholic Church, Social Justice, and the Rights of Workers, 1979–1996*. Waterloo: Wilfrid Laurier University Press.

Schüssler Fiorenza, Elisabeth. 1983. *In Memory of Her: A Feminist Reconstruction of Christian Origins*. New York: Crossroad.

Sen, Amartya. 1999. *Development as Freedom.* New York: Knopf.

Skocpol, Theda. 1992. *Protecting Soldiers and Mothers: The Political Origins of Social Policy in the United States.* Cambridge, MA: Belknap Press of Harvard University Press.

Smith, Adam. [1790] 2009. *The Theory of Moral Sentiments.* New York: Penguin Books.

Smith, Christian. 1991. *The Emergence of Liberation Theology: Radical Religion and Social Movement Theory.* Chicago: University of Chicago Press.

———1996. *Resisting Reagan: The U.S. Central America Peace Movement.* Chicago, University of Chicago Press.

———2002. "*Las Casas* as Theological Counteroffensive: An Interpretation of Gustavo Gutiérrez's *Las Casas: In Search of the Poor of Jesus Christ.*" *Journal for the Scientific Study of Religion* 41(1): 69–73.

Smith, Christian and Robert Faris. 2005. "Socioeconomic Inequality in the American Religious System: An Update and Assessment." *Journal for the Scientific Study of Religion* 44(1): 95–104.

Smith, Gary Scott. 1999. "Reformed Tradition in America" and "Presbyterians and Social Reform." Pp. 212–216 and 243–246 in *Dictionary of the Presbyterian and Reformed Tradition in America*, edited by D. G. Hart and Mark Noll. Downers Grove, IL: Intervarsity Press.

Snow, David, Louis Zurcher and Sheldon Ekland-Olson. 1980. "Social Networks and Social Movements: A Microstructural Approach to Differential Recruitment." *American Sociological Review* 45(5): 787–801.

Somers, Margaret. 1994. "The Narrative Construction of Identity: A Relational and Network Approach." *Theory and Society* 23(5): 605–649.

Spalding, Rose J. 2007. "Civil Society Engagement in Trade Negotiations: CAFTA Opposition Movements in El Salvador." *Latin American Politics and Society* 49(4): 85–114.

Stafford, Tim. 2005. "Good Morning, Evangelicals." *Christianity Today.* November.

Steensland, Brian. 2002. "The Hydra and the Swords: Social Welfare and Mainline Advocacy, 1964–2000." In *Faith-Based Activism and the Public Role of Mainline Protestantism*, edited by Wuthnow and Evans. Berkeley: University of California Press.

———2007. *The Failed Welfare Revolution: America's Struggle over Guaranteed Income Policy.* Princeton: Princeton University Press.

Stotts, Jack. 1989. "'By What Authority…?' (Matthew 21:23): An Unscholarly Foray into Acts 2:44–45; 4:32–35." In *Reformed Faith and Economics*, edited by Robert Stivers. Lanham, MD: University Press of America.

Swedberg, Richard. 1998. *Max Weber and the Idea of Economic Sociology.* Princeton: Princeton University Press.

Swidler Ann. 1986. "Culture in Action: Symbols and Strategies." *American Sociological Review.* 51(2): 273–286.

Szollosy, David. 2000. *Stay with the One Crucified: Theology and Ecclesiology Represented in the Statements of Canadian Diocesan Social Justice Commissions.* Master's Thesis, University of St. Michael's College.

Thévenot, Laurent and Michael Moody and Claudette Lafaye. 2000. "Forms of Valuing Nature: Arguments and Modes of Justification in French and American Environmental Disputes." Pp. 229–271 in *Rethinking Comparative Cultural Sociology: Repertoires of Evaluation in France and the United States.* New York: Cambridge University Press.

Thompson, John and Stephen Randall. 1994. *Canada and the United States: Ambivalent Allies*. Athens, GA: University of Georgia Press.

Thuesen, Peter J. 2002. "The Logic of Mainline Churches: Historical Background since the Reformation." Pp. 27–53 in *The Quiet Hand of God: Faith-Based Activism and the Public Role of Mainline Protestantism*, edited by Robert Wuthnow and John H. Evans. Berkeley: University of California Press.

Tyndale, Wendy. 2011. "Religion and Millennium Development Goals: Whose Agenda?" Pp. 207–230 in *Religion and Development: Ways of Transforming the World*, edited by Gerrie ter Haar. New York: Columbia University Press.

UNCTAD. 2004. *Beyond Conventional Wisdom in Development Policy: An Intellectual History of UNCTAD 1964–2004*. New York: United Nations.

U.S. Catholic Bishops. 1986. *Economic Justice for All: Pastoral Letter on Catholic Social Teaching and the U.S. Economy*. Washington, D.C.: U.S. Catholic Conference Bishops.

Vaisey, Steven. 2009. "Motivation and Justification. A Dual-Process Model of Culture in Action." *American Journal of Sociology* 114(6): 1675–1715.

Volf, Miroslav. 2011a. *Allah: A Christian Response*. New York: HarperOne.

———2011b. *A Public Faith: How Followers of Christ Should Serve the Common Good*. Grand Rapids, MI: Brazos Press.

Wagner-Pacifici, Robin. 1994. *Discourse and Destruction: The City of Philadelphia versus MOVE*. Chicago: University of Chicago Press.

Warren, Mark R. 2001. *Dry Bones Rattling: Community Building to Revitalize American Democracy*. Princeton: Princeton University Press.

Weber, Max. 1958. *The Protestant Ethic and the Spirit of Capitalism*. Translated by Talcott Parsons. New York: Scribner.

Wells, Sidney. 1969. "The Developing Countries, GATT, and UNCTAD." *International Affairs* 45(1): 64–79.

Wibbels, Erik and Moisés Arce. 2003. "Globalization, Taxation, and Burden-Shifting in Latin America." *International Organization* 57(1): 111–136.

Wilde, Melissa. 2007. *Vatican II: A Sociological Analysis of Religious Change*. Princeton: Princeton University Press.

Williams, Philip. 1989. *The Catholic Church and Politics in Nicaragua and Costa Rica*. Pittsburgh: University of Pittsburgh Press.

Wood, Richard. 1999. "Religious Culture and Political Action" *Sociological Theory* 17(3): 302–332.

———2002. *Faith in Action: Religion, Race, and Democratic Organizing in America*. Chicago: University of Chicago Press.

Woodberry, Robert. 2012. "Missionary Roots of Liberal Democracy" *American Political Science Review* 106(2): 244–274.

World Bank. 2004. World Development Indicators. www.worldbank.org/data.

Wuthnow, Robert. 1987. *Meaning and Moral Order: Explorations in Cultural Analysis*. Berkeley: University of California Press.

———1989. *Communities of Discourse: Ideology and Social Structure in the Reformation, the Enlightenment, and European Socialism*. Cambridge, MA: Harvard University Press.

———1994a. *God and Mammon in America*. New York: Free Press.

———1994b. *Producing the Sacred*. Chicago: University of Chicago Press.

———1996. *Poor Richard's Principle: Recovering the American Dream Through the Moral Dimension of Work, Business, and Money*. Princeton: Princeton University Press.

———2005. *America and the Challenges of Religious Diversity*. Princeton: Princeton University Press.

Wuthnow, Robert and John Evans, eds. 2002. *The Quiet Hand of God*. Berkeley: University of California Press.

Yergin, Daniel and Joseph Stanislaw. 1998. *Commanding Heights: The Battle for the World Economy*. New York: Free Press.

Zelizer, Viviana. 1979. *Moral and Markets: The Development of Life Insurance in the United States*. New York: Columbia University Press.

———1994. *The Social Meaning of Money: Pin Money, Paychecks, Poor Relief, and Other Currencies*. New York: Basic Books.

———2005. *The Purchase of Intimacy*. Princeton: Princeton University Press.

———2007. "Ethics in the Economy." *Journal for Business, Economics and Ethics* (zfwu) 1: 8–23.

Index